Investm
Appraisa
Non-Fina
Managers

The Institute of Management (IM) is at the forefront of management development and best management practice. The Institute embraces all levels of management from students to chief executives. It provides a unique portfolio of services for all managers, enabling them to develop skills and achieve management excellence.

If you would like to hear more about the benefits of membership, please write to Department P, Institute of Management, Cottingham Road, Corby NN17 1TT.

This series is commissioned by the Institute of Management Foundation.

SMARTER SOLUTIONS

The finance pack

Investment Appraisal for Non-Financial Managers

A step-by-step guide to making profitable decisions

KATE MORAN

Prentice Hall

London • New York • Toronto • Sydney • Tokyo • Singapore •
Madrid • Mexico City • Munich • Paris

PEARSON EDUCATION LIMITED

Head Office:
Edinburgh Gate
Harlow CM20 2JE
Tel: +44 (0)1279 623623
Fax: +44 (0)1279 431059

London Office:
128 Long Acre
London WC2E 9AN
Tel: +44 (0)207 447 2000
Fax: +44 (0)207 240 5771
www.business-minds.com

First published in Great Britain in 1995

© Pearson Education Limited 2000

The right of Kate Moran to be identified as author of this work has been asserted by her in accordance with the Copyright, Designs, and Patents Act 1988.

ISBN 0 273 62682 5

British Library Cataloguing in Publication Data
A CIP catalogue record for this book can be obtained from the British Library.

10 9 8 7 6 5 4 3 2 1

Typeset by Northern Phototypesetting Co. Ltd, Bolton
Printed and bound in Great Britain by Biddles Ltd, Guildford and King's Lynn

The Publishers' policy is to use paper manufactured from sustainable forests.

Contents

Preface

Who should read this book

I have written this book for all non-financial managers who are involved in appraising new investment proposals. You need to be familiar with the main concepts used in investment appraisal even if this is not your area of functional expertise. Perhaps you have an investment proposal that you want to champion and take to senior management, or you may be part of a cross-functional project team evaluating a new investment.

The intention of this book is to demonstrate why you should not leave investment appraisal solely to the finance department. There are many elements to detailed investment appraisal and the involvement of non-financial managers enhances the quality of the appraisal process. It increases the chances that a successful investment chosen in theory, will be a successful investment in reality.

How to use this book to your best advantage

This book is for all non-financial managers who want to know more about investment appraisal. Your existing knowledge may range from sketchy to substantial and so each chapter is written as a discrete entity. If you are already familiar with investment appraisal methods and just want to brush up on some specific issues, you can simply read the relevant chapters. Investments vary considerably in their complexity and your investment project may not require you to estimate a terminal value for example, or to assess the tax implications in detail.

> The intention of this book is to demonstrate why you should not leave investment appraisal solely to the finance department.

Use this book as a workbook and later on as a source of reference.

What are the objectives for this book?

When you have read this book you will know:

- The main investment appraisal methods used by managers.

- The advantages and disadvantages of those methods and when you should use a particular method.

- Why I believe that Net Present Value is the most versatile and robust method to use.

- What cashflows should be included in the investment appraisal.

- How you can minimise uncertainty through simulation and other risk analysis methods.

- How to assess the appropriate cost of capital for your investment appraisal.

- How to sell the investment proposal successfully.

Style and structure of this book

This book focuses on developing your confidence and decision-making skills when reviewing investment projects. There is naturally some analysis involved in investment appraisal but I don't believe in analysis for its own sake. You will usually be under some time constraints and so I have been pragmatic, indicating short cuts wherever possible.

A schematic flow of investment appraisal is given below. Each chapter of the book addresses a specific step in the appraisal process.

In Chapter 1, we discuss some of the questions to be asked *before the main analysis of the project is initiated*. By asking these questions before time and effort have been committed, the investment appraisal is at its most effective. An overview of the broader investment selection process is given alongside a discussion on the capital budgeting environment. The various types of investments that you are likely to encounter are also outlined. You are then ready to consider what type of appraisal method best suits your needs. This question is addressed in Chapters 2 and 3 when we look at Net Present Value and other appraisal methods. I should say now that I believe that the Net Present Value

> Use this book as a workbook and later on as a source of reference.

method is the most useful and comprehensive but there are specific circumstances when it may be more appropriate to use a slightly different method.

Once you have decided on the method you are going to use, you will need to identify all the *inputs* for the process. Chapters 4 and 5 look at the cashflows of the investment; Chapter 6 provides some case studies to review your understanding. Chapters 7 and 8 look at measuring the risk of the investment through the appropriate use of a discount rate. Chapter 9 examines methods for valuing the end of an investment.

Once you have completed your analysis, there are two more critical steps to take and these are covered in the final chapters. You have to *test the validity of the results* and you have to *sell the investment proposal*, assuming of course that it still looks attractive after the detailed analysis. Chapter 10 looks at these final steps and Chapter 11 provides some conclusions.

Case studies

The use of examples and case studies in this book will introduce you to a range of different investment scenarios. Their purpose is to confirm your understanding. They begin very simply and become more complex as the book progresses.

At the end of each chapter, one or two hypothetical cases are given for you to consider how to tackle them. Furthermore Chapter 6 is devoted to seven longer case studies which bring together several of the issues already discussed in Chapters 2 to 5. Look at these case studies and decide how you would have approached the problem. I recommend that you get some paper and a calculator, or turn on your computer, and work through the analysis needed for some of the case studies. The numbers are straightforward and it won't take much time. This is really the only way to test and develop your understanding. I have given some possible solutions but it's all too easy to read my answer, nod sagely and read on. You won't get the most out of this book if you do that every time.

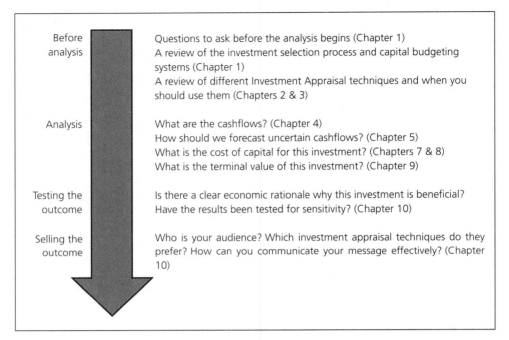

Before analysis	Questions to ask before the analysis begins (Chapter 1)
	A review of the investment selection process and capital budgeting systems (Chapter 1)
	A review of different Investment Appraisal techniques and when you should use them (Chapters 2 & 3)
Analysis	What are the cashflows? (Chapter 4)
	How should we forecast uncertain cashflows? (Chapter 5)
	What is the cost of capital for this investment? (Chapters 7 & 8)
	What is the terminal value of this investment? (Chapter 9)
Testing the outcome	Is there a clear economic rationale why this investment is beneficial?
	Have the results been tested for sensitivity? (Chapter 10)
Selling the outcome	Who is your audience? Which investment appraisal techniques do they prefer? How can you communicate your message effectively? (Chapter 10)

Flow diagram for investment appraisal

The overriding purpose of new investments is to enhance the return on the investment made by shareholders.

CHAPTER ONE

What is investment appraisal?

- Why do companies invest?

- The eight steps in an appraisal process

- Questions to ask

- Reviewing types of investments

- Examining the capital budgeting process

- Considering the environment – Cost–Benefit Analysis

CHECKLIST OF KEY POINTS

1 The overriding purpose of new investments is to enhance the return on the investment made by shareholders. This return must be greater or equivalent to the returns they can get by investing elsewhere. Investment appraisal is about selecting investments where the benefits outweigh the costs. In this case, the cost is the lost opportunity to invest in other projects.

2 Before beginning a detailed investment appraisal you should ask yourself three questions:

- Does the investment fit the strategic direction of the company?
- Does the company have any budgetary constraints?
- Is there a way to improve the attractiveness of the investment even further?

In addition, you should consider the impact of the investment on the other stakeholders in the company, such as the employees or the local community.

3 A summary of the different stages in the wider process of selecting investments is given here. It takes the strategic objectives of the company as the starting point. The search for investment ideas should be in line with these objectives. The investment project undergoes an initial screen, before detailed investment analysis takes place. The different possible outcomes of the investment are outlined and the cashflows measured. The investment projects selected are those whose benefits outweigh the costs, when compared in a common currency, that is to say, in today's money. Authorisation is then obtained for the investment, and after the initiation of the investment, a post-audit is conducted to ensure that it remains viable.

4 There are three different types of investment: those that involve an expansion of existing facilities, or a diversification into new products or new markets; cost-reduction investments; and safety and maintenance investments. Although the same investment appraisal methods are used to evaluate them, the different facets of the process vary in importance depending on the type of investment.

Introduction

This chapter considers what you need to know and think about before you begin any investment appraisal. It is divided into the following sections:

- an overview of the appraisal process; what it is and why it is important
- a list of key questions to ask yourself
- a review of the main types of investments
- an examination of the capital budgeting process.

Once you have digested all this, you will be ready to consider what method you want to use to analyse an investment (Chapters 2 and 3).

Why do companies invest?

The overriding purpose of new investments is to enhance the return on the investment made by shareholders. The shareholders in a company have a range of other investment opportunities as Figure 1.1 highlights. Shareholders are looking for either a stream of dividends from their shares, or capital growth in those shares (or a combination of both) which exceeds the returns they could have gained elsewhere. Thus the ultimate aim of new investment is to increase shareholders' wealth, by increasing the value of the company's shares on the stock market, and by maximising the stream of dividends. This will only be done if new investments made by the company are more valuable to a shareholder than taking his money and investing it somewhere else. An alternative source of capital for new investments is a bank loan. The bank receives interest on the loan at a set rate along with loan repayments.

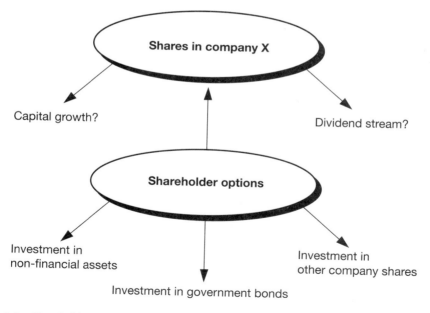

Figure 1.1   Shareholder investment opportunities

> Investment appraisal is about selecting investments where the benefits of the investment outweigh the costs and where the cash generated by the project more than outweighs the lost opportunities for shareholders and banks to invest elsewhere.

Investment appraisal is an *art* as much as a *science*

What do I mean by 'the benefits should outweigh the costs'? Behind this simple concept lies a multitude of questions. What is the *true* cost of an investment? What are the benefits of the investment, and how should they be measured? How do I know whether benefits that occur in the future *do* actually outweigh the current cost of the investment? To answer these questions correctly, today's managers need to understand what information should go into the appraisal model as well as knowing about the process of investment appraisal itself. They must be able to use their judgement to include both the obvious, tangible costs and benefits, but also the less tangible or hidden costs and benefits. Furthermore managers need to understand which investments are likely to be attractive and acceptable to their company *before* investing significant time, effort and money in evaluating them in detail.

The eight steps in an appraisal process

Now I will review the overall process of appraisal so that you know what you are embarking upon! There are a number of stages in investment appraisal. Some can be undertaken simultaneously but many follow logically from the steps already taken. Figure 1.2 demonstrates the major stages in investment appraisal. This book will be concentrating on the middle steps: the identification of outcomes, the measurement of cashflows and the selection of investments. For many appraisals there are feed-back loops where the results from a later stage of the analysis may make you revisit an earlier stage in the process, to look at the assumptions or the rationale. These are indicated with a dotted line.

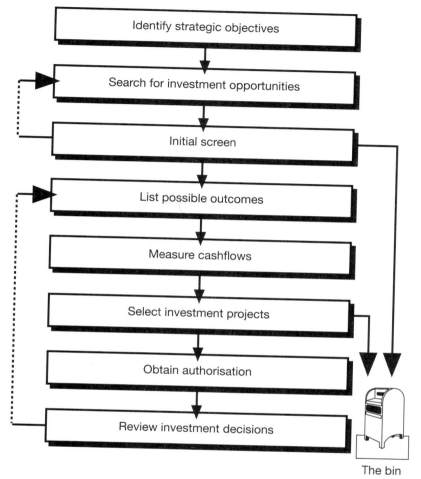

Figure 1.2   Investment selection

1 First **identify the company's strategic objectives**. As we have discussed, ensure that an investment project is in line with these strategic objectives. Ideally your systematic search process for likely investment projects will be designed with these strategic objectives in mind.

2 The next step is to **search for investment opportunities.** This book is concentrating on the process of investment appraisal. However, there is only value in managers understanding the appraisal process, if there is a good flow of potentially interesting investments coming into the review system in the first place! Many companies focus on the valuation process and do not pay enough attention to the search process that precedes it. The search process should be an integral part of business planning – managers in all functional areas should be continually scanning the environment for new opportunities. This has a second benefit – it can also act as an 'Early Warning System' by identifying an absence of new opportunities for investment in the future.

PRACTICAL TIPS: THE SEARCH PROCESS

- Widen the pool of people who are actively looking at new investment possibilities.

- Create an environment where investment ideas are more likely to be on the right track, that is to say, ensure that people understand the strategic direction of the company, explain the budgetary constraints imposed on new projects (see later) and whether these are negotiable or not.

- Ensure that the generation of new investment ideas is rewarded, both verbally and financially, and involve the proposer in the analysis as far as possible.

- Concentrate your search process on the areas of the company where a competitive advantage is enjoyed. This is more likely to generate beneficial investments in the future.

---

3 In many companies, investments identified by the search process are subjected to an **initial screen** which assesses their likely attractiveness. Whether this occurs will be a function of the capital budget environment of that company, the budget constraints, and whether there are people available to give attention to new project investments. The initial screen should ensure that the company does not engage in detailed analysis of a number of projects if it does not have the resources to spare for such analysis, or the money to invest extensively once the analysis is complete.

4 & 5 For those investment proposals that are going forward to detailed analysis, the reviewer must **consider all the possible outcomes of each investment**, and then **measure the cashflows** associated with those outcomes, together with the initial investment cost.

6 **Investments are selected** according to investment criteria which have been agreed upon by the company (and which the following chapters will review in detail).

7 The next step is to **present the appraisal for authorisation** from the appropriate capital budget committees within the company.

8 One step which is often overlooked when considering investment appraisal is the final step of reviewing investments that have been accepted, and **monitoring to what extent the actual outcomes have mirrored the forecasted outcomes**. This valuable information can be fed back into all the relevant stages of the process, especially new investment projects that are being forecasted and measured. This should ensure that the investment appraisal process continues to improve in its forecasting and decision-making abilities.

Questions to ask

Before you decide what appraisal method you should use, and what information you will need to make a good decision, step back from the process and ask yourself three fundamental questions:

- Does the investment fit the strategic direction of the company?
- Does the company have any budgetary constraints?
- Is there a way to improve the attractiveness of the investment even further?

Does this project fit with the strategic direction of the company?

This would not be a major issue in an ideal world. The senior management of the company would try to maximise shareholder value and their strategic direction would be in line with that objective. Any investment project that increased shareholder wealth would be accepted automatically. In reality, there are three problems with this utopian view.

Firstly, the management of a company may seek to make their lives comfortable by not taking risks, or not pursuing all opportunities that could increase shareholder wealth, if a good return will be achieved anyway. This is the so-called *satisficer theory of corporate life*.

Secondly, senior management may not have the same opinions as you as to what will increase shareholder wealth and thus your investment proposal may not be considered in the strategic interests of the firm. This may be due to different perceptions of the full costs of the investment.

CASE STUDY 1.1

The senior management of a successful company does not believe that acquisitions of competitive companies are an appropriate way to grow the business. It believes that organic growth will lead to the best return on shareholders' wealth in the long run, due to the considerable problems associated with integrating two company cultures and management teams, and the time taken up by senior management sorting out teething troubles. If an acquisition is proposed as a profitable investment for this company, without taking into consideration the opinions of senior management, the investment proposal will be rejected at an early stage. A more successful approach may be to address the concerns of the management directly. They may be concerned about the *hidden* costs of acquisitions. Alternatively, consider another investment such as a strategic alliance, which has some of the advantages of the acquisition proposal but which may be more palatable. By firstly proposing a strategic alliance the manager may ensure that the investment proposal is at least considered and then some of the advantages of an acquisition can be brought into the discussion.

Thirdly, the company, as represented by its senior management, may not be solely motivated by profit. Such management may have additional objectives that may, or may not, be shared by a majority of the shareholders.

CASE STUDY 1.2

Take a company such as The Body Shop. A new investment is proposed, a night cream with a premium price, the justification of which rests largely on its expensive packaging. Given the corporate ethos of The Body Shop, and its avowed position on the wasteful nature of ostentatious packaging in the cosmetics industry, this investment proposal is highly unlikely to be accepted by the senior management! In cases such as this, the company is accepting that it has obligations not only to its shareholders but to the community or to society as a whole.

Summary: If your investment proposal does not fit with corporate strategy for whatever reason, decide whether there is any chance of it being accepted and, if so, how you can sell it most effectively (see Chapter 10).

Does the company have any capital budgetary constraints?

If the company does not have access to additional sources of capital, then it is under a hard capital constraint or is said to have a *hard ceiling* on capital investment. (In efficient capital markets this should not occur if the investment will be beneficial. However, there are imperfections in the market that make this a possibility for small or medium-sized companies. It is rarely the case with major corporations.) If the capital investment budget has been imposed by senior management and represents what they want to spend on capital investment, then it is considered to be a *soft ceiling* on capital investment.

In the case of a hard ceiling on investments, managers use specific methods to identify the combination of projects which will maximise shareholder wealth. If you are proposing a project whose minimum investment in one year exceeds the hard capital ceiling, perhaps you should put the idea aside until more capital is available, or consider whether the project could be reduced, and still remain a profitable investment. If you are operating under a soft capital constraint, then there may be ways to overcome the problem. However, it is worth remembering that it is going to be harder to sell this project compared to one which falls comfortably within the capital budget.

> **Summary:** Don't invest much time until you know whether the senior management is sufficiently interested in your project to waive the soft ceiling.

Is there a way to improve the attractiveness of this project even further?

Most projects do not have only one way of being formulated. Ask yourself whether the timing is optimal, whether it could be done on a different scale and, if so, whether there are economies of scale that might make it even more attractive. (This might work the other way round with diseconomies of scale occurring once a project becomes too large.)

> **Summary:** Take time to review the outline and scope of the project to investigate any potential improvements.

Reviewing types of investments

There is a vast array of investment types that must be evaluated in the course of running a business. Any investment appraisal method used must be robust enough to cope with the varying dimensions of investment size, length and complexity. It is useful to look at types of investments and to put them into broad categories before looking at specific case studies. Though the same investment appraisal process is used regardless of the type of project, each investment type does reflect different complexities that the investment reviewer should be aware of at the outset.

(Different investment types are used in a number of case studies given in Chapter 6.)

Expansion or diversification investments

An expansion investment is an expansion of existing or similar product lines in order to gain greater sales, whereas a diversification may be an investment in totally new product lines or into a new geographical market, or a combination of both. Such investments will rely on considered forecasting of not only operating costs but also expected demand, technology changes and competitor responses. You must ensure that both tangible costs and benefits and qualitative intangible costs and benefits are considered. If it is a large investment it may be worthwhile developing a project team of specialists in different functional areas, so that all the potential cashflows are accurately assessed. For example, if a company is considering an investment in a new product, it needs to consider investments in machinery and plant, assess production costs, assess the size of the market, assess the likely demand for the project and devise a marketing and sales strategy. A project team consisting of a marketing manager, a production manager, a specialist engineer and an accountant would be appropriate for such an investment appraisal.

In diversification investments, the investment project may not seem beneficial when viewed as a stand-alone project. However, if the investment is seen as an entry point into a new market, which will then allow the company to initiate other profitable investments, the investment is giving the company a valuable *option* to expand through further investments, if the market looks promising. This option has a value and this strategic advantage should be weighed up alongside the tangible cashflows.

Cost-saving investments

Here the premise of the investment is that by investing in new machinery or in new processes, whether they are technological or managerial processes, the company will gain cost savings in the future. This may be through a reduction in operating costs of a particular machine, or it may be through increasing the versatility of the production process, thus reducing overall production costs.

In such investments you should look at cost savings throughout the lifetime of the investment. Two alternative pieces of machinery can be assessed for a factory – one may be cheaper to buy but lead to higher maintenance and running costs over its lifetime.

It is important to note that an investment may be in people rather than in machinery. A company may be considering whether spending £20,000 on training its workforce will lead to greater productivity and improved quality. It may be assessing whether spending £30,000 on an incentive scheme, to reward productivity and quality control, will also save costs. It will be necessary to consider not just the investment cost, but the hidden costs or benefits of introducing this cost-saving investment – for example, how much time will it take to train your staff to act in a different way, will labour morale improve or deteriorate etc?

Cost-reduction investment decisions are often a question of deciding between two courses of action. If the costs are the same but the potential benefits are different, it would be easy. But more usually you have to decide between two investments of differing costs and benefits. You may need to evaluate two machines with different life expectancies – so your appraisal method must be able to compare these investments across similar time-frames. The decision between which investment to choose may come down to converting the intangible benefit of improved quality into a measurable benefit. For example, you may be able to say that improved quality produced by a more expensive machine will lead to additional sales and calculate the increased cashflow coming from this more expensive investment alternative.

Safety and maintenance investments

This group of investments can be sub-divided into those with tangible costs and benefits, and those of a more qualitative nature.

Tangible costs and benefits

In the case of replacement or maintenance investments, the question is not just whether to replace one piece of machinery with another piece of machinery but the timing of that replacement. It is not just whether the cost savings achieved will outstrip the investment cost, but whether there is an even greater cash surplus to be made if the replacement is left for a couple of years.

In some cases the company may have no choice as it may be required by law to carry out necessary maintenance and/or replacements. These investments do not necessarily have to pay their own way, but investment appraisal can determine how the safety standards can be achieved at minimum cost in today's money. The decision may often depend on the engineering analyses of alternative technologies.

Qualitative decisions

Some safety investments do not have clear-cut outcomes that can be measured, for example, any investments in safety equipment in the workplace where there is a danger of injury, or even loss of life, if that equipment is not installed. This investment decision can be turned round, and the question restated – does the company believe that the investment of £200,000 in safety equipment is justified given it prevents injury to its employees?

Large and small investments

When many managers think of investment appraisal, they think of the large-scale investments; a major investment in a new product line, an expansion to new markets and so on. However, many of the techniques discussed in this book are equally appropriate for smaller-scale investment projects. For example, whether to buy a piece of machinery outright or to lease it; whether to replace a piece of machinery now or in a couple of years' time, or whether to use an internal taskforce to look at a management problem or to appoint outside consultants. This book will use both large- and small-scale investment examples.

Examining the capital budgeting process

As already indicated, the investment appraisal will depend partly on the system of capital budgeting that is in place in your company so it is worth reviewing the context of investment appraisal at this stage.

Most companies have a capital budgeting process, either formal or informal. An informal process would examine each investment proposal on its individual merits, without a set capital budget being put aside.

A more formal capital budgeting process takes place when a capital budget is agreed for the year. Investment proposals are put forward from the company's management team, or from each of its divisions. Each proposal is screened and gradually a large pool of projects is reduced to those which seem to have the greatest net benefit. In other words, the resulting benefits outweigh the initial investment cost. The number of projects left after the review process will broadly be a function of two factors:

- the quality of the projects, i.e. how many projects actually show a net benefit
- the constraint on the capital budget.

If a company has a set capital budget it must ensure that this resource is spent not only on new investments but also on supporting existing investments which may require two or more years of capital investment before the benefits start coming through.

Some companies break down their capital budget into categories of investment. They may consider projects under three headings: investments for expansion or diversification; cost-saving investments; and safety and maintenance investments.

For example, a company or division may have ten projects which show a net benefit and require a total investment of £400,000 but it may have only £250,000 available in its capital budget. Thus the company has to choose which projects have the highest net benefit.

Example

Investamor Ltd has a capital budget of £600,000 for the coming year. It divides potential investments into the three categories given above and has decided that investing in growth projects is a strategic priority for them, that safety and maintenance are also of critical importance and that cost-saving investments, though important, will have to wait until next year. A list of investment proposals is put forward.

Proposed investments ranked in order of net benefit*

Growth investments	Safety and maintenance investments	Cost-reduction investments
Project 1 – £80,000	Project A – £50,000	Project X – £125,000
Project 2 – £150,000	Project B – £30,000	Project Y – £60,000
Project 3 – £70,000	Project C – £40,000	Project Z – £95,000
Project 4 – £100,000	Project D – £55,000	
	Project E – £25,000	
Total £400,000	£200,000	£280,000

* the investment cost is given in the example but the net benefit, that is the resulting benefit minus the investment cost, has determined the ranking of the investment project within each budget category.

Given Investamor's strategic objectives the company selects the following investments.

Capital budget

Total	Growth investments	Safety and maintenance investments	Cost-reduction investments
£600,000	£300,000	£175,000	£125,000
Projects accepted			
	1	A	X
	2	B	
	3	C	
		D	

In this case Investamor Ltd allocates £300,000 of the total budget of £600,000 to new growth investments, £175,000 to safety and maintenance and the remaining £125,000 to cost-reduction investments. Then it reviews the projects that have a net benefit for the company and accepts the most beneficial projects up to their capital budget. As a result 75 per cent of investments that fell into the growth category were accepted, all the investments, except one, that were associated with safety and maintenance, but under 50 per cent of the cost-reduction investments.

> **Note:** By assigning budgets within the overall budget, Investamor may have decided to forgo choosing the optimal mix of projects (in terms of maximising the net benefit to the company) in favour of pursuing particular strategic objectives.

Considering the environment – Cost–Benefit Analysis (CBA)

As a manager, your prime responsibility is to your shareholders. However, at the beginning of any investment appraisal, it is worthwhile considering other environmental factors involved. There are other *stakeholders* in the company as well as shareholders, such as the employees of the company and the local community. Consider the impact of the investment proposal on the employment patterns of your company. Will it provide new job opportunities or will it lead to redundancies, or a reduction in promotion possibilities? How should you sell this to the company's employees?

Sometimes *Cost–Benefit Analysis* is used as an alternative description for investment appraisal. However, strictly speaking, it is the term used for the wider investment appraisals conducted by public bodies when considering, for example, whether a new bypass should be built or a hospital extended.

Similarly, investing money to improve safety on the factory floor will not directly lead to increased shareholder wealth, but it does improve the environment for another major group of stakeholders.

An investment of any reasonable size will have environmental or qualitative aspects to consider. The cost of improving safety may be clear to see, but what about the *opportunity cost* of not improving safety? If a company does not invest in improving the safety of its workforce the morale of the workforce will gradually decline, as they perceive that their safety is not a high priority for their company. They may decide to strike over the issue; new people would be dissuaded from joining; more enterprising employees might leave to go elsewhere; the company's image in the community might suffer. Primarily we will be discussing the financial aspects of investment appraisal in the rest of this book, but qualitative aspects are important, especially when selling an investment proposal internally.

Sometimes *Cost–Benefit Analysis* is used as an alternative description for investment appraisal. However, strictly speaking, it is the term used for the wider investment appraisals conducted by public bodies when considering, for example, whether a new bypass should be built or a hospital extended. They take into account all interested parties such as users, employees, local government and so on. Cost–Benefit Analysis is looked at briefly in Chapter 4.

CHECKLIST OF PRACTICAL TIPS

This chapter has concentrated on issues requiring consideration before the investment appraisal takes place and on giving an overview of investment selection.

1 Before investment appraisal begins, ask yourself the following questions:
- Does the investment fit the strategic direction of the company?
- Does the company have any budgetary constraints?
- Is there a way to improve the attractiveness of the investment even further?
- Have I considered the broader environmental aspects of this investment?
- Can the search process be improved to ensure a continuous stream of good quality investment proposals?

2 Depending on your answers to the above questions, you must decide how much time you should spend on the investment evaluation. Other factors which will influence that decision will be:
- How large is the possible benefit to the company?
- Is the investment within the scope of the capital budget? If not, is there a possibility that the capital budget can be increased?

There are four components to assess when conducting an investment appraisal using the Net Present Value method: the initial cash outflow or investment cost; the net cash inflows; the lifespan of the project; and the cost of capital.

CHAPTER TWO

Using Net Present Value (NPV)

- The four components of investment appraisal

- Introducing the jargon – the time value of money and present values

- Understanding the NPV method

- Short cuts

- Setting criteria for any investment appraisal technique

- Why managers don't use NPV

CHECKLIST OF KEY POINTS

1 There are four main components to assess in the Net Present Value method: the initial cash outflow or investment cost; the net cash inflows; the lifespan of the investment, and the cost of capital.

2 The Net Present Value method compares today's cash outlay with future cash inflows coming from the investment, by converting the future cash inflows into today's currency i.e. converting them into their *present values*. This is done by discounting the cashflows at their *opportunity cost of capital*.

3 The opportunity cost of capital is the market interest rate prevailing for investments of a similar risk profile.

4 The Net Present Value is found by taking the present values of the future cash inflows and adding these to the investment cost. If the NPV is positive, this investment will add to shareholder wealth as it earns a greater return than shareholders could earn elsewhere. The present values represent the market price for the investment and a positive NPV indicates that the investment is worth more than the company has to pay for it, that is, the initial capital outlay.

5 Every investment appraisal method should take into account the time value of money; the risk of the investment and the whole of the economic life of the investment. It should be an objective measurement and it should focus on cashflows rather than accounting profit.

Introduction

In Chapters 2 and 3, we will be concentrating on reviewing the methods of investment appraisal. In Chapters 4 to 9, the inputs into the investment appraisal process will be considered.

The four components of investment appraisal

There are four components to assess when conducting an investment appraisal using the Net Present Value method: the initial cash outflow or investment cost; the net cash inflows; the lifespan of the project; and the cost of capital (see Figure 2.1).

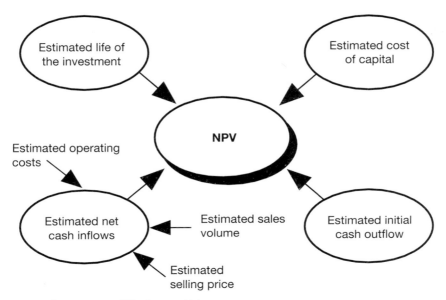

Figure 2.1   Components of Net Present Value

The initial cash outflow

In most investments there is an initial cash outflow as money is spent on plant or equipment, on training the labour force, on marketing a new product. This may take place during one year or there may be two or three years of cash outflow, if it is a sizeable or phased investment. If machinery needs replacing during the lifetime of the investment, there may be an additional one-off cash outflow once the investment is underway. At the end of the investment's life, any residual value

An important component of the initial cash outflow will be the initial *working capital* requirements.

in the capital investment is shown as a cash inflow either in the last year or the following year depending on how easy it will be to sell the assets.

An important component of the initial cash outflow will be the initial *working capital* requirements. The working capital is the additional resource that is needed to get the investment started, before the cash inflows from the investment begin. For example, if the investment project is an expansion of an existing product line, new stock has to be bought and some of the initial purchases are made on credit thus tying up the company's resources even more. This working capital resource is shown as a cash *inflow* at the end of the economic life of the project when those resources are released for use elsewhere. This is usually included in the last year of cashflows under the assumption that stocks will be gradually depleted towards the end of the investment's life and debtors will pay soon after the last year-end.

Net cash inflows

After one or two years of operation, the company will expect to see a net inflow of cash resulting from the investment project. This net inflow is the additional revenue coming from the investment minus the additional running costs. The running costs will be the direct costs together with any additional tax burden as this is also a cashflow. (Of course not all investments will have this pattern of cashflows – an investment by a pharmaceutical company to research a promising compound will have several years of cash outflow before any resulting net cash inflows.) As the investment project expands there may be further changes in working capital requirements of the investment. For example, as sales increase we can expect to see a similar increase in credit sales that will delay the inflow of cash into the business.

Note: In Chapter 3 when discussing the Net Present Value method and other appraisal methods, the periodic cashflows generated by an investment will be examined. These cashflows can be estimated for regular intervals throughout the investment's life, for example, every year or every month. Unless otherwise specified, we will assume that cashflows are estimated on a **yearly** basis.

In most of the examples used in the first few chapters of this book, investment is described as occurring in Year Zero and by this we mean occurring at the end of Year Zero (or the beginning of Year One). The first year of cash inflows is shown as occurring in Year One and taken to be all the cash inflows occurring during the year.

Depreciation

It is important to mention depreciation briefly at this stage. We will return to it in Chapter 4, when we look at cashflows in more detail. Depreciation is an accounting concept that seeks to apportion the costs of a major capital outlay over the economic life of that investment. Typically an investment is depreciated over a set number of years and a depreciation expense is added to the profit and loss account after running expenses. However, in investment appraisal we are looking at *cash* outflows and *cash* inflows and so we must ignore depreciation. We have already included the full cost of the initial investment in Year Zero – if we added depreciation to our operating expenses, we would be double-counting. The net cash inflows are just that – *cash* inflows and not accounting profit.

'Opportunity' costs

In some cases of expansion or diversification investment projects, the cash inflows may be actual increases in cash – the business has expanded and there is more money coming into the business than before the investment took place. However, in many cases the cash inflow that you are trying to measure is the flow of cash compared with the *alternative state of nature*. What do I mean by this? If a company is considering building a factory on a piece of land that it already owns, it must consider what it would do with the land if it did not build the factory. If it sold the land, then the market value of that land should be considered an opportunity cost. This is the forgone cash inflow that would occur if the investment does not take place. Similarly, an investment in machinery may result in cost savings. These are costs that would occur if the investment does not take place. Fully appreciating the 'opportunity costs' is an important component of investment appraisal, and is further explored in Chapter 4.

The lifespan of the investment

This depends on the investment's physical, economic and technological life. Some investments have a fixed life of a certain number of years. Others can go on indefinitely, for example, a new product introduction. In such cases, you can take one of two approaches:

- You can take the investment project life as being the plant or factory life used to make the new product. If you believe the product life will be shorter than the plant life, you can include a residual value for the plant in your final year of cashflows.

- You can forecast the cashflows for the first six to eight years and then use a terminal value to assess the worth of the new product investment in the later years. Chapter 9 looks in detail at how to assess the terminal value of an investment.

The cost of capital

Many words are used to describe the cost of capital. Investment appraisal methods, such as the Net Present Value method, use the term 'discount rate'. Others use the opportunity cost of capital. Once the cost of capital for an investment has been determined by a company (dealt with in detail in Chapters 7 and 8), it is often called the 'hurdle rate' or the 'minimum required rate of return'. I think the *opportunity* cost of capital is a good way to think of it, because that is exactly what it is. It corresponds to the market rate of interest for an investment, with a similar risk level. In Chapter 1, we discussed that any new investment must earn a return which at least compensates the shareholder for the lost opportunity to invest their money elsewhere, either on the capital markets, or in other non-financial assets. If new investments do not earn a return that matches this market return, they should take their money and invest it themselves.

Introducing the jargon – the time value of money and present values

Investments in new projects do not take place in a vacuum. In order to be able to evaluate whether an investment project is worth investing in, we must have a way of comparing the future returns of the investment with the initial capital outlay, in other words, a way of converting different values into a common currency. We must also have alternatives with which to compare the investment project. A comparison of alternatives is not necessarily a comparison of two different investment projects but rather a consideration of what the alternative uses for the capital would be if the investment did not take place.

We need to know whether having a certain stream of cashflows in future years is worth the investment we are putting in today. One way of doing this is to ask: if you could have £1 today or more than £1 in a year's time, how much more would you have to receive for you to be *indifferent* between taking £1 today and waiting a year for the larger amount? Your answer will partly be determined by the perceived risk of not receiving the money tomorrow and the alternative uses you may have for £1 today.

Compound interest and discounting

The interest rate is the exchange rate between money in today's currency and money in tomorrow's currency. It acts as the means of conversion between different time periods. The Net Present Value model seeks to bring all future cashflows back into today's money so that they can be compared with the capital outlay made today. It does this by *discounting*. Discounting can be seen as the corollary of compound interest. If £62.10 were invested for five years at an interest rate of 10 per cent, it would be worth £100 in Year Five. This is because it earns compound interest, that is interest on the initial sum invested and interest on the interest already accrued. The formula is shown as:

Money in Year Five = (Money in Year Zero) × (1 + interest rate) no. of years

$$= £62.10 \times (1 + 0.1)^5$$
$$= £100$$

If one wanted to take the £100 that is received in Year Five and convert it back to what you would have to invest in Year Zero, the inverse is taken:

$$\text{Money in Year Zero} = \frac{\text{Money in Year Five}}{(1 = \text{interest rate})^5}$$

$$= £100/(1 + 0.1)^5$$
$$= £62.10$$

$$\frac{£100}{(1+0.1)^5} = £62.10$$

25

This can be shown graphically (see Figure 2.2).

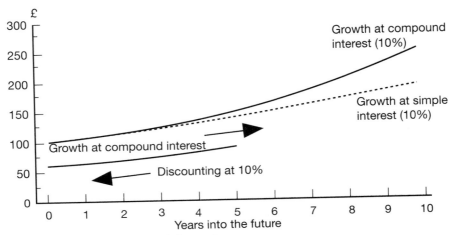

Figure 2.2   Compound interest and discounting

The inverse of the discount rate is called the *discount factor*.

$$\text{Discount factor} = \frac{1}{(1 + r)}$$

The concept of present value

By using discounting at an appropriate rate, we can convert future cash inflows into their equivalent worth today – their present value.

$$\text{Present Value} = \text{Cashflow in future} \times \text{Discount factor}$$

Thus the present value of £100 received in one year's time if the discount rate is 10 per cent is:

Present value   = £100 × 0.909

       = £90.90

(Discount factor   = $1/(1+10\%) = 0.901$)

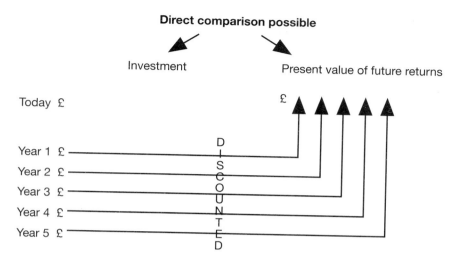

Figure 2.3   The basic model

Understanding the NPV method

The method

The Net Present Value method is a very simple process:

■ First the initial cash outflow is estimated.

■ Then the periodic net cashflows which will result from the project are calculated.

■ If the project does not have a discrete end, a *terminal value* is calculated and added to the last year's cashflow or the following year depending on when this flow of money will be realised.

■ An opportunity cost of capital is calculated and used as the discount rate (see later).

■ These cashflows, including the terminal value, are then discounted back to their equivalent present value using the formula below.

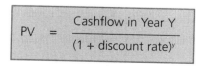

$$PV = \frac{\text{Cashflow in Year Y}}{(1 + \text{discount rate})^y}$$

- The sum of all the present values of the future cashflows is calculated and added to the initial investment and this sum is called the Net Present Value.

$$\text{Net Present Value*} = -C^0 + \frac{C^1}{(1+r)^1} + \frac{C^2}{(1+r)^2} + \frac{C^3}{(1+r)^3} + \frac{C^4}{(1+r)^4}$$

* where C = cashflow.

- If the Net Present Value is positive, this indicates that we should accept the investment project as it will add to shareholders' wealth. The present value represents the market price for the investment and thus a positive NPV suggests that the company will pay less, in terms of capital outlay, than the investment project is worth.

Why can we make this last assumption? We have chosen a discount rate that represents the opportunity cost of capital, i.e. at this rate of return, shareholders could have taken their money and invested in other shares, with a similar risk, and recouped their initial investment. By not only recouping the initial investment, but adding to it (the present value of future cashflows exceeded the initial investment), we have earned a greater return than shareholders could earn anywhere else and thus increased their wealth.

Simplifying assumptions

You will realise that we have made some assumptions which simplify the process. These assumptions will be relaxed gradually as we add some of the complexities that inevitably accompany investments in the real world. For now, we have made three critical assumptions:

- Firstly, we have assumed that there is no inflation and no taxation. These assumptions will be relaxed in Chapter 4 onwards.

- Secondly, all cashflows are assumed to be known, measurable and certain. This is the case both for the initial capital outlay and the resulting cash inflows from the investment. These assumptions will be relaxed in Chapter 5 onwards.

- Thirdly, the opportunity cost of capital or discount rate is also assumed to be already calculated. In the worked examples we will refer to the discount rate as given. This assumption will be relaxed in Chapter 7.

The mechanics of discounting

Before we look at some worked examples, let us examine the different ways of carrying out the NPV calculations – the mechanics of the process. To discount future cashflows back to present values, you can use a number of methods:

- Firstly, you can use the formula given above and your calculator. This will give you a good feel for what you are doing, and it is worth working through a couple of examples in this way. However, it is very laborious and there are much quicker ways of doing it!

- You can use the PV factor tables (which appear in the appendices) to give you the present value of £1 at various discount rates and over different years. So to find the present value of £100 in five years' time at a discount rate of 10 per cent, you look up the PV factor which is 0.621 and multiply this by 100 to get £62.10.

- You can key in the 'ingredients' of the formula (the investment, the yearly cashflows and the discount rate) into a financial calculator and this will calculate the NPV for you.

- You can set up a *very simple* computer model. However, most computer spreadsheet packages now have a formula for NPV. For example in Lotus 123 you type:

@ NPV (discount rate; range of annual cashflows)

The Lotus formula provides the present value of the cashflows. You add the initial capital outlay in Year Zero to obtain the Net Present Value.

- Finally, if you have a set of identical net cashflows for each year, you can use a short cut method that I will outline in the next section.

Example

Bearings Ltd is considering whether to invest in a new plant to make ball bearings. The initial cost outlay will be £750,000 and the increased cashflows coming from the plant are shown below. It is assumed that the plant will be redundant after five years as new technological developments will require an investment in new plant and equipment. Bearings Ltd estimates that the machinery will have a scrap value of £60,000 and that the building can be sold for warehousing for £70,000. Both of these transactions will take place in Year Six. Assuming a discount rate of 10 per cent, the model sets out the calculation as follows:

Year	Investment	Cashflows	PV factors	Present values
0	−£750,000		1.000	−£750,000
1		£300,000	0.909	£272,700
2		£280,000	0.826	£231,280
3		£220,000	0.751	£165,220
4		£170,000	0.683	£116,110
5		£120,000	0.621	£74,520
6		£130,000	0.564	£73,320
Net Present Value				£183,150

As the Net Present Value is positive, this is an investment project that the company should strongly consider approving, if there are no capital budget restrictions.

Short cuts

Short Cut 1: Identical cashflows in each year

There is a short cut which makes calculating the Net Present Value of an investment even simpler *but it only works if cashflows from different years are identical* as in Figure 2.4.

One of the other properties of the NPV model is that present values are additive. As this is the case, it follows that the PV factors that are used to calculate the present values are also additive. By adding the PV factors together and multiplying the annual cashflow by this *cumulative PV factor*, the present value for all these cashflows is calculated.

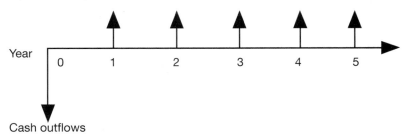

Figure 2.4   Identical cashflows or annuities

Take the cashflows given below:

Year	Cashflow	PV factors at 15%	Present values
1	£40,000	0.870	£34,800
2	£40,000	0.756	£30,240
3	£40,000	0.658	£26,320
4	£40,000	0.572	£22,880
		2.856	£114,240

You will note that if you multiply £40,000 by the cumulative PV factor 2.856 (0.870 + 0.756 + 0.658 + 0.572), you will reach the same answer – £114,240 – as if you calculated the present value of each year's cashflow and added them together.

Your task is made even simpler by cumulative present value tables or annuity tables (see the appendices). Remember you can only take this short cut if the cashflows are the same each year. This will probably only happen in specific cases such as lease payments for a piece of machinery or plant.

Example

QuickStore Ltd is considering whether to sell a warehouse that is surplus to their needs now for £100,000 or to lease the warehouse for three years at £20,000 per year and then sell it in four years' time for £80,000. The discount rate has been calculated as 9 per cent. When considering whether they should lease the warehouse or not, they should consider the alternative, i.e. selling the warehouse now for £100,000, as an *opportunity cost*. They have forgone the option of selling the warehouse for that price if they lease it. Thus when considering the lease, the £100,000 is seen as a cash outflow.

Year	Cashflows	PV factor	Present values
0	−£100,000	1.000	− £100,000
1 to 3	£20,000	2.531	£50,620
4	£80,000	0.708	£56,640
Net Present Value			£7,260

QuickStore Ltd would be better off by £7,260 if they lease the warehouse and sell it later rather than selling it now.

Short Cut 2: Investments which have no foreseeable end

Some investments do not have a foreseeable end to their economic life. For example, a new product extension to a well-known brand might be considered to be an investment with no clear end to its economic life, or an investment in a charitable trust for employees or the local community. A company wishing to invest in an educational trust for the local community that would generate a certain amount per year in scholarships and bursaries, is in an identical situation to a company wanting to invest in perpetuity (a bond that offers a fixed income every year in perpetuity). How much would they need to invest to ensure that this future income will always be available and will not run out? The return on a perpetuity bond is:

$$\text{Return} = \frac{\text{Cashflow}}{\text{Present value}}$$

Thus the cost of the investment (or the present value of the investment) can be reformulated from the formula above as:

$$\text{Present value of the investment} = \frac{\text{Cashflow}}{\text{Return}}$$

The company may wish to take into account the likely average inflation rate so that the real value of the annual scholarship fund does not decrease over time. If the rate of return is greater than the inflation rate (or growth rate), the formula can be restated as:

$$\text{Present value of the investment} = \frac{\text{Cashflow}}{\text{Return} - \text{growth rate}}$$

Example

Benefacto Ltd has decided that it wants to put something back into the local community. It decides that a trust fund, which provides money on an annual basis for sports events in the community, would be an appropriate investment. It wants to provide £20,000 per year growing at an average rate of 4 per cent per year in perpetuity. Its opportunity cost of capital is 12 per cent. The money it will have to invest to achieve its trust fund goal is as follows:

$$\text{Present value} = \text{Investment} = \frac{£20,000}{(12\% - 4\%)} = £250,000$$

Calculation of an annuity from a perpetuity

Earlier on we introduced the concept of annuities through the back door, when we discussed investments which had identical cashflows for a set period. You can use cumulative PV factors to calculate the value of these annuities (which is why they are also called annuity factors). Clearly, annuities are related to perpetuities. Benefacto Ltd could have decided to set up a trust fund for a limited period of time, say 15 years, rather than in perpetuity. One way of calculating the investment required for this would be to use annuity or cumulative PV factors. The discount rate is 12 per cent and the growth rate is 4 per cent which leaves an adjusted discount rate of 8 per cent.

Cumulative PV factor at 8% for 15 years is 8.559
Investment = £20,000 x 8.599 = £171,180

Another way to look at annuities is as the difference between two perpetuities; one perpetuity that begins now and one perpetuity that begins in 15 years' time. The difference is an annuity for 15 years.

$$\text{Present value} = \text{Cashflow} = \frac{1}{r} - \frac{1}{r\,(1+r)^t}$$

Taking this formula, we have already calculated the present value of a perpetuity beginning today (£250,000). The value of a perpetuity beginning in 15 years is:

$$\text{Present value} = \frac{£20,000}{(8\%)(1+8\%)^{15}} = £78,820$$

Thus the cost of annuity is £250,000 minus £78,820 = £171,180.

Short Cut 3: For alternative timing of cashflows

So far we have assumed that the annual cashflows are achieved throughout the year and are converted back to their present values. However, this is not always realistic. Take the example of an investment that lasts one year. The initial cash outflow of £100,000 results in a regular cash inflow every month of £10,000. The discount rate on an annual basis is 12 per cent. We can take each month to be the discounting interval rather than each year. Instead of having one present value for the year, we would now have 12 present values, one for each month.

This is shown graphically in Figure 2.5.

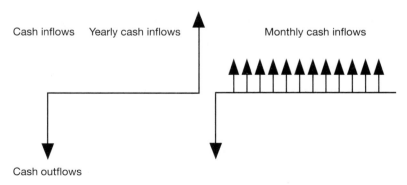

Figure 2.5   Using different time periods

The discount rate for each month would be the annual discount rate divided by 12 months and, in this case, it would be 1 per cent per month. Let us compare the NPV on an annual basis and on a monthly basis.

Year	Yearly cashflows	PV factor	PV	Monthly cashflows		PV annuity factor	PV
0	£100,000	1.000	£100,000	0	£100,000	1.000	£100,000
1	£120,000	0.893	£107,160	1–12	£10,000	11.26	£112,600
NPV			£7,160				£12,600

By discounting the monthly cash inflows rather than the annual cash inflow, the Net Present Value of the investment project increased from £7,160 to £12,600.

You may wish to be more precise than annual discount rates allow, if you need to be very accurate and precise in your calculations or if you *know* that the cashflows will be coming in at monthly intervals during the year for example.

Be careful. Usually you do not need to be this accurate in the mechanics of discounting, as so many other elements of the process, such as the cashflow forecasts themselves, are unlikely to be completely accurate. Also, by adding this level of sophistication, you are making the NPV method more complex and therefore more difficult to explain to other people. **Wherever possible, keep it simple!**

Setting criteria for any investment appraisal technique

Given what has been said about investment evaluation so far, some broad rules can be made by which *any investment appraisal method can be evaluated.*

- It should take into account the time value of money. In other words it must have some way of comparing cashflows at different times in a similar 'currency'.

- It should take into account the risk of the project and calculate an opportunity cost of capital that reflects the interest rate achievable in the capital markets for an investment with a *similar risk level.*

■ It should take into account the whole of the economic life of the investment, that is, attribute value not only to the early years of the investment but also to the later years and the end of the investment's useful life.

Given what has been said about investment evaluation so far, some broad rules can be made by which any investment appraisal method can be evaluated.

■ It should be an objective measurement, that is to say, not based on arbitrary rules set by management which depend on their personal attitude to risk, on their remuneration system or simply on *past* performance rather than *best* performance.

■ Finally, it must focus on cashflows rather than accounting profit so that the attractiveness of a project is not obscured by the accounting conventions used by a particular firm.

Why managers don't use NPV

In this chapter, I have set out the basic model of Net Present Value. It is a logical and straightforward model and one that can cope with a number of additional complexities as later chapters will demonstrate. Yet, in many studies conducted during the last few years, it has been shown that discounted cashflow methods such as Net Present Value or Internal Rate of Return (discussed in the next chapter) are not used by the majority of managers in assessing potential investment projects. The vast majority of UK managers still prefer to use the Payback method or Accounting Rate of Return. The next chapter identifies the strengths and the many weaknesses of such approaches but the empirical evidence shows that the *perceived* strengths make them satisfactory methods. Why? To put it simply – *they are easy to understand and they are easy to use.*

The Net Present Value method is often made to seem more complex and elaborate than it should be. This is not necessary and makes it more difficult for the investment appraiser to sell the investment proposal to senior management. The section on practical tips below gives some ideas on how to ensure that your NPV analysis is seen as straightforward and simple to understand.

Flow chart summary

The flow chart (Figure 2.6) summarises some of the questions which should have been generated by this chapter. Make sure that you have an answer for each of them before reading the next chapter.

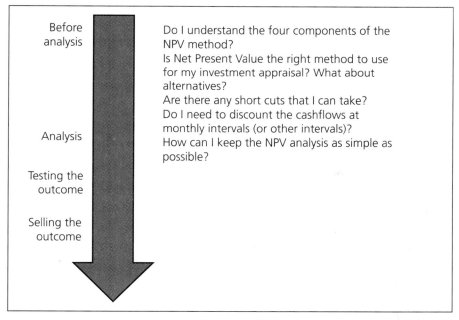

Before analysis

Do I understand the four components of the NPV method?
Is Net Present Value the right method to use for my investment appraisal? What about alternatives?
Are there any short cuts that I can take?
Do I need to discount the cashflows at monthly intervals (or other intervals)?
How can I keep the NPV analysis as simple as possible?

Analysis

Testing the outcome

Selling the outcome

Figure 2.6   Flow diagram for investment appraisal

CASE STUDY 2.1

James Williams has been asked to evaluate the attractiveness of a new investment idea. Williams & Jenkins Ltd sell a range of industrial equipment to large corporate clients. They are considering offering leasing contracts on a bi-annual basis to certain key customers. James has spent some time compiling all the relevant information that he needs to build a simple cashflow model, and that information is

> The cost of capital is 12 per cent for this investment and the economic life of the lease will be five years.

Cashflows

H0	(£200,000)
H1	£20,000	← *A lower lease payment while any teething problems are sorted out*
H2	£30,000
H3	£40,000
H4	£40,000
H5	£40,000
H6	£40,000
H7	£40,000
H8	£40,000
H9	£40,000
H10	£40,000

H = Half a year.

Solution

As the lease payments will be coming in every six months, it is more appropriate to use six months as the discounting period rather than one year. Thus instead of using 12 per cent as the discount factor we will use 6 per cent. We can also make use of the cumulative PV factors for the cashflows in H3 to H10 as they are identical.

The calculation is as follows:

Half year	Cashflows	PV factor	Present values
H0	(£200,000)	1.000	(£200,000)
H1	£20,000	0.943	£18,860
H2	£30,000	0.890	£26,700
H3 to H10	£40,000	5.527	£221,080
NPV			£66,640

How to calculate the cumulative PV factor

The cumulative factor for H3 to H10 is *not* 6 per cent for eight periods. That would be assuming that the company was going to get £40,000 every six months starting *now*. Rather, to calculate the cumulative PV factor required for H3 to H10, you take the cumulative PV factor for ten periods and take the cumulative PV factor for two periods to get the equivalent cumulative PV factor for three to ten periods:

$$7.360 - 1.833 = 5.527.$$

A short review of the theory behind the Net Present Value technique

So far I have discussed the Net Present Value method as if it were merely a logical and commonsense approach to investment appraisal. However, as you may find that it is not the only, or even the most common, method of appraisal in your own company, it is worthwhile demonstrating that it is soundly based on the economic theory of consumption and investment.

The capital market and consumption patterns

The Net Present Value method assumes the existence of efficient capital markets. The existence of capital markets allows people to spend or save their money as they wish. It allows for the transfer of money across time, through the use of interest rates. By enabling people to trade money today for money tomorrow (lending), or money tomorrow for money today (borrowing), it releases people from the obligation of matching their current consumption to their current cashflow. This can be demonstrated with the aid of a diagram.

In Figure 2.7, current cashflow is indicated by AD and the cashflow that will be received in one year's time is indicated by AB. The Capital Market Line is the line CE. Its slope shows the rate of exchange between money today and money in one year's time and its slope represents $1 + r$ where r is the one-year interest rate. Someone with current cashflow AD and future cashflow AB can choose to trade some or all of these resources *in either direction* along the Capital Market Line. Thus if a person wishes to save all their money, he or she can reduce current expenditure to zero and trade it on the capital market to maximise their money later. In one year's time they will have increased their money by BC on the diagram, which equates to AD(1+r). On the other hand, if a person wishes to spend all their money today *and* borrow against the money they will receive in one year's time, they can also do so, and increase today's consumption by DE which equates to AB/(1+r).

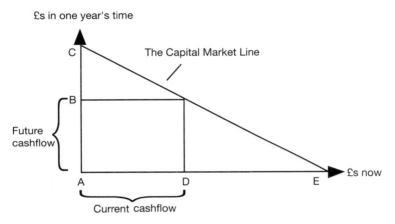

Figure 2.7   The Capital Market Line

Example

Let us take some real numbers and put these into an example. Figure 2.8 shows this graphically.

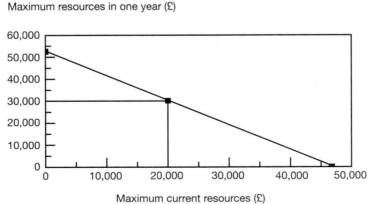

Figure 2.8   Worked example

Let us suppose that Jack Brown has resources of £20,000 today and resources of £30,000 in one year's time. The market interest rate is 10 per cent. He can lend his £20,000 now and get £20,000 × (1+0.10) = £22,000 in a year's time thus giving him total resources of £30,000 plus £22,000 = £52,000. Alternatively, he can borrow against the £30,000 he is going to receive next year and receive £30,000/(1+0.10) = £27,273 today which gives him total resources of £20,000 plus £27,273 = £47,273 today.

Investing in real assets

Individuals can also invest in real assets – land, machinery, buildings etc. This is shown by drawing an Investment Opportunities Line.

Unlike the Capital Market Line, the Investment Opportunities Line is not a straight line as the returns on investment projects get gradually lower as the *best* investments are taken up. The first investment may have a higher return than investing in the capital markets but as more and more investments are taken up, the pool of interesting projects starts to dry up and the returns get lower. This is the law of diminishing returns.

Figure 2.9 demonstrates this and shows how the first investment of £20,000 achieved a return in one year of £30,000. However the second investment of £20,000 only achieved a return of £15,000 and the third investment gained only £5,000. This process continues until there are no future returns for current investment opportunities.

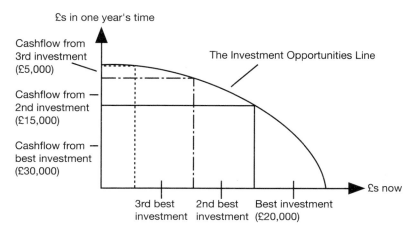

Figure 2.9   The Investment Opportunities Line

How can individuals gain from using both the capital markets and opportunities to invest in real assets?

It has already been established that an individual can attain any point on the line AE, the Capital Market Line, by a combination of consumption, saving or borrowing.

If the Capital Market Line and the Investment Opportunities Line are placed on the same diagram, it becomes clear that, by using the capital markets to borrow money and then using that money to invest in real assets, Jack Brown can earn a greater return than he can earn in the capital markets. He would be able to repay the money he owed at the market interest rate and still have money left over.

For example: Jack Brown has maximum resources of £47,273 today, partly by borrowing against future resources. If he invests DE of this money, which is worth £27,273, in real assets he can attain a better return (AF or £45,000) than if he lent it on the capital market (return of AB or £30,000). He can repay the money that he borrowed (AB) and be left with a profit of BF (£15,000) in one year's time which equates to EH (which is £15,000/(1 + 0.10) or £13,636) in today's money.

Figure 2.10 also demonstrates Net Present Value graphically. The maximum sum that could be realised today from the investment in the future cashflow is DH; this represents the *Present Value* of the investment. The maximum that this investment would cost would be DE. The difference between DH and DE is EH and this is the *Net Present Value* of the investment.

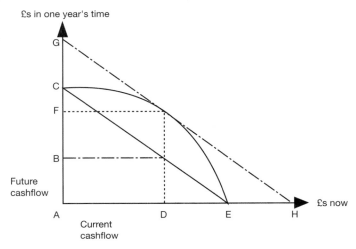

Figure 2.10   Maximising your resources

CHECKLIST OF PRACTICAL TIPS

There are many lessons to be learnt from examining why other methods are used which can be usefully incorporated into your investment appraisal analysis, using the Net Present Value method.

1 Don't complicate your NPV analysis. Always keep in mind what stage of the evaluation you have reached. Don't get bogged down in the finer details if this is merely the initial screen.

2 If it is the final analysis for a major investment proposal, you may wish to do a more thorough analysis, but concentrate only on the major points for the meeting. Keep the detail in reserve to be used to answer questions and to be incorporated in the report appendices.

3 Talk in the language that your reviewers understand. If they are used to looking at the payback time for projects, then having completed your analysis, and ensured that it is a project with a positive NPV, calculate how many years it will take to recoup the original investment (using discounted cashflows), and use this analysis. If they like to know the Internal Rate of Return, calculate this and use this to sell the project even though the analysis has been conducted using NPV methods rather than the Internal Rate of Return. (These methods are examined in the next chapter.)

Many companies use a range of appraisal methods to *evaluate* a project and another to *justify* the investment.

CHAPTER THREE

Using alternative appraisal methods

- The Payback method

- Improving on the Payback method: Discounted Payback

- The Average Return on Book Value method or Accounting Rate of Return

- The Internal Rate of Return (IRR) method

- The Profitability Index

- Ranking projects

- When to use each technique (or not at all!)

- Ranking projects under capital constraints

CHECKLIST OF KEY POINTS

1 In addition to NPV, there are four other appraisal methods which are commonly used: the Payback method and its variant, the Discounted Payback method; the Accounting Rate of Return; the Internal Rate of Return and the Profitability Index. Of these, Payback is the most commonly used with the IRR and the Profitability Index being the least popular.

2 The Payback method and the Accounting Rate of Return method have serious flaws in that they do not take the time value of money into account and they do not look at the full economic life of the investment.

3 Furthermore, the Accounting Rate of Return measures profitability and not cashflow and thus can be manipulated by changing accounting methods which have nothing to do with the underlying investment.

4 However, there is scope for using Discounted Payback at the early stages of an analysis, as a screening method. It is also useful when technological changes make forecasting cashflows after a set number of years highly speculative. In such cases, Discounted Payback can be seen as a form of truncated Net Present Value analysis.

5 The IRR and the Profitability Index use the discounted cashflow approach which is also used by the NPV method. They give less than perfect results when mutually exclusive projects, or investment projects of differing size and scope, are being considered.

6 One of the potential drawbacks of the NPV method is that it favours large investments over smaller ones. For this reason, the Profitability method is the preferred method of appraisal when the company is under a budget constraint and investment projects have to be chosen which maximise the overall Net Present Value.

7 Although the Net Present Value method is the most robust method, with the above exception, the use of phrases such as the 'rate of return' and the 'payback period' are good communication tools when selling an investment project to senior management.

Introduction

A study of UK companies conducted by Pike and Wolfe in 1986 discovered that over 90 per cent of managers use methods other than NPV to evaluate new investments whilst only 68 per cent of managers use Net Present Value. Many companies use a range of appraisal methods, choosing one method to *evaluate* a project and another method to *justify* the investment. Let us review some of the most commonly used methods so that you can draw your own conclusions as to their attractions, but also as to their viability as robust tools for appraisal. We will start with the simplest.

The Payback method

Outline

Some companies require that an investment should be recouped within a specified time
– one that has been decided upon by senior management prior to the investment
proposal. For example, it may have been decided that four years will be taken as *the
payback cut-off point*. This decision rule is usually decided upon after reviewing past
experience of successful investments. Or it may be based on the management's opinion
of the forecasting accuracy of later cashflows. An investment is put forward for review
which outlines the likely cash investment and cash outflows, together with their timing.
The payback period of this project is calculated by adding together the cash inflows from
successive years until the cumulative cash inflow is the same or more than the cash
outlay required – the cash outflow. If the payback period is less than or equal to four
years, then the project is accepted.

CASE STUDY 3.1

Easy Company Ltd is reviewing a proposal for investment in some machinery. It has an
investment decision rule that all investment projects must show a payback on the
original capital outlay in three years. This investment project is for a piece of machinery
which will speed up the production of their supercharged widgets. The investment and
the resulting cash savings are shown below:

Year		Investment	Cash savings
	0	£50,000	
	1		£15,000
	2		£20,000
	3		£25,000
Total		£50,000	£60,000

The project will recoup the £50,000 investment within three years and so the
management decide to undertake the project.

A critique

In the Pike and Wolfe study, as in many other recent surveys, the Payback method was used by approximately 90 per cent of the companies in some capacity. Payback has a number of advantages. It is very easy to understand and to explain to other people. It requires the proposer to consider and collect only the forecasts of the initial capital outlay and estimated cash inflows in the next few years, typically no more than five years. It gives a 'result' very quickly without much analysis needed. (There is no need to compute a discount rate for example.) Finally if forecasts into the future are unlikely to be accurate, due to rapid technological change for example, it is considered 'less risky' because it is only taking into account those cashflows which are easier to forecast well.

However its disadvantages outweigh the advantages cited above and hopefully are fairly obvious to you as well. In Chapter 2 we concluded that any good appraisal method will incorporate the following features:

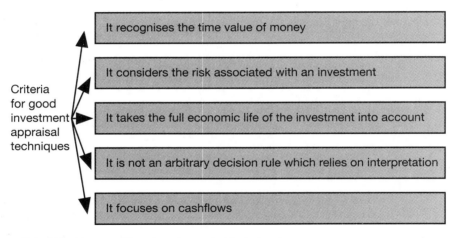

Figure 3.1   What is a good investment appraisal technique?

The Payback method seems to conflict with four out of five of these criteria!

■ Payback takes no account of the time value of money. That is to say it assumes that, if a company has an investment decision rule which sets payback on projects at, say, four years, the company will be indifferent as to whether its investment is recouped in the first year of the project or the third year of the project.

■ It ignores any cashflows which might occur outside the 'Four-Year Rule'. Thus it may reject a very lucrative project, in favour of a less profitable one, because the former recoups its investment over a six-year period whilst the latter recoups much less cash, but within the four-year payback period.

■ The payback period automatically favours short-term over long-term investment. Ideally a company should have a range of investment projects with differing time horizons, thus retaining a flexible approach to new opportunities while capitalising on long-term projects, which ensures that the company keeps pace with technological or other research developments that affect its future viability.

■ Payback does not have clear decision criteria as to whether to accept or reject an investment project. The cut-off point is ambiguous. For example, when is the investment stage of a project considered to be finished? When the investment project begins to generate cash or automatically after the first year? This ambiguity leads to subjective decision-making rather than clear-cut decision rules.

■ Furthermore, the concept that Payback is 'less risky' is misleading. The opportunity cost of capital takes into account the increased risks associated with forecasting in future years whereas Payback just ignores these cashflows altogether. This is not 'less risky' just more inaccurate!

Improving on the Payback method: Discounted Payback

Outline

This appraisal method takes the basic structure of the Payback method, and then deals with one of the major disadvantages of that method by discounting the future cash inflows at an appropriate discount rate. Thus the initial investment is compared with future cashflows given in today's money. The cut-off decision rule remains and it is wholly at the management's discretion to choose three, four or any number of years as the cut-off point.

CASE STUDY 3.2

Taking the example of Easy Company Ltd given earlier, they have now decided to use a Discounted Payback method to evaluate this project. The discount rate has been set by the company at 10 per cent.

		Cashflows	PV factor	Present value
Year	0	−£50,000	1.000	−£50,000
	1	£15,000	0.909	£13,635
	2	£20,000	0.826	£16,520
	3	£25,000	0.751	£18,775
Total				−£1,070

Using this method the project does not recoup the £50,000 investment within three years. The present value of the three years of cash inflows is only £48,930 (£1,070 short of the initial investment) and so the management decides not to undertake this project.

A critique

Although this appraisal method is a considerable improvement on straight Payback, it still ignores the economic life of the potential investment after the arbitrary cut-off point. Taking the last example – under their three year cut-off rule, Easy Company Ltd rejected the project. But the economic life of that piece of machinery was not necessarily three years. It would only have needed to bring in another £1,567 in incremental cashflows in Year Four (which equates to £1,070 when discounted back with a discount factor of 0.683), to recoup the full investment. This may be very feasible but it is ignored by Easy Company Ltd.

However, there is a role for the Discounted Cashflow method. In Chapter 1, the importance of tailoring the amount of effort that goes into the analysis to the stage of evaluation was highlighted. At the initial stages of evaluation, a quick estimate of the initial investment, the early incremental cashflows together with the company discount or hurdle rate normally used will give you enough to determine whether this is an investment project that deserves more analysis. In this way you do not have to spend time estimating later cashflows or salvage/scrap values before you know that it looks promising.

A second occasion when you may wish to use Discounted Payback is when an industry is undergoing such technological change that a new product may be obsolete after a few years. In this case taking cashflows for only three or four years (or whatever is the maximum period that the company thinks it can be sure of a cash inflow), and using the Discounted Cashflow method is appropriate. However, this is exactly the same as using the Net Present Value method and saying that the economic life is no more than four years! In this case, the Discounted Payback method should be viewed as a truncated form of the Net Present Value method.

The Average Return on Book Value method or Accounting Rate of Return

Outline

An alternative to Payback is to look at the Average Return on the Book Value of the investment. This method goes by a number of names: Return on Investment (ROI), Return on Capital Employed, Accounting Rate of Return and so on, which can lead to confusion in itself.

The average forecasted profits of an investment project, after depreciation and taxes, are divided by the average book value of the investment. This method, or a variant of it, is used by over half of the companies interviewed by Pike and Wolfe and by Drury *et al.*

$$\text{Return on book value} = \frac{\text{Average profits of the investment}}{\text{Average book value of the investment}}$$

CASE STUDY 3.3

Tradecloth Ltd, a company selling cloth to the clothing industry, is considering investing in an expansion of its activities, to sell throughout the country rather than in just one region. There will be a considerable investment in plant and equipment to increase production, and in its fleet of vans which distribute the cloth to its customers. In return Tradecloth Ltd has forecast substantial increases in profitability. The increases in Tradecloth's book value and net profits are given below:

Book value	Year 0	Year 1	Year 2	Year 3
Gross book value of the investment	£100,000	£100,000	£100,000	£100,000
Depreciation*		£20,000	£20,000	£20,000
Accumulated depreciation		£20,000	£40,000	£60,000
Net book value of the investment	£100,000	£80,000	£60,000	£40,000

Average book value = £280,000 divided by 4 = £70,000

* assumes a five-year single declining depreciation period

Profits	Year 1	Year 2	Year 3
Revenue	£40,000	£50,000	£100,000
Costs	£15,000	£16,000	£25,000
Cashflow (Revenue – Costs)	£25,000	£34,000	£75,000
Depreciation	£20,000	£20,000	£20,000
Net profit	£5,000	£14,000	£55,000

$$\text{Average book rate of return} = \frac{\text{Average annual income}}{\text{Average annual investment}} = \frac{£24,670}{£70,000} = 35.2\%$$

A critique

The advantage of the Return on Book Value method is that it is a familiar concept to managers. When discussing an interesting project in broad outline with a colleague, their first question may well be 'So what's its return on investment?' But herein lies a problem. The Return on Investment is an ambiguous phrase and will be interpreted differently by different adherents – some people will calculate the Average Return on average Capital Employed (in other words the capital outlay together with retained earnings); others will calculate the return on the *initial* capital employed (in other words just the initial capital outlay).

The Average Return on Book Value (or Investment or Capital Employed) method has a multitude of flaws. It is worth looking at this in more detail because these flaws are not so glaringly obvious as in the case of the Payback method.

As with Payback, this method does not take into account the time value of money, i.e. that early forecasted profits are worth more than later profits. In the example above, the increase in revenue, and hence cashflow and net profit, occurred gradually over three years. If these flows were discounted to take into account the time value of money, then the average profit shown would be much lower. By averaging both forecasted profits and book value, this important distinction is lost.

The advantage of the Return on Book Value method is that it is a familiar concept to managers. When discussing an interesting project in broad outline with a colleague, their first question may well be 'So what's its return on investment?' But herein lies a problem.

I have used the term *Accounting* Rate of Return to remind you that the forecasted profits depend, not only on the underlying cash generation, but also on the accounting systems that the company uses, such as which depreciation methods they use, or how they account for their inventories. For example, by using a different valuation method for inventories, a company would be able to reduce the book value of the investment and so enhance the perceived return on book value even though there had been no underlying change in the attractiveness of the investment. Accounting decisions such as these will affect both the profit forecasts and the book value, but have nothing to do with cashflow generation. They are statistical illusions – they do not indicate whether a particular project is a good or a bad investment.

Taking the example given above, if the company used an accelerated form of depreciation, rather than straight depreciation as given in the initial example, the average book value and the average net profit would both be restated with an accompanying change in the rate of return calculated from 35.2 per cent to 37.2 per cent. But *nothing would have changed* – it would still be the same underlying investment opportunity generating the same cashflows.

Book value	Year 0	Year 1	Year 2	Year 3
Gross book value of the investment	£100,000	£100,000	£100,000	£100,000
Depreciation*		£25,000	£18,750	£14,060
Accumulated depreciation (accelerated)		£25,000	£43,750	£57,810
Net book value of the investment	£100,000	£75,000	£56,250	£42,190

Average book value = £273,440 divided by 4 = £68,360
* assumes a five-year reducing balance accelerated depreciation period

Profits	Year 1	Year 2	Year 3
Revenue	£40,000	£50,000	£100,000
Costs	£15,000	£16,000	£25,000
Cashflow	£25,000	£34,000	£75,000
Depreciation	£25,000	£18,750	£14,060
Net profit	£0	£15,250	£60,940

$$\text{Average book rate of return} = \frac{\text{Average annual income}}{\text{Average annual investment}} = \frac{£25,397}{£68,360} = 37.2\%$$

Another flaw in this method is that the Return on Book Value does not take any account of working capital requirements that are needed for the investment as working capital is not captured in accounting profit.

Finally having calculated an average return on the book value of the investment, how can a firm know whether the return is acceptable or not? It can compare the return to its company-wide return on book value, or to the industry average. However, other companies may be using differing accounting conventions so you may not be comparing like with like. Furthermore, who is to say that the average for the company or the industry is a *good* investment? If the average return is very high due to successful invest-ments in the past, the company may reject investment projects which would still be profitable for them.

The Internal Rate of Return (IRR) method

Now let us consider two other methods which do share the *discounted cashflow approach* of the Net Present Value method. The first is the Internal Rate of Return, or IRR for short.

Outline

Using the Internal Rate of Return is similar to Net Present Value in that it uses a discounted cashflow approach. Indeed an alternative name used by accountants for the Internal Rate of Return is the Discounted Cashflow Yield.

The Net Present Value model takes the opportunity cost of capital (in other words the discount rate), the initial cash outflow and ensuing cash inflows, and then assesses whether, at the opportunity cost of capital, the cash inflows measured in today's money outweigh the cash outflows. Using the IRR method, the problem is approached in a different way. Taking the cash outflow and the forecast cash inflows, it calculates what the rate of return *would have to be* to make the Net Present Value of the investment zero, i.e. at what rate of return will the NPV of the investment equate to zero? A company using IRR as a way to assess investment projects will accept all projects if the oppor-tunity cost of capital required by the company is *less* than the IRR generated by the investment project. In other words the Internal Rate of Return is the maximum cost of capital that a company could use to finance an investment without harming the share-holders.

How to calculate the Internal Rate of Return

There are three main methods of which the latter two are most commonly used:

- interpolation
- using a calculator
- using a computer model.

Interpolation

This can either be done graphically or numerically. In Figure 3.2, the Net Present Value of an investment project is shown as a function of its discount rate. As the discount rate increases, so the NPV of the investment decreases until, at a discount rate of approximately 13 per cent, the NPV is zero.

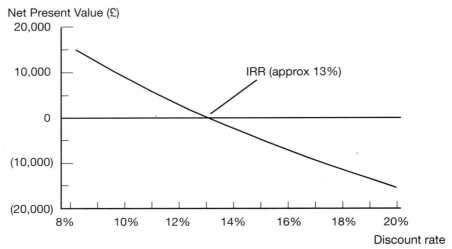

Figure 3.2   Net Present Value and the discount rate

Taking Figure 3.2 as an example, by plotting the changing NPV as the discount rate is altered on a graph, the point at which the NPV is zero can be read off and will give an approximate indication of the Internal Rate of Return for the investment project.

Alternatively, you can take two discount rates, one rate that gives a positive NPV and another discount rate that gives a negative NPV, and interpolate the IRR. Using the figures from Figure 3.2, at 11 per cent the NPV was £5,400 but at a discount rate of 15 per cent the NPV was negative at – £4,700.

$$11\% \ + \ \frac{\{£5,400 \ \times (15\%{-}11\%)\}}{\{£5,400 \ + \ £4,700\}} \ = 13.1\%$$

Note: As the calculations involved in Internal Rate of Return involve compound interest, they are based on a geometric progression rather than a linear one. Thus any line shown graphically between two points is actually slightly curved. The further apart the interpolation is between two sets of data either graphically or numerically, the less accurate that interpolation will be. (For simplicity's sake, the interpolation is substituting a linear relationship for a geometric one.)

The calculator or computer

By using a financial calculator or a computer model, you can calculate the Internal Rate of Return more quickly and to a greater degree of accuracy. On a Lotus spreadsheet using the formula @IRR (guess, range of cashflows) the computer will calculate the IRR. For the guess section, you have to supply the computer with your best approximate guess as to the value of the IRR and this allows it to reduce the number of iterations that it goes through before providing an accurate answer. (However it is important to be able to do a rough approximation if you are away from your calculator or have lost its manual!)

CASE STUDY 3.4

A company is deciding whether to invest in a new product extension to an existing brand of frozen foods. The initial investment will cost £65,000 and the project will generate the following cashflows in each of the subsequent years until Year Six. The company has calculated that its required cost of capital is 18 per cent and thus any project that has an Internal Rate of Return above 18 per cent will be accepted.

Years	Investment	Cashflows (not discounted)
0	£65,000	
1		£20,000
2		£20,000
3		£25,000
4		£35,000
5		£30,000
6		£25,000

These figures were fed into a computer model that gave an IRR of 29.4 per cent. As this is considerably more than the 18 per cent return that the company requires, the investment is accepted.

A short cut

We have seen in Chapter 2 how we can make use of the Cumulative Present Value or Annuity Tables with investment projects which yield identical cashflows in each year. We can also use these tables to identify the Internal Rate of Return. For example, suppose we are reviewing an investment which requires a capital outlay of £100,000 initially but which then yields £30,000 each year for five years. The cumulative PV factor which gives a Net Present Value of zero must be equal to £100,000 divided by £30,000, in other words, 3.33.

This is the cost of the investment divided by the annual cash inflow. The cumulative PV factor when compared to the PV factors for five years (see tables at end of Chapter 9), is very similar to 3.352 which is the cumulative PV factor for 15 per cent. Thus this investment has an Internal Rate of Return of approximately 15 per cent.

A critique

There are two main reasons why the Internal Rate of Return method is useful for managers. Firstly, they do not need to specify an opportunity cost of capital, especially if the company has specified a 'hurdle rate' or a required cost of capital that new projects must achieve to be accepted. They can just calculate the IRR either manually or using their calculators, and they know whether it is acceptable to their company. Even if there is no company hurdle rate, if the investment project is showing a very high IRR such as 30 per cent, managers will decide that the investment is sufficiently profitable to go ahead with the investment, or at least to warrant further analysis. This is because the rate of return is much more than the *probable* opportunity cost of capital.

The second reason it is popular is that it shows the results of the analysis in percentage form as the *true* return on the investment, as opposed to the accounting rate of return, and this is an easy way of communicating its attractiveness to other managers.

However, this advantage of communication also highlights one of its disadvantages. The IRR method tells you nothing about the size or scope of a potential investment. This is important to note when you are choosing between two mutually exclusive investments, where only one of the investment projects can be chosen. For example, if you were choosing between two investment projects with capital outlays of £500 and £5,000 and the IRR of the £500 investment was higher, by this method you would choose this one as the more attractive. However, the NPV of the other investment could be much higher and so you may make a less than perfect decision. Thus, the IRR method is not suitable for making comparisons between investment projects of different scope or differing time horizons. This can be demonstrated in a worked example.

Example

Alternator Ltd has to choose between two alternative proposals for a capital investment. Their cashflows and NPVs and IRRs are given below.

Year	Project A investment	Cashflows	Project B investment	Cashflows
0	−£160,000		−£80,000	
1		£45,000		£20,000
2		£55,000		£20,000
3		£50,000		£25,000
4		£45,000		£35,000
5		£40,000		£30,000
6		£30,000		£25,000
NPV at 10% discount rate		£33,125		£27,400
IRR		18.0%		21.1%

Project A would be chosen if the NPV method was used whilst Project B would be chosen according to its IRR. But, by taking the remaining cashflows and calculating the NPV and the IRR, we can see that this would have been a less than perfect decision.

Investment (A–B) Year	Investment	Cashflow
0	−£80,000	
1		£25,000
2		£35,000
3		£25,000
4		£10,000
5		£10,000
6		£5,000
NPV at 10% discount rate		£5,725
IRR 13.5%		

There is still value to be gained for the shareholders by investing the differential.

There are also a number of technical disadvantages to using the IRR method which you must be aware of if you are dealing with unconventional cashflows. It is often assumed that the NPV of an investment project declines consistently as the opportunity cost of capital or discount rate increases. This is not necessarily the case; for example, it depends on whether you are lending or borrowing money. If you are lending money and then recouping your investment, the NPV of the project will increase as the discount rate increases.

Secondly, it is perfectly possible for one project to have more than one IRR depending on the form of the cashflows. Due to the fact that the IRR is determined by mathematical iterations, it is possible to have *two IRRs* when there is more than one change in the direction of the cashflows. Most investment projects have negative cashflow for one or more years followed by several years of positive cashflow. However, if an investment was to incur another negative cashflow at the end of its economic life, the investment would actually have two Internal Rates of Return. For example, if a company is processing radioactive material, it will have to invest heavily at the end of the investment's life to dispose of the radio-active waste products. Figure 3.3 shows this graphically:

> There are also a number of technical disadvantages to using the IRR method which you must be aware of if you are dealing with unconventional cashflows.

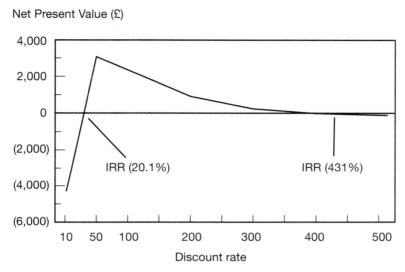

Figure 3.3   More than one Internal Rate of Return

This is why the computer asks you to guess the IRR. If you have an investment with cashflows that change in this way, look at the more logical of the two IRRs and scrap the other one.

The Profitability Index

Outline

An alternative way of stating the Net Present Value rule is the Profitability Index. It takes the present value of the investment project's cashflows and divides them by the initial capital outlay (typically the cash outflow in Year Zero). If the Profitability Index is more than one, then managers should invest in the project as it represents a positive Net Present Value.

$$\text{Profitability Index} \quad = \quad \frac{\text{Present value of cashflows}}{\text{Initial cash outflow}} \quad = \quad \frac{PV}{C^0}$$

CASE STUDY 3.5

GlosterBus Ltd is a bus company considering whether to buy a new bus this year. The cost of the bus will be £38,000 and the present value of the cash inflows, due to its increased capacity to carry more customers on its routes, is £55,000 at a cost of capital of 14 per cent. The Profitability Index will be:

$$\frac{£55,000}{£38,000} = 1.45$$

A critique

Though the Profitability Index is just a logical rearrangement of the Net Present Value rule, it can lead to less than perfect decisions, if a company is having to choose between two mutually exclusive projects which both have positive NPVs and Profitability Indices of more than one. Taking the example of Alternator Ltd again, the management now has to choose between two investment strategies, one a low investment and another, more ambitious strategy involving high capital outlay on buildings, personnel, marketing and selling expenses. Both investments have the same risk. The initial cash outflow, the Present Value of the cash inflows (discounted at 12 per cent), the Profitability Index and the NPVs of the two alternative investment strategies are shown below.

	Initial investment	Present value	Profitability Index	Net Present Value
Project A	£5,000	£8,000	1.6	£3,000
Project B	£25,000	£35,000	1.4	£10,000

If the managers of Alternator Ltd were using the Profitability Index as the method of investment appraisal, they would choose Project A over Project B as the project that gives the highest index, but Project B has a much larger Net Present Value.

As with the Internal Rate of Return, this can be demonstrated by taking the incremental cashflows, that is, the difference between Project A and Project B, and seeing whether they also fulfil the Profitability Index decision rule.

	Initial investment	Present value	Profitability Index	Net Present Value
Differential	£20,000	£27,000	1.35	£7,000

This highlights that if Alternator Ltd had taken Project A, they would have missed out on the larger opportunity.

> **Note:** Here we have been looking at a case of choosing between two **mutually exclusive** investments which are one-off investments. If this is not the case, and you are trying to maximise total Net Present Value, then by taking five Project As rather than one Project B, you can gain an NPV of £15,000 for the same investment of £40,000. I will look at the impact of capital budget constraints later on in the chapter.

Ranking projects

In an ideal world all projects that look beneficial, that is to say where the benefits outweigh the initial cost, would be accepted. However, in many cases, you have to choose between proposals. It is a useful exercise to compare the different results given by the various appraisal methods of a hypothetical investment proposal.

CASE STUDY 3.6

Indecis Ltd has three mutually exclusive investments for machinery to review. The cashflows associated with the three investments are given below:

Year	Project A	Project B	Project C
0	−£200,000	−£95,000	−£80,000
1	£30,000	£35,000	£30,000
2	£50,000	£30,000	£30,000
3	£60,000	£25,000	£20,000
4	£60,000	£22,000	£10,000
5	£70,000	£20,000	
6	£64,000	£18,000	

Some common assumptions: Each of the three projects has the same risk profile. Taxes have not been included for simplicity's sake.

Appraisal 'results' from different methods:

Payback (Cut-off at 3 years):	4 years	3.2 years	3 years
Rate of Return on Book Value:	26.1%	22.5%	4.9%
Average profits	£22,333	£9,167	£1,667
Average book value	£85,714	£40,714	£34,286
Depreciation	£40,000	£19,000	£16,000
Internal Rate of Return:	15%	17.1%	5.8%
NPV at 10% discount rate:	£17,525	£11,080	−£7,775
Initial cashflow	−£200,000	−£95,000	−£80,000
PV of cash inflows	£217,525	£106,080	£72,225
Profitability Index:	1.09	1.12	0.90

As can be seen, the different methods all give very different results.

■ Payback shows Project C to be the most attractive, but this ignores the short life of the project *after* the cut-off point of three years.

■ Accounting Rate of Return indicates that Project A should be the investment project chosen. This is because the *average* rate of return is 26.1 per cent, which is the highest average return. However, it can tell the company nothing about *when* the profits of the project occur. The Internal Rate of Return does tell us this and looks at the *true* rate of return. The IRR indicates that Project A actually has a true rate of return of 15 per cent which is lower than the IRR of Project B at 17.1 per cent.

■ The IRR and the Profitability Index both suggest that Project B should be taken because the IRR of 17.1 per cent and the Profitability Index of 1.12 are the highest of the three projects.

This is implicitly assuming that there is a capital budget constraint. If there is *no* capital constraint, then Project A would be the most attractive because it has the highest NPV of all the projects. This can be demonstrated by a simple check. Assume that Project B was accepted. Is the hypothetical project (A–B) an investment that has a positive NPV?

Year	Project A–B
0	−£105,000
1	−£5,000
2	£20,000
3	£35,000
4	£38,000
5	£50,000
6	£46,000
NPV	£6,445
Profitability Index	1.06

This demonstrates the lost opportunity of further gains if Project B is taken rather than Project A.

Note: If there is a capital constraint, the Profitability Index is the preferred technique to use as we see in a later section.

When to use each technique (or not at all!)

The surveys mentioned earlier indicate that many companies do not just use one appraisal method. A two-stage process is often used, with Payback or Discounted Payback used for the initial screen, and then Net Present Value, IRR or Return on Book Value used for the detailed analysis. Ease of understanding, and hence communication, was seen as very important when considering which appraisal method to adopt. I hope that this chapter has demonstrated that in most cases the best way of examining investments is by calculating the Net Present Value. However some companies are particularly attached to their traditional appraisal methods and it may take time for a company to change. What should you do in this case? There is a variety of options which all stem from one approach:

> Try to carry out the appraisal using the Net Present Value method as far as possible but making allowances for your company's culture.

CHECKLIST OF IDEAS

- If they use Payback, persuade them to discount the future cashflows and to change the cut-off period according to the type of investment they are considering, so that it mirrors the economic life of the investment more closely.
- Persuade your management to use a two-step process; the first screen to be based on discounted Payback, and if acceptable, the more detailed evaluation to be conducted using Net Present Value.
- Assess the investment on the basis of Net Present Value but use the terms of reference that your company's management feels comfortable with. Thus, talk about the Internal Rate of Return that the investment generates, or the high Profitability Index (assuming the investment project has a positive NPV). By using NPV, you have avoided the possible pitfalls of those methods and ensured that the underlying analysis is correct but you can still *communicate* in your audience's language.

We will return to some of these issues in Chapter 10 when we look at how to sell a profitable project.

Ranking projects under capital constraints

There is one time when the use of an alternative method to Net Present Value will yield a better result and that is in the case of hard budget constraints.

So far we have assumed that all projects with a positive Net Present Value will be accepted. However, in reality, a company is often operating under budgetary constraints, either fixed by the markets or by senior management. As you will have noticed, the NPV method tends to favour large investments over smaller ones. However, this can lead to a lack of flexibility when operating under a capital budget constraint, as the following example indicates.

Example

A company has an active screening process for new investment ideas and has generated five projects all of which have positive NPVs at the company cost of capital of 15 per cent (and Profitability Indices of more than 1 and Internal Rates of Return of over 15 per cent). There is a budget constraint of £300,000 but the total investment cost of the five projects far exceeds this at £575,000. The management has to decide which of these projects should be accepted. The obvious answer would be to take the projects with the highest NPVs but is this correct? Let us look at the cashflows, the NPVs and the Profitability Indices:

Project	Investment	Present value	Profitability Index	Net Present Value
A	£100,000	£142,000	1.42	£42,000
B	£200,000	£240,000	1.20	£40,000
C	£75,000	£110,000	1.47	£35,000
D	£150,000	£170,000	1.13	£20,000
E	£50,000	£80,000	1.60	£30,000

If the projects which have the highest Net Present Values are taken, the ranking is A, B, C, E and D, with only A and B within the £300,000 budget limit. This would give a total

Net Present Value of £82,000. However, if the Profitability Index is used to rank the projects, the ranking is very different with projects chosen in the order E, C, A, B and D. Only E, C, A and part of B are within the budget limit. The Net Present Value of E, C and A alone is £107,000 which far exceeds the NPV of A and B. Furthermore, if these projects are divisible and Project B can be reduced to a smaller investment project, the NPV can be increased. By taking a £75,000 investment in Project B, to fully utilise the capital budget allowance, an additional £15,000 in Net Present Value can be realised.

Project B	£200,000 investment leads to £40,000 NPV
→ Project B × 0.375	£75,000 investment leads to £15,000 NPV

The timing of the cash outflows will also be of critical importance when looking at a capital constraint. Some of the investments with an early return of cash inflows could be used to finance the later cash outflows of phased investments or investments which are only due to start at a later date. Chapter 4 looks at this in further detail.

Flow chart summary

Having read this chapter, you should be in a position to decide which appraisal method is most appropriate for your purposes. The flow chart summary in Figure 3.4 suggests what questions you should now be asking.

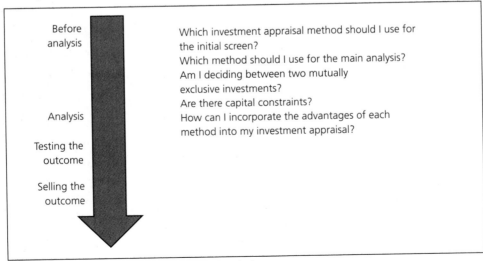

Before analysis

Which investment appraisal method should I use for the initial screen?
Which method should I use for the main analysis?
Am I deciding between two mutually exclusive investments?
Are there capital constraints?

Analysis

How can I incorporate the advantages of each method into my investment appraisal?

Testing the outcome

Selling the outcome

Figure 3.4   Flow diagram for investment appraisal

CASE STUDY 3.7

Thomas Robinson has to present a list of the most attractive investment prospects for his division of Robarts Ltd. There is a capital budget limit, which has been imposed by the board, of £400,000. He has been presented with a number of projects, and as many opinions, from his project team, as to which of these investment projects should be on the shortlist. A summary of the projects and any salient features has been given below. If you were Thomas Robinson, which investment projects would you propose in order to maximise the total NPV of the investments combined?

Project A

Capital outlay: £120,000   Present Value of annual cashflows at
                                  14%: £160,000

This is a one-off investment project.

Project B

Capital outlay: £30,000   Present Value of annual cashflows at
                                 14%: £48,000

This is a one-off investment project.

Project C

Capital outlay: £80,000   Present Value of annual cashflows at
                                 14%: £90,000

This is one of two mutually exclusive proposals. The alternative proposal is Project D.

Project D

Capital outlay: £95,000   Present Value of annual cashflows at
                                 14%: £106,000

This is one of two mutually exclusive proposals. The alternative proposal is Project C.

Project E

Capital outlay: £200,000   Present Value of annual cashflows at
                                  14%: £250,000

This is a one-off investment project, but which can be reduced in scope in £50,000 blocks.

Project F

Capital outlay: £50,000   Present Value of annual cashflows at
                                  14%: £65,000

This proposal can be replicated.

Project G

Capital outlay: £60,000   Present Value of annual cashflows at
                                  14%: £65,000

This proposal can be replicated.

Project H

Capital outlay: £75,000   Present Value of annual cashflows at
                                  14%: £95,000

This is a one-off investment project.

CHECKLIST OF PRACTICAL TIPS

1 Decide upon the requirements for your analysis – is it a quick review or a detailed evaluation? Does it have an economic life of several years? Are you comparing two mutually exclusive projects? Are you trying to rank projects within a fixed capital budget? The answers to these questions should help you to decide which method to use.

2 In most cases, the Net Present Value method is the safest and most robust method to use. But if your company uses other methods, try to incorporate as much of the NPV method into your analysis as you can.

3 In particular do not use the other discounted cashflow methods, Internal Rate of Return and the Profitability Index, if you are choosing between two mutually exclusive investment projects.

4 If you are having to rank investment projects *under budgetary constraints*, conduct your analysis using the NPV method and then compute the Profitability Index. Rank the investment projects according to their Profitability Indices not according to the overall NPV of each project.

5 Use the methods of Return on Investment or Payback to sell the project if these are the methods, or even phrases, that your management is comfortable with.

6 Be familiar with your company's current appraisal methods and make sure that you do not antagonise people by highlighting too aggressively the inadequacies of their favourite methods! Use Net Present Value to conduct your analysis but use their language to sell the analysis.

It is of absolutely no value to have a theoretically correct method of investment appraisal, when the information you are feeding into the process is not of good quality, or is just plain wrong!

CHAPTER FOUR

Estimating cashflows

- Part I – Types of cashflows

- Part II – Relevant cashflows over differing time horizons

- Part III – The impact of tax

CHECKLIST OF KEY POINTS

This chapter has three parts: the first part looks at what are the relevant **cashflows** to be included in investment appraisal; the second part looks at what cashflows to compare when evaluating investment projects over **different time horizons**; the final part takes a more detailed look at how to deal with **taxation** in your investment appraisal.

Part I

1 There are four criteria that govern which cashflows are relevant, and thus should be included in investment appraisals: they should be cash and cash alone; they should be related to the investment; they should be incremental, and they should include both tangible costs and benefits, and those intangible costs and benefits that can be converted into cash values.

2 Investment appraisers must collect information and forecasts on cashflows, not on operating profit. Cashflows measure when cash comes in and out of the business whereas profit takes account of sales only when they are earned (and this is not necessarily when the customers pay), and costs only when they are incurred (and this is not necessarily when your suppliers get paid, or you pay your taxes). In addition, a depreciation expense is added to the operating expenses which should be ignored when looking at cashflows.

3 Only cashflows directly related to the investment should be included. Thus allocated overhead costs, for example, should not be included, but opportunity costs, which give a value for an alternative use of an asset used in an investment, should be included.

4 Only incremental costs are relevant when considering cashflows relating to a new investment project. Sunk costs, costs already incurred, are irrelevant to the investment appraisal. If taking this investment allows the company to utilise their capital allowances, that tax saving is an incremental benefit and should be included in the investment appraisal.

5 Less tangible costs and benefits are included in investment appraisal wherever reasonable assumptions can be made that allow these to be converted into commonly accepted cash values. Care should be taken to ensure that the conversion is reasonably conservative, so as to not jeopardise the credibility of the overall appraisal.

6 If an holistic approach is taken which seeks to evaluate the attractiveness of a particular investment, not just for the shareholders, but for other stakeholders as well, the appraisal process is often termed Cost–Benefit Analysis (CBA). CBA is usually undertaken by public bodies seeking to understand the effect of a public investment on the whole community.

Part II

7 Nearly all investments have alternatives, one of the most common ones being whether to invest in a project now or later? In these cases, you need to compare how the cashflows of the project will change as the start date is delayed, and compare the NPVs of different start dates.

8 Often you need to choose between two projects of not only different NPVs but also different time horizons. The only way to compare 'apples with apples' is to compare the benefits across the same time-frame. This can be done by taking the lowest common denominator in terms of years. Alternatively, you can compute an equivalent annual cashflow, which is really an annuity for the life of the investment. This corresponds to the present value of the investment. You can then compare the two projects easily.

9 Using Equivalent Annual Cashflows (EAC) also makes the task of deciding when to replace a piece of equipment easier. The annual cash inflows of an existing machine, together with its salvage value, can be compared with the EAC of a new machine. When the EAC is greater than the lost opportunity to continue with the old machine, it is time to replace.

Part III

10 Finally we look at taxation in more detail. There are two main tax implications for investment appraisal. The first one is to ensure that tax cashflows are included when they are actually paid, and not when the tax is incurred.

11 The second major tax implication is that the company can use capital allowances and thus obtain a tax shield. The tax shield that is provided by these capital allowances is a cash saving and thus a cash inflow for the investment and its Present Value should be computed alongside all other cashflows.

Introduction

So far, we have paid most attention to the process of investment appraisal – how to select potentially attractive projects; the questions to ask before investing time and effort in investment appraisal and which methods of investment appraisal should be used. In this chapter, and in Chapter 5, we focus on the **inputs** into the process rather than the process itself. It is of absolutely no value to have a theoretically correct method of investment appraisal, when the information you are feeding into the process is not of good quality, or is just plain wrong!

Most people who argue against formal investment appraisal methods are criticising the ways in which these methods are applied, not the underlying theory behind them. For example, they point to an inconsistent use of inflation or taxation, a failure to compare investments with relevant alternatives, or an inability to include the intangible costs and benefits of an investment.

This chapter aims to ensure that these flaws will not appear in *your* analysis. So far we have been operating under some very convenient assumptions. We have assumed the following:

■ all cashflows are relevant and known

■ there are no project timing issues

■ there is no taxation

■ all cashflows are certain

■ there is no inflation

■ the cost of capital is known.

In the next two chapters we are going to relax all but the last assumption. This chapter will look at the first three issues: how to select relevant cashflows to use in investment appraisal; the ways in which varying investment time horizons can affect your analysis; and the impact of taxation. Chapter 5 will look at other cashflow forecasting problems such as the impact of inflation and how to evaluate uncertain cashflows.

Part I – Types of cashflows

Figure 4.1 indicates the broad categories of cashflows to be included in an investment appraisal.

Often the manager appraising a possible investment uses a variety of sources for data, not all of them consistent. He or she has to check the validity of the data thoroughly before submitting the investment proposal for scrutiny.

Initially...	Capital investment Other expenses Working capital	Plant, machinery People, market research Stocks, credit
Ongoing...	Sales increases Cost savings Tax shields	
At the end...	Working capital Scrap values	Stocks, outstanding sales and bills Plant, machinery

Figure 4.1   Cashflow types

Criteria to establish relevant cashflows

First we shall set up some ground rules for what should and shouldn't be considered relevant cashflows. They fall into four categories as shown in Figure 4.2:

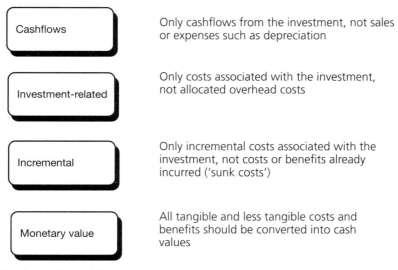

Cashflows — Only cashflows from the investment, not sales or expenses such as depreciation

Investment-related — Only costs associated with the investment, not allocated overhead costs

Incremental — Only incremental costs associated with the investment, not costs or benefits already incurred ('sunk costs')

Monetary value — All tangible and less tangible costs and benefits should be converted into cash values

Figure 4.2   Criteria for cashflows

Cashflows not accounting profit

We have talked, in Chapter 2, about the need to differentiate cashflows from accounting profit. Cashflow is the profit from the investment project after tax but before depreciation, interest charges and dividends. Over the life of an investment project, the cashflow and the profit will be identical but the timing will be different. When we are considering the time value of money, the timing of payments can be highly important. Net cashflows are a measure of what cash comes into the investment and what cash goes out. The cashflows indicate whether the investment is worthwhile, not the accounting decisions such as how fast capital investments should be depreciated. We ignore depreciation because we have already accounted for the capital outlay in the first year(s) of the investment project. We ignore interest charges because these are embraced by the discount rate that is used to discount the cashflows (see Chapters 7 and 8).

There are two other reasons why the cashflow from an investment does not equal accounting profit. Firstly, in the profit and loss account in Year One tax payable is deducted from the profit *in that year*, but in practice most tax is paid the following year. Secondly, the profit and loss account does not take into account working capital outlay. The differences are summarised in Figure. 4.3.

	Cashflows	Accounting profit
Revenues	When cash comes in	When sale occurs
Operating expenses	When cash goes out	When expense occurs
Depreciation	Not included	Included in P&L accounts added back for tax accounts
Capital allowances	Tax shield included as cash inflow	Included in tax accounts
Taxes	When tax is paid (one-year time lag)	Recognised when tax incurred

Figure 4.3 Cashflows vs accounting profit

However, arriving at the projected cashflows is seldom easy. There are two main ways to derive cashflows for investment appraisals:

- from the raw data
- from pro-forma financial statements such as the profit and loss statement and the balance sheet.

Deriving cashflows from raw data

Ideally you should put together your own cashflow forecasts and not take figures from a pro-forma profit and loss forecast. As you consider your sales forecasts and operating cost forecasts, remember the following pointers:

- include a cash outflow when it is likely to go out of the business, not when it will be shown as an expense.
- include a cash inflow from sales when your customers will actually pay, not when the accountants will recognise the sale.
- include *incremental tax*, which has occurred due to the incremental cashflow from the investment. Do not include a cash outflow for tax in the year in which the tax expense occurred. Rather forecast the tax outflow for the following year when those taxes will actually be paid. For a further discussion on tax, see Part III of this chapter.

By concentrating on cash you should automatically include *working capital expenses*. Working capital is the capital needed by any new project, for example, to pay for inventories or to allow for customers paying on credit, indeed all the expenses required by the investment before cash is received from the customers. The longer the production cycle and the longer your customers take to pay, the greater your working capital requirements are likely to be.

Deriving cashflows from projected financial statements

As there are these differences between cashflow and profit that we've mentioned, it is tiresome to have to calculate cashflow from the profit and loss forecast. However, this may be the form in which the information comes to you, especially if it comes from a company accountant.

Generally working capital requirements can be derived from the balance sheet. Take stocks and debtors, i.e. when a sale has been made but no money has been received as the customer paid on credit, minus creditors, i.e. when you have paid for supplies on credit and have not parted with your cash yet. It is likely that as the investment increases its sales through its lifetime, there will be additional expenditure on working capital each year, the reason being that the ratio between accounts receivable and accounts payable will remain fairly constant. (If you do not have this information broken down into these components, a reasonable proxy from working capital is current assets minus current liabilities.)

> **Note:** You will only need to add in working capital requirements if you are deriving cashflows from the profit and loss account.

Here is a worked example to identify the main changes you need to make.

Example

Information from the forecast P&L and the balance sheet

Year	0	1	2	3	
From the balance sheet:					
Investment	−£60,000				
Stocks	£0	£40,000	£50,000	£55,000	
Debtors	£0	£20,000	£24,000	£28,000	
Creditors	£0	£30,000	£36,000	£42,000	
From the profit and loss statement:					
Revenues	£0	£200,000	£240,000	£280,000	
Operating profit	£0	£30,000	£48,000	£60,000	
Depreciation (straight line)	£0	−£20,000	−£20,000	−£20,000	
Interest charges	£0	−£5,000	−£4,000	−£3,000	
Tax payable at 33%	£0	−£1,650	−£7,920	−£12,210	
Net profit		**£3,350**	**£16,080**	**£24,790**	
Dividends	£0	£0	−£1,000	−£1,500	
Retained profit		**£3,350**	**£18,430**	**£41,720**	
Add back:					
Depreciation, interest charges & dividends	£0	£25,000	£25,000	£24,500	
Delay tax charge*	£0	£1,650	£6,270	£4,920	−£12,210
Add investment	−£60,000				
Add changes in working capital†		−£30,000	−£8,000	−£3,000	£41,000
Cashflows	**−£60,000**	**−£3,350**	**£23,270**	**£26,420**	**£28,790**

* this shows the difference between tax payable in one year, and when the tax is actually paid in the next year. So in Year Two tax is paid on Year One's profits (£1,650) and not on Year Two's profits (£7,920) and the difference is added back (£7,920 minus £1,650 is £6,270).

† add in the initial working capital expenses in Year One (stocks plus debtors minus creditors), and then any changes in working capital. Add back the working capital outlay for the investment to Year Three's cashflow, as those funds are released at the end of the investment.

Cashflows must be incremental

Forget 'sunk costs'. This is money that has already been spent and should have no bearing on whether, if further money was invested, it would gain a good return for shareholders. This maxim is the same whether the money already invested is considered to have gained a poor return, or gained a very good return. It is of no relevance. Thus if Mr Jones is considering whether to build a block of flats on some land that he already owns, you do not need to include the cost of the original land purchase as part of the investment cost, as that is a sunk cost.

All incidental costs and benefits should be included. An example of incidental cost that is often overlooked is the management time involved in the investment project that leads to a temporary decline in sales elsewhere in the business. That cost (lost sales) should be included as an incidental cost.

Incidental costs and benefits occur when new investment in one area of the company may improve the performance of other products within the company. For example, a diversification into a new product area may bring new customers into a retail store who will then be introduced to the other products on offer. An example of this might be Marks & Spencer's move into premium quality foods which brought a different sector of the market into the shops who had to walk past all the clothing stock to get to the food department, and thus made 'incidental' purchases en route.

Forget 'sunk costs'. This is money that has already been spent and should have no bearing on whether, if further money was invested, it would gain a good return for shareholders. This maxim is the same whether the money already invested is considered to have gained a poor return, or gained a very good return. It is of no relevance.

Incidental costs and benefits such as these can have far-reaching consequences, and are not always easy to spot. So take time to think broadly around the proposed investment to ensure these costs and benefits are included.

Example

Talkative Toys Ltd is a retail toy company specialising in interactive toys for children aged from four to ten years. They are keen to extend their product range to include toys and educational gadgetry for children up to the age of fourteen. They are particularly keen to enter the interactive computer game market. One strategy is to launch a new product, an interactive video, at a particularly attractive price. Taken by itself, it is a loss leader. It will cost £120,000 upfront in additional launch advertising and new window displays promoting the product. The expected increase in cashflow coming from this product is thought to be £10,000 for the first three months declining to £5,000 per month, once the promotion ceases, with an estimated lifespan of only 1½ years, or 18 months. The cost of capital is taken to be 12 per cent per year, which is equivalent to 1 per cent per month. The Net Present Value is as follows:

Month	Cashflows	PV factor at 1%	Present values
0	(£120,000)	1.000	(£120,000)
1 to 3	£10,000	2.941	£29,410
4 to 18	£5,000	13.459*	£67,295
Net Present Value			(£23,295)

* the cumulative PV factor was found by taking the 18-period PV factor, 16.40, minus 2.941.

However, the purpose of this new product introduction, at such a reasonable price, is to get new children of the right age (accompanied by their beleaguered parents) into the stores, where they will be tempted by the range of interactive video and computer games. Talkative Toys believe that the promotional activity in the first three months surrounding the launch will lead to a sales increase of 10 per cent on their range for the first three months which equates to an additional £15,000 in cashflow each month. Given the principle of conservatism, they decide not to include any increase in sales after that period (as the sales increase could be due to other factors). The new Net Present Value looks rather different:

Month	Cashflows	PV factor at 1%	Present values
0	(£120,000)	1.000	(£120,000)
1 to 3	£25,000	2.941	£73,525
4 to 18	£5,000	13.459	£67,295
Net Present Value			(£20,820)

Cashflows should be investment-related

This would seem so obvious that it hardly needs mentioning. Yet many new investment appraisals are saddled with extraneous costs, which can obscure our vision as to whether the underlying investment is attractive or not. For example, an investment should not have a share of overhead costs allocated to it as part of the appraisal. Such a practice could lead to potentially beneficial investments being rejected, because the company itself has too heavy a corporate structure, or owns too many executive jets! If the company has a headquarters staff of 50, and no new employees will be needed if an investment in a new product line takes place, then there is no incremental headquarters cost.

Opportunity costs

Investment appraisal is all about comparing one investment with another. Many people erroneously assume that when considering a new project, they should compare 'Before' and 'After' rather than 'Either-Or'. Why is this? If Mr Jones is considering whether to build a block of flats on a piece of land, the alternative to consider is whether to sell the land. That is an opportunity cost for the investment. To establish the opportunity costs of the alternative use of an asset, use the market value, wherever possible.

Include tangible and intangible cashflows

Investment appraisal takes into account less tangible costs and benefits that affect the company. Cost–Benefit Analysis on the other hand, takes a far more holistic approach than most investment appraisals and seeks to establish costs and benefits for *society as a whole*, for all stakeholders involved, not just the company. Cost–Benefit is reviewed briefly in the next section.

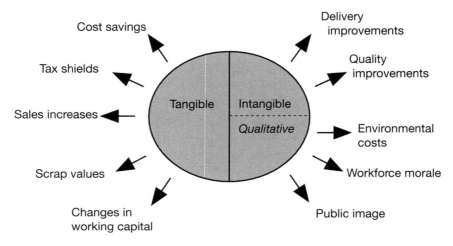

Figure 4.4   Tangible and intangible costs and benefits

Intangible costs and benefits include safety issues, quality improvements, labour morale and company image. I will put such intangible costs and benefits into two categories: those which can, with some thought, be converted into reasonable cash values, and those which cannot because they are truly of a qualitative nature.

Conversion into cash values

Improvements in product quality or delivery time, for example, can often be converted into cash values. A proposal is put forward, say, for an investment in new machinery. This machine will lead to some cost savings but its prime advantage is the improvement in product quality that it will provide. If you do not include this benefit in the analysis, you will seriously underestimate the value of the project. So the company thinks how the improvement in quality leads to monetary benefits, for example, quality improvements lead to cost savings through the reduction in scrap and wastage, the amount of rework that is needed and the time it takes to inspect each product. As the quality has improved, the company can expect to have fewer cash outflows from its warranty service, as fewer products will need to be repaired within the warranty period. It can also lead to an increase in sales as customers perceive that the quality has improved. The project appraiser must collect enough information to allow him to make informed judgements on how the increased quality will affect cashflows.

Of course some product improvements resulting from investments are quite difficult to quantify. For example, if a new investment in machinery allows the company to be more versatile, this may lead to economies of scope and will give a strategic advantage to the company. But how do you quantify 'strategic advantage'? In some cases, you must treat the project as having non-quantifiable benefits (see below).

> **A word of caution:** When converting less tangible costs and benefits into monetary values, think carefully about your audience, to whom you will have to sell the project. Make sure you can show clearly how you derived these monetary values. Preferably try to use only those assumptions that will be generally accepted. Some discussion of these assumptions with colleagues will show you whether they are generally agreed upon.

Separate out the more debatable costs and benefits, and treat these as part of the upside/downside scenarios for the investment. Do not jeopardise a sound investment appraisal by over zealous inclusion of all potential benefits.

Qualitative costs and benefits

Costs and benefits that affect the wider community often fall into this category. Examples could be an investment that affects the air quality of the surrounding community, or an investment that gives benefits that affect the workforce, such as improving the working environment (adding restaurants, shops, sports facilities and so on). Net Present Value analysis is still useful in these circumstances – it allows a company to see the 'value' that it is placing on these qualitative elements. For example, a company can calculate the present value of the *cost* of an investment, and evaluate whether the intangible benefits are worth this net outlay.

Example

A company may decide to shut down a waste processing plant that operates close to a town even though the plant is operating profitably. The plant is affecting the surrounding community and this generates much negative publicity. By computing the present value of closing the plant, that is, the lost profits of the future, the company has imputed a value to the negative publicity. In effect, what it is saying to shareholders is that the negative impact of poor public relations has a greater value than the opportunity cost of closing the plant. Thus it would be in the company's best interest to close down the plant.

Cost–Benefit Analysis

Cost–Benefit Analysis is really an extension of evaluating intangible, as well as tangible, costs and benefits. The term 'Cost–Benefit Analysis' is given to investment appraisals which seek to identify all the social costs and benefits arising from an investment project, both tangible and intangible. However, a word of warning – though this holistic approach may be the most 'correct' method to use, always remember who your *prime audience* is.

CASE STUDY 4.1

In the pharmaceutical industry, the price of new prescription drugs is often supported by pharmaco-economic studies, which seek to justify the price of the drug by identifying and costing the benefits to society. These might be in the form of cost reductions for hospital care or surgery, if the drug is reducing the need for surgery, or if the new drug is curative and replaces older drugs (which would need to be taken for the rest of a patient's life). It may be reducing the costs to employers through reducing the indirect costs of lost productivity and sick leave. In the UK the main audience for these pharmaco-economic studies is the government, as it is responsible for approving all new drugs. Given that it is primarily interested in reducing the healthcare budget, it will be mainly interested in potential reduction in hospital costs or the costs of long-term drug use. The government, and hospital administrators and doctors, are only moderately interested in cost reductions for *employers*, especially if the effect on them is an increase in their immediate drug budget! A drug that will increase the healthcare budget may be rejected by the government even though the savings made by employers far outweigh the increased costs incurred by the government.

Cost–Benefit Analysis is usually undertaken in public sector investments. It considers the costs and benefits to the wider community. For example, in the case of a new road the appraisal would consider the impact not only on the local government but on the potential road users; on businesses and residential areas located near to the road; on people who are forced to sell their houses to make way for the road. Such Cost–Benefit Analyses have their own unique set of problems. The boundaries of the investment project are less clear-cut, there are more costs and benefits which do not have easily definable monetary values and finally there is no obvious way of establishing what discount rate should be used in the analysis.

A checklist of costs and benefits

Before we look at the timing of investments, I have included (see Figure 4.5) a checklist of the major costs and benefits to be included in an investment appraisal, and the main ones which you may have been tempted to include but which are not part of investment appraisal. I know it has no surprises for you at this stage! It takes the building of a new manufacturing plant as its example, but the checklist is useful for a range of potential investments.

Costs	Relevant?
Cost of the site?	
Cost of demolition of the buildings?	
Market value of the site and existing buildings?	
Cost of site lighting installed last year?	
Proportion of head office accounting costs?	
Depreciation of new plant and equipment?	
Increased stock costs?	
Money spent on the feasibility study?	
Relocation costs of key personnel?	

Figure 4.5   Checklist – building a new manufacturing plant

Part II – Relevant cashflows over differing time horizons

The second important issue to consider when formulating the inputs for your investment appraisal is the effect of differing time horizons on your investment proposal. This can have many manifestations – we shall consider the three most common forms outlined in Figure 4.6.

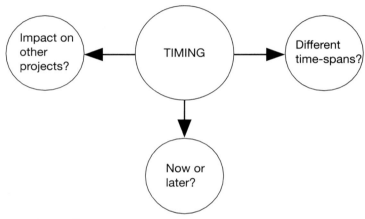

Figure 4.6   How timing affects investment decisions

To invest now or later?

As was stated earlier, every project has an alternative of some shape or form. If the investment you are considering is a stand-alone investment, you must consider *when* you will get the greatest benefit from it – now or if you wait for a year, or two, or three.... That is your alternative investment. First you must calculate the different NPVs of the investment as the start date changes from Year Zero to Year One to Year Two, and so on. Of course, this sounds much easier than it often is, as you will rarely have certain information on how your environment is going to change. For example, if you are considering a diversification, you will need to consider how your entry costs will change with time as well as the parameters of the market-place: the market demand, prices, potential market share achievable, and so on. Then you can select the start date that has the highest NPV. Make sure that your NPV is the value of each investment *today* not when each investment is forecast to start.

Usually the arguments for initiating an investment now are that the 'opportunity' might disappear and that it's a profitable project with a positive Net Present Value. On the other hand, the risks may be diminished if the project is delayed for a year. The 'opportunity' may still be there, and the market may be even larger as demand picks up. This could be the case when a company is considering entering an emerging market. (There is also a value in flexibility, being able to start small and expand, though this is not a timing issue.)

Example

A travel company is considering entering a new holiday market. The country has had a difficult past due to an old political regime. A new government is in power and the country, which is very beautiful and unspoilt, is now open for tourism. The travel company has analysed the investment required to establish a presence in this market and to sell holidays. The project has a positive NPV of £200,000 with a discount rate of 15 per cent. However, the company decides to consider what the project NPV would look like if it waited a year or more. The NPV rises steeply at first, because the market is growing rapidly and, by waiting a short while, they gain many more customers over the same time-span. Their marketing costs are also lower as the destination becomes more well known. Later, the NPV growth slows as they are no longer one of the early travel companies to enter the market and consequently their market share is more difficult to retain.

The costs of investment also grow so that the resulting NPVs of the different start dates are as follows.

Begin in Year	1	2	3	4	5
Net Present Values (£000s)	200	260	300	320	280
Growth of NPVs	–	30%	15.4%	6.7%	−12.5%

Choosing between investments of differing time horizons

A common investment decision is between two alternatives which have differing time horizons. If two machines will provide an equivalent output, all you need to decide is which investment minimises your costs. In other cases, you are trying to maximise the Net Present Value of an investment over a set time horizon. For example, one machine may have a lower annual NPV than another but also a shorter life, and thus needs to be replaced more often. How can we say which is the most beneficial investment to take? We have to find a way of comparing them across the same time horizon. This can be done in one of two ways:

■ compare the investments over the lowest common denominator in terms of time

■ compute the Equivalent Annual Cashflow or the Equivalent Annual Cost.

Taking the first method, the NPV analysis is conducted to find the investment with the highest NPV over an identical time horizon. Each investment is assumed to be repeated once it comes to an end.

If you are comparing two pieces of machinery – one with a two-year life and a Net Present Value of £12,000, the other with a three-year life and a Net Present Value of £9,000, the lowest common denominator is to look at the NPVs over six years. That is, you assume that the first machine has to be replaced once, whilst the second machine has to be replaced twice in this period. The NPV of Machine A over six years is £24,000 whereas the NPV of Machine B is now £27,000 and thus Machine B seems to offer the best return for the shareholders as it maximises the value in today's money.

This method is fine if you are comparing investments of one and two years or of two and three years. However, if you are comparing two investments with lives of four and six years respectively, the lowest common denominator would be 24 years. This is unlikely to be a realistic time horizon over which to assume machinery is replaced with identical machinery every time!

A second method is to convert the Present Values into an Equivalent Annual Cost or Equivalent Annual Cashflow. This is done with the aid of the annuity method that we discussed in Chapter 2. As we discussed then, the annuity method allows us to ask what investment (Present Value) will give us a regular payment every year for a set period? We can turn this around and ask what is the regular annual payment that equates to this Present Value?

$$\text{Equivalent Annual Cost} = \frac{\text{Net Present Value}}{\text{Annuity factor for N years at r\%}}$$

Now we can calculate the Equivalent Annual Cashflow, the EAC, for each investment and choose the one with the highest EAC without having to find a common time-frame. Alternatively, if the benefits are identical, we can compute the Equivalent Annual Cost and take the lowest.

Example

Thriftco Company is renewing its cleaning and maintenance contract and is considering quotations from two service suppliers. Cleanco Ltd has put in a quotation for a three-year contract that has a cost of £60,000, whilst Dustfree Ltd has put in a quotation for four years for £80,000. Which contract is the cheapest on an annual basis if the cost of capital for Thriftco is 14 per cent?

$$\text{Cleanco's EAC} = \frac{£60,000}{2.322} = £25,840 \text{ per annum}$$

$$\text{Dustfree's EAC} = \frac{£80,000}{2.914} = £27,454 \text{ per annum}$$

Thriftco decides to take up a contract with Cleanco Ltd.

Life-Cycle Costing (LCC)

The above comparison of two investments across different time horizons is utilising the concept of Life-Cycle Costing. This is the assessment of the costs of an investment, usually in a piece of machinery, over the whole of its economic life (or the whole of its life until it is divested). Life-Cycle Costing is useful when you have to compare two investments which have different capital outlays and also differing maintenance and running costs on a yearly basis.

Example

Office Boy Ltd is an office services supplier. It is considering a new investment in some fax/plain paper copier machines which it will then lease out to small businesses. They are reviewing two alternative models which provide an identical service but which have the following costs per machine.

	Machine A	Machine B
Acquisition cost	£1,500	£2,000
Installation cost	£100	£50
Annual costs		
Maintenance	£200	£150
Paper	£200	£180
Life of machine	4 years	5 years
The real cost of capital is 8%		

The Equivalent Annual Cost for Machine A is:

$$\frac{\text{Purchase \& installation cost}}{\text{Cumulative PV factor at 8\%}} = \frac{£1,500 + £100}{3.312} = £483 \text{ p.a.}$$

The EAC for Machine B is:

$$\frac{£2,000 + £50}{3.993} = £513 \text{ p.a.}$$

To complete the review, we must add the annual maintenance and running costs, £400 in the case of Machine A making a total annual cost of £883, and £330 for Machine B making a total annual cost of £843. It would seem that Machine B is actually the cheaper machine when we consider the total life of the investment.

To replace now or later?

A variation on the 'Now or later?' decision is the decision of *when* to replace a piece of machinery. It is important always to remember what is the appropriate comparison. You must compare how the future net cashflow of the existing machine compares with the net cashflows of the best available alternative machine. Of course, in the case of the old machine, there are only the net cashflows and the salvage value (that will decline as the machine continues to be used) to consider. On the other hand, any new machine is a capital outlay, but it usually has higher net annual cashflows, as it is more efficient and requires lower maintenance. In order to compare the two investment alternatives, you need to convert them into Equivalent Annual Cashflows. This can be done using the EAC method discussed in the previous section. It does not matter that we are looking at the net cash inflow rather than the net cash outflow – the reasoning is the same.

Example

Cobbles Company is considering whether to replace a trusty but antiquated steel compressing machine, 'Trusty Sue', that is unlikely to last more than two more years. The annual cashflow that it contributes and its likely salvage value that would be attainable if sold today, next year or the following year are given as well. The cost of a new compressor would be £15,000 but it would contribute £7,000 in net cashflows each year for the next five years. It is the best alternative on the market. When should Cobbles replace 'Trusty Sue'? The Equivalent Annual Cashflow for the new machine is:

Year	Cashflows	PV factor at 12%	PV
0	(£15,000)	1.00	(£15,000)
1 to 5	£7,000	3.605	£25,235
NPV			£10,235

The Equivalent Annual Cashflows, that is to say a five-year annuity, would be £10,235/3.605 which equals £2,839 per annum. Now let us compare the old and the new machines.

Year	1	2	3
Trusty Sue cashflows	£4,000	£3,000	£2,000
Scrap value	£1,000	£500	Zero
Opportunity cost*		−£1,120	−£560
Total annual cashflows	£5,000	£2,380	£1,440
OR			
New machine EAC	£2,839	£2,839	£2,839

* the opportunity cost is calculated by taking the salvage value in one year and the interest payable on that cash at 12 per cent.

Looking at the figures, it seems clear that 'Trusty Sue' has at least one more year of grace before she goes to the scrapyard herself. However, the net cashflows in the following year are lower, her salvage value is lower and Cobbles has lost the opportunity to sell her for £1,000 in Year One and invest the money at 12 per cent, an opportunity cost of £1,120. Though the annual cash inflows are still higher than the EAC of the new machine, the lost opportunity of not selling earlier means that the net annual cashflows would be lower than the EAC. Thus 'Trusty Sue' should bid her farewells.

The impact on future projects

So far we have viewed all projects as either stand-alone or as direct comparisons between two, mutually incompatible, alternatives. The timing of cashflows can have, however, a further repercussion. Two investment projects may have similar NPVs, but one investment may receive cashflows in the early years which allows the company to take a further project later on. The alternative investment may not release cash until much later, and thus a third project cannot be taken on as the available cash is already tied up in the earlier investment. Project appraisers must always consider the impact of capital availability for any future known investment projects.

The use of Linear Programming (LP)

In Chapter 2 we stated that if the capital budget was constrained, then the Profitability Index should be used to rank investment projects according to the present value return on the initial cash outlay. However, Profitability Index will only be appropriate if there is one and only one constraint, such as a capital limit on the first year of cashflows, i.e. on the capital outlay. Once companies have to think about the impact on future projects or the need to stay within a capital budget for a second year of capital outlay, we must use another technique, Linear Programming. Linear Programming takes all the constraints on the capital investment budget and transforms them into equations which it proceeds to solve.

Why more companies don't use linear programming

There are three main reasons. Firstly, LP is very expensive to use. Secondly, its use suggests that the company knows of all future potential investments. Thirdly, often companies have only a very hazy idea of investments in the future and so do not want to spend valuable money working on the perfect solution for an investment decision which is merely hypothetical. However, simple LP models can be used to choose between two or three mutually exclusive projects where more than one resource is constrained.

Part III – The impact of tax

Tax has two main implications for investment appraisals. On the one hand, if the investment is successful and has a net profit, company taxes will increase. On the other hand, if the investment has involved capital expenditure, the company may be able to claim capital allowances from the government and this will help to reduce its tax burden. The purpose of this section is to show you how you can calculate the forecast tax burden for an investment project, and when you should assume this tax burden has to be paid.

Taxable profit

We have discussed how important it is to consider only cashflows when forecasting the benefits of an investment. However, to calculate the tax cashflows accurately, you will need to forecast the profit of the investment as well. How accurate this estimate needs to be will depend on how large the investment is, and how far the investment proposal has progressed through the review process. Once the incremental cashflow has been forecast, the payment of taxes should automatically be included in your cashflow forecasts.

Timing of tax cashflows

In the UK, the actual payment of corporation taxes, payable on the profits of one year, does not normally occur until the following year. It is currently due six months after the end of the financial year. Thus, on average, a company only pays tax one year after the tax expense was incurred.

Depreciation

Companies have to capitalise certain expenditures rather than claiming them as expenses in the profit and loss statement for the year in which they occur. The justification for this is that the economic life of a piece of machinery is longer than a single year. A depreciation expense is then deducted on a yearly basis according to a prescribed schedule. This schedule could be a straight-line depreciation for five or ten years, i.e. the cost of the investment is divided by five and a fifth of the investment is recognised as an expense each year. Or the company's accountants may decide to use a form of accelerated depreciation such as reducing balance depreciation. In these circumstances, a greater proportion of the investment is recognised as an expense in the earlier years.

> Tax has two main implications for investment appraisals. On the one hand, if the investment is successful and has a net profit, company taxes will increase. On the other hand, if the investment has involved capital expenditure, the company may be able to claim capital allowances from the government and this will help to reduce its tax burden.

A comparison of how the depreciation will vary for these two methods is shown below, when we take an investment of £20,000 that has a life of five years.

Year	Straight-line depreciation		Reducing balance depreciation	
	Asset value	Expense	Asset value	Expense
0	£20,000		£20,000	
1	£16,000	£4,000	£15,000	£5,000
2	£12,000	£4,000	£11,250	£3,750
3	£8,000	£4,000	£8,432	£2,813
4	£4,000	£4,000	£6,323	£2,109
5	–	£4,000	£4,742	£1,581*

* during the fifth year, the remaining asset value is shown as a depreciation expense.

It is largely up to the financial management of a company to choose their depreciation policy. Accelerated depreciation will reduce the profits seen in the annual report, in the early years. But the method chosen will not affect the *amount* of tax that a company must pay.

Capital allowances

In the profit and loss statements prepared for the annual report, the depreciation expense for capital assets is deducted from operating profit, as are other items such as provisions for bad debts and political contributions. However, for the purposes of the tax man, these deductions are not allowed and are therefore added back to operating profit in the tax accounts. In this way, a company cannot reduce its profits, and hence its tax burden, by changing its depreciation system. However, the government does allow companies to deduct capital allowances which are specified by the government for different types of investment. Figure 4.7 highlights the capital allowances for the three capital asset categories.

	Industrial Buildings	Plant & Machinery	Motor vehicles
Straight line	✓		
Reducing balance		✓	✓
Number of years	25	Life	Life
Same as depreciation	✓	Possible	Very possible
Example – Yr 1	£400	£2,500	£2,500
Yr 2	£400	£1,875	£1,875
Yr 3	£400	£1,406	£1,406
Yr 4	£400	£1,055	£1,055
Yr 5	£400	£791	£791

Figure 4.7   Capital allowances

Balancing charges and allowances

If an asset is sold before all the capital allowances are taken, the difference between the net book value (after these capital allowances) and the price received for the asset is settled with the government. If the asset is sold for more than its net book value, there is a balancing charge due to the government as it claims back the excess capital allowance that it has previously given. However, if the asset was sold for less than its taxable book value, the government gives an additional capital allowance. These allowances or payments are known as balancing charges.

Timing of tax savings from capital allowances

The capital allowances are only available in the year following the purchase of the asset. This means that on average the tax savings will be available a year after that (as that is when the company will pay the tax). Depending on the timing of the asset purchase, this capital allowance can lag behind by as little as nine months or as much as a year and a half. As a general rule, take any capital allowances as cash inflows beginning two years after the capital outlay. You may be able to be more precise about when the capital investment is made during the year, and therefore, when the tax savings from the capital allowances can be forecast.

How this affects investment appraisal

So far in this section we have looked at the company as a whole when considering depreciation and capital allowances. It is important to remember that the cash impact of these capital allowances will depend on two factors:

■ when the investment begins to make a profit so that the capital allowances can be offset against this; and

■ whether the company as a whole can offset the capital allowances against other profits made even if they do not come from this investment project.

The impact of inflation on tax for investment appraisals

The impact of inflation is twofold. One consequence makes the investment project more attractive, the other decreases its appeal. On the one hand, because tax payments lag behind when taxable profits actually occur, in times of high inflation, the *real* cost of those tax payments is decreased. On the other hand, capital allowances for the purchase of fixed assets such as plant and equipment, vehicles and buildings are unchanged by inflation and thus the *real* benefit of these capital allowances also decreases over time.

Financial leases and tax

We have discussed how the investing decision must be separated from the financing decisions. This is particularly the case when considering whether to buy or lease a piece of equipment. A lease is a series of fixed payments made to a lessor who has leased a company a piece of equipment or a building. There are two main types of lease. The first form is an *operating lease*, where a company decides to lease a piece of equipment on a quarterly or monthly basis, and where it is a cancellable contract. There can be a distinct benefit in the option to cancel a lease on equipment that is not available if the equipment is bought outright. Case study 7 in Chapter 6 looks at this issue in more detail. The second type of lease is a *financial lease*. A financial lease is a non-cancellable lease that should be seen as a form of financing. The lessor leases the equipment to the company and in return receives lease payments for the lease period. It is rather like obtaining a secured loan. The difference is that instead of borrowing the money to buy the equipment, against which the loan is then secured, the lessor owns the equipment and the company uses it for the contract period.

How does tax affect leases?

Tax affects leasing in two ways. Firstly, a company that chooses to lease a piece of equipment rather than buy it loses the opportunity to offset any capital allowances against tax. On the other hand, the lease payments themselves are deducted before tax and so create a *tax shield* themselves. This is illustrated in Figure 4.8.

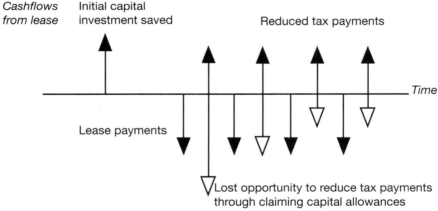

Figure 4.8   Impact of tax on leases

Given that lease payments are rather like paying interest on a secured loan, the appropriate discount rate is the interest rate that would be incurred if the company borrowed the money to buy the equipment rather than leasing it. Furthermore, as the net return to the lessor is dependent on the after-tax interest rate, and the cost to the lessee is determined by the after-tax interest rate, the discount rate should be *after tax*. Let's look at an example.

Example

Farmer Brown is deciding whether to borrow money to buy a new combine harvester or to lease the machine from a leasing company for five years. The cost of borrowing the money to make the purchase would be 10.5 per cent which equates to an after-tax rate of 7 per cent. It is assumed that the machine will have no salvage value after five years. It is also assumed that the lease payments are payable in advance on a yearly basis.

Year	Cost of harvester	Lost capital allowance	Tax shield	Lease payments	New tax shield	Net cashflow
0	£60,000					£60,000
1		£15,000		(£15,000)		(£15,000)
2		£11,250	(£4,950)	(£15,000)	£4,950	(£15,000)
3		£8,438	(£3,713)	(£15,000)	£4,950	(£13,763)
4		£6,328	(£2,784)	(£15,000)	£4,950	(£12,834)
5		£18,984	(£2,088)	(£15,000)	£4,950	(£12,138)
6			(£6,265)		£4,950	(£1,315)
NPV at 7%						£2,324

When would a company choose to lease equipment?

A company would choose to lease a piece of equipment if the financing provided by the leasing company exceeded the financing provided by the equivalent loan. Where the lessor and the lessee are both paying the same rate of corporation tax, it is a zero sum game; if the deal is good for the lessee, it is bad for the lessor and vice versa. The only winner in this case is the tax man. However, if the lessee is not earning sufficient profits to utilise the tax shield from capital allowances or from the tax deductible lease payments, then the lessee and the lessor can both be winners.

Consistency

There is one overriding rule which governs both the treatment of taxation in project appraisal, and the treatment of inflation: *be consistent*. If cashflows on an after-tax basis are included in your analysis, ensure that the discount rate used is also after tax, as we did in the Farmer Brown example above. We will examine how to derive this discount rate in Chapters 7 and 8 but keep in mind the rule of consistency as you consider the effect of inflation in the next chapter.

Flow chart summary

The flow chart in Figure 4.9 below summarises some of the questions that you should be asking when deciding which cashflows are relevant to your investment appraisal.

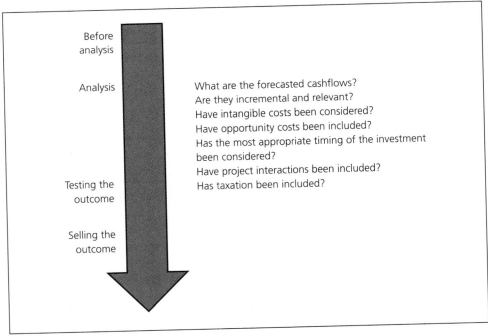

Figure 4.9   Flow diagram for investment appraisal

CASE STUDY 4.2

Genima Ltd is a manufacturing company producing a range of construction and tunnelling machinery. It is considering a capital investment to introduce a new product and the research team have already done some preliminary analysis. It is now September 1999 and they want to decide whether to make the capital investment so that they can have the new process line ready for a launch during 2000. Below is some of the information that they have amassed. The opportunity cost of capital for this investment is 10 per cent and inflation, for the purposes of this case study, is assumed to be zero. What is the NPV of the investment?

Estimated life of the product

- Four years (2000–2003); they assume they will need to bring out a newer model by this time.

New equipment cost

- £200,000, purchased in quarter 4 this year.
- It will have a residual value of £45,000 at the end of the investment.

Research and development

- £90,000 in total; £50,000 already spent, the remainder spent in quarter 4.

Factory capacity

- Allocated costs of £75,000 starting in 2000. This site is already owned and will be used for existing product lines if it is not used by the new investment.

Capital allowances

- Available on double declining basis beginning the year after the capital investment is made.

Management time

- Genima has hired a new operations manager to oversee this investment. He has already spent 75 per cent of his time evaluating the viability of the investment for the last three months. It is forecasted that this investment will continue to take 75 per cent of his time in 1999 and 50 per cent of his time until the end of 2000. His cost to Genima is £40,000 per year.

Working capital

■ Genima will have to buy in certain components and their customers, who are mostly corporations, will be paying 30 days after delivery. The initial net working capital will be £60,000 and will increase by approximately £20,000 per year.

Fixed overheads

■ Fixed overheads of £100,000 will be charged to this investment at the current allocated overhead rate which is calculated on factory space used. The cost of additional fixed costs due to this investment are £40,000 per year, excluding the cost of the operations manager.

Other issues

■ The selling price is £250 per unit and Genima has forecasted to sell 2,000 units in 2000, 3,000 units in 2001, 3,400 units in 2002 and 3,600 units in 2003.

■ The variable cost per unit is £175.

■ Genima's corporate tax rate is 33 per cent.

Solution

The yearly cashflows are as follows:

Year	Net cashflow	PV factor	PV
1999	(£307,500)	1.000	(£307,500)
2000	£46,667	0.909	£42,400
2001	£126,667	0.826	£104,627
2002	£142,500	0.751	£107,018
2003	£256,042	0.683	£174,876
2004	£7,031	0.621	£4,366
2005	£19,701	0.564	£11,111
NPV			£136,918

In 1999, Genima will have spent £200,000 in capital outlay, £40,000 in research, £60,000 in working capital outlay and £7,500 in fixed overheads (operations manager).

Let's look at these cashflows in more detail from 2000 onwards:

Year	2000	2001	2002	2003	2004
Sales	£500,000	£750,000	£850,000	£900,000	
Fixed costs	(£60,000)	(£40,000)	(£40,000)	(£40,000)	
Variable costs	(£350,000)	(£525,000)	(£595,000)	(£630,000)	
Change in WC	(£20,000)	(£20,000)	(£20,000)	£120,000	
Capital allowance	£50,000	£37,500	£28,125	£21,094	£59,102*
Tax saving		£16,667	£12,500	£9,375	£7,031
Tax at 33%	(£23,333)	(£55,000)	(£65,000)	(£123,333)	
Cashflows	£46,667	£126,667	£142,500	£256,042	£7,031

* the capital allowance for 1999 includes a balancing charge to balance the accumulated capital allowance with the value of the capital assets.

Comments

- The sunk costs of management time and research costs are not included.

- The factory allocated costs are not included (sunk cost).

- The allocated overhead cost is not included, only those fixed costs which are incremental to existing costs (£20,000 in 2000).

- Half of the new operations manager's costs are included but not the time already spent.

- Tax savings due to capital allowances are included and a balancing charge of £18,281 is made when the equipment is sold at the end of the investment life (£63,281 – £45,000).

- Working capital in the project is included as a cash inflow in the final quarter.

CHECKLIST OF PRACTICAL TIPS

1 First, decide on the appropriate alternative to the investment project; are there any opportunity costs which should be included in the analysis?

2 Then write down all the tangible and intangible costs and benefits of this project that are *incremental* to existing expenditure. Can the intangible costs and benefits be converted into monetary values *in a way that is acceptable to others*? Concentrate on the incremental costs and benefits that are most relevant to your immediate audience. Leave the other quantifiable benefits as icing on the cake.

In Part I we will consider how to deal with inflation. In Part II, we will look at how to use various tools to evaluate the uncertainty of cashflow forecasts.

Forecasting cashflows

- Part I – How to deal with inflation
- Part II – Dealing with uncertainty

CHECKLIST OF KEY POINTS

1 Part I of this chapter considers how to deal with inflation. The overriding rule is that inflation should be treated on a consistent basis, that is, if cashflows are given in real terms then the discount rate must be given in real terms as well. Similarly, if cashflows are nominal then a nominal cost of capital must be used to discount these cashflows in the Net Present Value analysis.

2 If all cashflows increase in line with inflation then the NPV analysis will yield the same results whether nominal cashflows with a nominal discount rate are used or real cashflows with a real discount rate. However, in reality, this is rarely the case. It is more likely that only some of the cashflows will rise directly with inflation. Sales growth can lag behind inflation whereas some costs such as labour costs often rise ahead of the Retail Price Index. Other costs such as lease payments may be fixed and should not be forecast as increasing with the general inflation rate. Thus it is recommended that cashflows are forecasted in nominal terms and a nominal discount rate used to convert them into present values.

3 In Part II, the question of how to deal with uncertain cashflows is addressed. Many cashflows are uncertain and there are a variety of ways of exploring these cashflow scenarios. These tools can help you to examine what could go wrong and will give you a greater insight into the drivers of the positive Net Present Value of an investment project.

4 These tools range from the relatively unsophisticated sensitivity analysis through scenario modelling to sophisticated simulation models using complex decision trees.

5 The more static models for looking at variable cashflows do not indicate that managers can change the direction of an investment project once it has been initiated, either by expansion or contraction, or even abandonment. This ability to alter the course of the investment depending on the early response of the market or the environment can have significant value. The use of decision trees, to identify the major strategic choices, can enhance your analysis.

6 However, all these techniques carry the risk that the manager loses 'sight of the wood for the trees'. The investment appraiser must retain a firm grip on what the key variables in the investment project are and not get bogged down in detail.

Introduction

This chapter builds on Chapter 4, where we looked at the question of relevant cashflows, and asks, how can we best *forecast* those cashflows? We will now relax the remaining assumptions governing the cashflows in investment appraisal; we are no longer going to assume that there is no inflation and we are no longer going to assume that the cashflows are known and certain. In Part I we will consider how to deal with inflation. In Part II, we will look at how to use various tools to evaluate the uncertainty of cashflow forecasts.

Part I – How to deal with inflation

Inflation affects investment appraisal in two main ways. It affects the cashflow forecasts in the investment proposal. It also affects the cost of capital that investors require. They want to ensure that they are making a return in real terms and so will adjust their expectations on the return of an investment upwards if there is high inflation.

How inflation affects cashflow forecasts

Generally the impact of inflation in financial statements is that asset values are *understated* in the pro-forma balance sheet because their market value rises with inflation, and profits are *overstated* in the pro-forma profit and loss statement as depreciation, which is deducted, does not rise with inflation. Inflation creates particular problems for forecasting cashflows: inflation increases uncertainty and makes estimating sales revenues, operating costs and working capital requirements more difficult. The increase in working capital requirements actually lowers the return on an investment as it means more money is being tied up in the investment that could have been used elsewhere. If a customer gets two months' credit for goods, the real value of that sale is reduced because you have lost the opportunity to invest that money for two months.

> Inflation affects investment appraisal in two main ways. It affects the cashflow forecasts in the investment proposal. It also affects the cost of capital that investors require.

The components of the discount rate

So far in this book we have talked about the time value of money – the opportunity cost of money that could have been invested and earning a return rather than being tied up in an investment project. There is a second component to the discount rate when inflation is a factor. That is *the change in the value of the money itself* as inflation reduces its purchasing power. Thus one hears economists talking about the real return on an investment and the nominal return on the investment, which takes inflation into account. For example, the average real return of the stock market has been stable for many years but the nominal return has varied markedly with inflation. A nominal discount rate has two components, the real discount rate that takes into account the time value of money and inflation.

> 1 + Nominal discount rate = (1+ Real discount rate) × (1+ Inflation)

Thus if the inflation rate is 5 per cent and the real discount rate is 6 per cent, the nominal discount rate will be:

$$
\begin{aligned}
1 + \text{Nominal discount rate} \quad &= \quad (1 + 0.06) \times (1 + 0.05) \\
&= \quad (1.113) \\
\text{Nominal discount rate} \quad &= \quad 11.3\%
\end{aligned}
$$

Forecasting cashflows in an inflationary world

There are two courses of action for the manager forecasting cashflows in the real world. He can forecast cashflows in today's money, i.e. assume that the purchasing power of the money remains the same. In this case he must also discount these cashflows at the real discount rate, not the nominal one. His second course of action is to try to forecast how the cashflows will change with inflation. If he takes this route, he should discount those cashflows at the nominal discount rate. Let's look at both of these alternatives in greater detail.

Using real cashflows

A manager may decide to use real cashflows if he believes that all the relevant cashflows are going to increase in line with inflation. If this is the case, using real cashflows with a real discount rate or using nominal cashflows with a nominal discount rate would give an identical result in an investment appraisal.

As discount rates are nearly always stated as nominal, this nominal rate should be converted into a real discount rate. This is done by taking the above formula and reconfiguring it:

$$\text{Real discount rate} = \frac{1 + \text{Nominal rate of return}}{1 + \text{Inflation rate}} - 1$$

Example

Supposing Tradex Ltd, a company importing bananas from abroad, is evaluating whether to install a new packing line in its Kent depot. For the sake of simplicity, and easy numbers to play with, let's assume that inflation will be 4.6 per cent for the next five years and that all its main cashflows will increase in line with inflation. The real discount rate that it is using to evaluate this project is 8 per cent and therefore the nominal discount rate is said to be:

$$\text{Nominal discount rate} = \text{Real discount rate} \times \text{Inflation}$$

$$= (1 + 8\%) \times (1 + 4.6\%) - 1$$
$$= 0.13$$
$$= 13\%$$

Note: This gives a slightly higher figure than just adding 4.6 per cent to the real discount rate of 8 per cent.

The company decides to calculate the NPV using both real figures and nominal figures.

Year	Real cashflows	PV factor at 8 %	Present value	Nominal cashflows	PV factor at 13%	Present value
0	(£20,000)	1.000	(£20,000)	(£20,000)	1.000	(£20,000)
1	£4,000	0.926	£3,704	£4,185	0.885	£3,704
2	£6,000	0.857	£5,142	£6,568	0.783	£5,143
3	£7,000	0.794	£5,558	£8,018	0.693	£5,557
4	£7,000	0.735	£5,145	£8,389	0.613	£5,144
5	£5,000	0.681	£3,405	£6,270	0.543	£3,405
NPV			£2,954			£2,953*

* the slight differences are due to rounding.

Critique of using real cashflows

In the above example all the cashflows changed directly in line with inflation so it did not matter which method was used as they yielded equivalent results.

However, there are two main reasons why companies choose to use nominal cashflows rather than real cashflows. Firstly, senior management may state the required rate of return for all new investment projects in nominal terms. Though you can convert the nominal discount rate into a real discount rate using the above formula, you may run into problems when selling your investment appraisal to senior management. The discount rate will not be instantly recognisable as the required stipulated rate of return.

A second and much more serious concern is whether it is always realistic to assume that all cashflows will change with inflation.

Take the simple example given above. Given that this company is an importer of goods, its costs of goods sold will be determined more by factors occurring in the country of origin such as their inflation rate and climatic conditions, rather than by the inflation rate in the home country. Other operating costs may not necessarily be in line with inflation. The shipping costs will be highly correlated to the oil price which is only one component of the general inflation rate. Even if sales do follow inflation in the broadest sense, there may be seasonal variations.

The above case is a very obvious one but in most situations there will be differences in how the different cashflows adjust for inflation. For example, sales increases often lag behind an increase in inflation as suppliers have to honour fixed price contracts for a time. Salary and wage growth often exceed the Retail Price Index because of productivity increases and an underlying increase in real wages. Other important cashflows that are often inflated incorrectly are lease payments and capital allowances, and therefore the tax shield that is derived from them. (If the nominal cashflows are being derived from nominal profit forecasts, it is important to remember that depreciation should not be inflated.)

It is important to appreciate these differences because even small differences can have quite an impact on the attractiveness of a project as the simple worked example below shows.

Example

Snuggles Company is considering whether to expand its baby clothes product line. At first it decides that the major cashflows associated with the increased production will increase in line with inflation which is 4.6 per cent and so it conducts the investment appraisal using real cashflows and a real discount rate of 8 per cent. However, on closer examination of its cashflows, the manager decides that sales growth will lag behind the inflation rate and that operating costs would increase slightly above the general inflation rate. The net result is that nominal cashflows are projected to grow at 3.5 per cent rather than 4.6 per cent. Comparing the investment analysis taking a 'real' approach and a 'nominal' approach, we see that the real approach would have over estimated the NPV of the investment by £3,314.

Year	Real cashflows	PV factor at 8%	Present value	Nominal cashflows	PV factor at 13%	Present value
0	(£80,000)	1.000	(£80,000)	(£80,000)	1.000	(£80,000)
1	£20,000	0.926	£18,520	£20,700	0.885	£18,320
2	£30,000	0.857	£25,710	£32,137	0.783	£25,163
3	£35,000	0.794	£27,790	£38,805	0.693	£26,892
4	£30,000	0.735	£22,050	£34,426	0.613	£21,103
5	£20,000	0.681	£13,620	£23,754	0.543	£12,898
NPV			£27,690			£24,376

Forecasting nominal cashflows

The above discussion might explain why generally it is more accurate to take nominal discount rates with nominal cashflows, but it still doesn't really help with estimating those nominal cashflows! The job of estimating future inflation is one of the most difficult ones for an economic forecaster and so you use the economic forecasts available for your analysis.

PRACTICAL TIPS: FUTURE INFLATION

- Agree among the project team what general inflation level you will be assuming for the investment appraisal. This is useful both for the smaller cashflows which do not warrant separate review and as a benchmark for the larger cashflows. (See next section.)

- You should try to project how inflation will vary over the next two to three years and then take a general estimate for the remaining years of the investment project.

- Next, take the main cashflows and think carefully about the drivers of their growth. Try to deal with each cost group separately. It may be helpful to use the general inflation forecast as a benchmark and adjust up or downwards. Are there any fixed contracts which will create a time lag in cost or sales adjustments?

- Remember to treat lease payments and capital allowances separately and not to increase them in line with inflation.

Using sensitivity analysis

If forecasting inflation is an area of uncertainty in your investment appraisal, it is often useful to use sensitivity analysis to ascertain how high inflation would have to be before a particular investment project no longer showed a positive NPV. In this way, if you have forecast inflation to be 5 per cent per annum for the next five years and sensitivity analysis shows that inflation would have to rise to 10 per cent per annum for the NPV to be negative, you can take comfort that your forecast would have to be very wrong indeed for the implications of the appraisal to change!

The use of sensitivity analysis will be reviewed in more detail in the next section.

Part II – Dealing with uncertainty

Inflation is just one area of possible uncertainty that could affect an investment appraisal. However, there could be many others, for example, the unit cost of production could be more than you forecast or the exchange rate could change thus altering the cost of imported supplies. So far we have assumed that there is just one set of cashflows from an investment and we have focused on the difficulty of identifying and quantifying those cashflows. But unfortunately this happens only occasionally in real life. More realistically there are a range of outcomes that could occur. Risk and uncertainty are used synonymously in this chapter. We could perhaps define risk by saying that *more can happen than will happen.*

There are two approaches to risk. The more modern approach to risk is to vary the discount rate depending on the degree of risk entailed by the investment. How we assess risk in this way and incorporate it in the discount rate is the subject of Chapters 7 and 8. What can be said here is that the discount rate implicitly accepts that risk increases with the length of the investment as the range of possible outcomes multiplies. By compound discounting the cashflows of the distant future, discounted cashflow methods such as Net Present Value automatically account for the increased risk as the investment continues.

> Sensitivity analysis takes the forecasted cashflows and looks at their major components such as the initial cash outlay, the sales and operating costs and the estimated time horizon for the investment. It seeks to ascertain which of the main cashflow components affect the overall Net Present Value of the investment in a significant way.

The more traditional methods of looking at risk, such as sensitivity analysis, scenario modelling and decision trees, all seek to identify the key areas of change within an investment project. But no manager will ever be able to simulate all the possible outcomes of a complex investment project, and thus these techniques do not eliminate the risk of the investment. However, they are still useful in helping you gain a greater understanding of the range of outcomes and the key drivers of an investment's cashflow. They cannot eliminate risk but they expose the risk to greater examination.

A number of tools have been developed to help us examine forecasted cashflows. They range from the relatively crude measurements, such as sensitivity analysis, to sophisticated use of computer simulation models.

Nowadays, computers can make what used to be a time-consuming and number crunching process, a painless and simple one. When developing a model of an investment on the computer, it is easy to include some sensitivity analyses which allow you to ask a number of 'what if' questions.

Using sensitivity analysis

Sensitivity analysis takes the forecasted cashflows and looks at their major components such as the initial cash outlay, the sales and operating costs and the estimated time horizon for the investment. It seeks to ascertain which of the main cashflow components affect the overall Net Present Value of the investment in a significant way. By identifying the main drivers of the NPV, managers can work out which areas need particular attention and perhaps do some further analysis to enable them to forecast that area with greater accuracy.

Sensitivity analysis asks what would happen to the Net Present Value of the investment if the capital outlay of that investment was actually x per cent higher, or if the sales resulting from the investment were y per cent lower than the initial forecast assumes? This analysis can be conducted at a second level of detail as well: instead of looking at sales, we can look behind the sales figures and consider the impact of changes in the selling price or in market share. The level of detail will be dependent on the stage of the investment appraisal and the size of the investment.

Sensitivity analysis is used to try to establish where investment projects might fail. Each of the critical variables is assessed as to whether there is a high likelihood that events could occur that would lead to a negative Net Present Value. The sensitivity analysis is thus reformulated to ask: by how much would the sales volumes need to decline before the NPV of the project was negative? Let us look at a simple example.

Example

Here the NPV was computed for an investment proposal under the base-case scenario. Then the reformulated NPV is shown when each component of the cashflows is changed for the worse. Thus with a 10 per cent decrease in the selling price, the NPV decreases to (£15,730) whereas if the sales and marketing costs were increased by 10 per cent, the NPV would only decrease to £14,607.

NPV under different conditions	Expected	5%	10%
Increase in initial investment cost	£17,977	£12,977	£7,977
Decrease in volumes sold		£12,318	£6,407
Decrease in selling price		£1,123	(£15,730)
Increase in production cost per unit		£8,708	(£562)
Increase in sales and marketing cost per unit		£16,292	£14,607

The initial investment cost would have to increase by 18 per cent before the NPV was negative. The selling price and the sales volumes would have to decrease by 5.4 per cent and 15.5 per cent respectively before the NPV was negative. The sales and marketing cost per unit and the unit production cost would have to increase by 53 per cent and 9.5 per cent respectively for the NPV to become negative.

Here we can see that the main variable that the company must look closely at is the sales price. A decrease of only 5.4 per cent results in a negative NPV.

The value of advanced information

If your sensitivity analysis has indicated that varying the value of one component, for example, the unit production cost, has a significant effect on the NPV, you could consider gaining some advanced information through prototype testing.

Example

The expected unit production cost is £420 and the Net Present Value of the investment is £150,000. However, there is some uncertainty as to whether the unit can be produced for this price. If the average unit cost increases to £490, the Net Present Value decreases to £10,000. The research department believe that a prototype research project which will cost £40,000 will eliminate this uncertainty. Thus the cost of the research project is £40,000 but its true value is much greater at £150,000 – £10,000 = £140,000.

Another use for sensitivity analysis – quantifying the unquantifiable!

We have already discussed the need to consider the qualitative aspects of an investment project, both beneficial or otherwise. However, there are some costs and benefits that cannot be estimated with any accuracy. One benefit of sensitivity analysis is that it allows us to turn the analysis on its head. Instead of trying to estimate a monetary value for a non-quantifiable benefit, we can ask what the possible maximum is, if it is a cost, for the investment still to have a small positive NPV. Or how low it can be, if it is a benefit, for the investment still to result in a positive NPV. A simple example will illustrate this.

Example

A doll manufacturer is considering a machinery investment. The machine will cost £120,000, will yield cost savings of £30,000 per year and has an expected life of five years at which point it will have no scrap value. However, the machinery uses a different method of assembly and each doll produced will be tougher and safer for children. The company believes that this improvement could have some impact on sales though they do not wish to forecast increased sales, as it is highly speculative. The NPV of the base case is (£6,276) using a discount rate of 10 per cent, assuming no impact on sales whatsoever. However, if the sales were increased by only 1 per cent per year (assuming a profit margin of 15 per cent), the NPV of the investment would be positive. All the plant management has to decide is whether there is any likelihood that the sales might not change at all? If not, then they can accept the project even though they may not know whether increased sales will be 1 or 2 per cent per year.

A critique of sensitivity analysis

The largest single criticism of sensitivity analysis is that the real world often doesn't work this way. To assume that only one variable will change at a time is often not satisfactory. Sometimes it is the case – the length of the project could change whilst everything else remains the same. In many cases, however, a change in one variable is caused by some change in the overall economic environment and this usually leads to change in other variables as well. For example, in the case of higher inflation than forecasted, this will lead to increased operating costs but the selling price will also change.

The first example given above used set changes of 5 per cent and 10 per cent in each of the main variables. This is an objective approach but it requires some careful thought as to what is an appropriate percentage change to take. The same percentage change across the board may be unrealistic. (A realistic downside sales forecast may be a decrease of 20 per cent but a realistic exchange rate change for the downside scenario may be more within a 10 per cent range.)

One way of avoiding this problem is to ask each of the specialists involved in the investment appraisal to estimate an optimistic, base-case or pessimistic forecast for their relevant area. So the production manager must supply an optimistic, base-case and pessimistic assessment for the operating costs, or the main components of operating costs such as the unit cost of production. The problem with this approach is that there is a high degree of subjectivity involved and this could lead to inconsistent forecasts. (One person's 'optimistic forecast' may be slightly better than base-case whilst another person's 'optimistic forecast' is the best possible outcome and assumes *everything* goes perfectly!)

> An adaptation of sensitivity analysis is scenario modelling. Here the investment appraiser considers what is the most likely change in the 'state of nature' and then adjusts the components of the investment appraisal simultaneously. This is more realistic in many investment scenarios and can give the Net Present Value on the range of possible outcomes.

Using scenarios

An adaptation of sensitivity analysis is scenario modelling. Here the investment appraiser considers what is the most likely change in the 'state of nature' and then adjusts the components of the investment appraisal simultaneously. This is more realistic in many investment scenarios and can give the Net Present Value on the range of possible outcomes. Different 'states of nature' in this context could be changes in the macro-economic environment, thus an investment is considered under the conditions of a recession or a period of high inflation.

The same methods could be used to evaluate how the Net Present Value of an investment project changes if different possible outcomes of an investment decision are forecasted such as high demand versus low demand.

Example

Opto Company is considering launching a new flavour ice cream tasting of peanut butter and jam. They have done their base-case scenario for the initial investment, sales, fixed costs, variable costs and so forth. They decide to consider two other scenarios: a pessimistic scenario, where the product 'bombs' in spectacular fashion, and an optimistic scenario, where the product starts a new craze among children and becomes *the* ice cream to buy. Both of these scenarios will affect a number of the variables that comprise the forecasted cashflows as is shown below. They affect the selling price achievable, the number of ice creams sold, the production cost per unit (due to economies of scale as production increases) and the actual life of the project (with the product being withdrawn after four years in the pessimistic scenario).

Criteria	Pessimistic	Base case	Optimistic
Initial investment	£100,000	£90,000	£80,000
Selling price	£0.60	£0.70	£0.70
Units sold in Year 1	50,000	90,000	140,000
Units sold in following years	30,000	70,000	120,000
Cost per unit	£0.38	£0.35	£0.32
(showing economies of scale)			
Life of the investment	4 years	5 years	6 years
NPV at 12%	(£76,000)	£4,570	£114,265

Opto realises that there is considerable variability in the potential outcome, and thus high risk. The base-case scenario results in a small positive NPV, the optimistic case results in a very heavy NPV whilst the pessimistic scenario leads to a large negative NPV. But it still leaves many unanswered questions... .

A critique of scenario modelling

There are two main criticisms of scenario modelling, both of which *are* avoidable. The first criticism is that different specialists often supply different parts of the scenario and, as with sensitivity analysis, this can lead to inconsistent results. If a project team is jointly responsible for the analysis, ensure that common assumptions have been agreed upon before providing scenarios.

The second criticism is that scenario modelling gives the range of possible outcomes but no more than that, as in the last example. It gives no indication of their likelihood. It may be that the pessimistic scenario may be twice as likely to occur than the optimistic scenario. This problem can be avoided if probabilities are attached to the different scenarios as in the case of Expected NPV analysis below.

Expected Net Present Values (ENPV)

The Expected NPV cashflows takes scenario modelling and attributes different probabilities to the range of likely outcomes. Taking a simple example when a project has two alternative scenarios – high demand or low demand. If there is high demand for the new product, the Present Value of the cashflows is £100,000 and there is a 70 per cent probability that this will be the case. If there is low demand for the project, the Present Values of the cashflows will only be £50,000 and there is a 30 per cent probability that this will occur. The initial cash outflow will be £50,000. The ENPV will be as follows:

$$
\begin{aligned}
\text{ENPV} \quad &= \quad -£50{,}000 + \{(£100{,}000 \times 0.70) + (£50{,}000 \times 0.30)\} \\
&= \quad -£50{,}000 + £85{,}000 \\
&= \quad £35{,}000
\end{aligned}
$$

Of course, with the use of computers it is easy to work on more sophisticated analyses. For example, each of the main components could have a set of probabilities attached to them and these are fed into a computer that then performs numerous reiterative calculations to achieve an Expected Net Present Value.

A critique of ENPVs

Though ENPVs are the end product of many investment appraisals, they still assume discrete courses of action which, once initiated, are unchanging. This may not be the case. Managers can change the nature of the investment once it has been started. Decision trees take into account the dynamic process involved in investment selection and management.

Using decision trees

So far we have simplified the environment and assumed that the course of the investment is predetermined at the beginning of the process, with set cashflows resulting from it. However, a manager may be faced with a choice of alternatives which in turn lead to further alternatives in future years. These subsequent decisions have a clear financial impact on the original choice of investment and you must be sure to include major subsequent choices in your analysis. Decision trees are useful tools to help you to do just that.

A decision tree is aptly named because it shows the various decisions and resulting outcomes diagrammatically in the form of a tree, usually a felled tree, as in Figure 5.1.

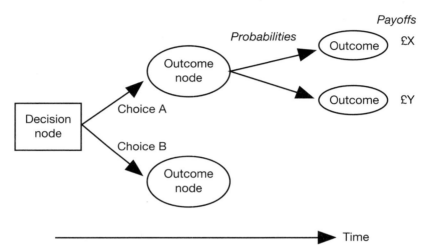

Figure 5.1   A simple decision tree

A decision tree is a series of 'nodes', where alternative courses of action are available, and branches which indicate the possible financial impact of those choices. There are two types of nodes: decision nodes denoted by a square and outcome nodes denoted by a circle and each relate to previous outcomes further down the tree, that is, earlier on in the life of the investment.

Let us take a simple one-period example so that you can become familiar with 'reading' a decision tree.

Example

Zappy Ltd is a Fast Moving Consumer Goods (FMCG) manufacturer that introduced a new product onto the shelves of the major supermarkets two years ago. It has not been an outstanding success and now the management must decide their next move. There are three possible alternatives for them. They can invest more marketing spend in the hope of stimulating latent demand. They can continue to invest at their current levels and hope that the product will finally take off, or they can cut their costs and withdraw the product from the shelves. An expansion in marketing spend to £40,000 is estimated to give an 80 per cent chance of High Demand* that will result in incoming cashflows at today's prices of £80,000. Maintaining a current investment of £20,000 also has a possibility of generating a High Demand but the chances are lower, only a 50 per cent probability. In both these scenarios, Low Demand will produce a present value payoff of (£40,000). The third alternative, withdrawing the product, will incur close-down costs of £5,000.

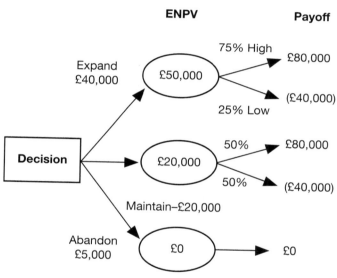

Figure 5.2   Zappy Ltd – decision tree

Figure 5.2 sets the problem out in a decision tree format. This format shows that the choice is between an ENPV of:

Expansion   £50,000 – £40,000   =   £10,000
Maintenance   £20,000 – £20,000   =   £0
Abandonment   £0 – £5,000   =   (£5,000)

The expansion option looks to be the most profitable route to take.

* for the sake of simplicity demand for the product has been divided into High Demand and Low Demand.

Decision trees for two or more periods

Now let us introduce a second decision in Year Two that is dependent on what takes place in Year One. This can get quite complex so hang in there.

How to read decision trees

You will make the initial investment decision based on which course of action, or branch in the decision tree, results in the greatest expected NPV. To find out which of the branches has the highest expected NPV, we need to work backwards from the end of each branch. In other words, we solve the question of what we should do today by considering what we should do when facing any subsequent decisions. Imagine you are now in Year One and you are faced with a second choice. There is no point concerning yourself with what has already happened. Your only decision is what you should do now – which course of action leads to the greatest expected PV in Year One. Having established this, you will discard the alternative course of action as less attractive and work backwards to incorporate the expected payoffs from the first year. Let's take an example.

Example

Delicious Deli Ltd is the name of a delicatessen owned by Marco Poloni. His existing shop is very successful and he is considering expansion – a chain of delicatessens in neighbouring towns and cities. He decides to open one store in Minchester, a neighbouring town, while finding sites for the other locations. He must decide between a large store in a prime location but with high overheads, or a smaller store not so close to the main magnet shops in town. As this is a new town for Marco Poloni, he is not completely sure of the demand for a delicatessen, but he thinks that if demand is strong, he will extend the small store. Marco's cost of capital is 11 per cent.

The major decision nodes, probabilities of success and payoffs are given in Figure 5.3.

In order to decide which size of shop Marco should invest in, we have to work back from the second decision; if demand is strong, Marco has the option to expand his smaller shop to larger premises. The additional cost will be £22,000.

Now let's imagine we are at the end of Year One which has been a successful year for Marco. If he expands, the expected payoff per year will be:

= (£40,000 per year × 80% probability) + (£3,000 × 20% probability)

HIGH DEMAND   LOW DEMAND

= £32,600

Now we have to convert this back to present values in Year One, so we take the cumulative PV factor for five years at 11 per cent and take away the PV factor for the first year (0.901) which leaves us with 2.795. We also have to account for the additional capital outlay of £22,000.

= (£32,600 × 2.795) – £22,000
= £69,117

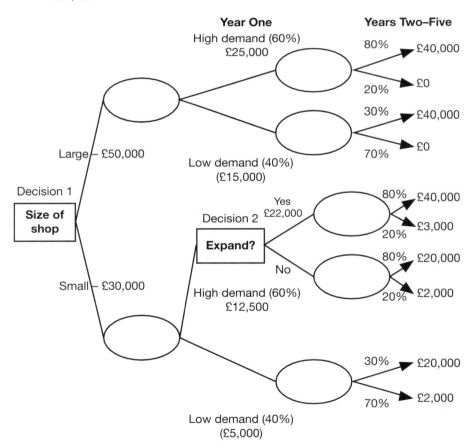

Figure 5.3   Delicious Deli Ltd

What is the payoff if he decides not to expand?

$\quad$ = $\quad$ (£20,000 per year × 80% probability) + (£2,000 × 20% probability)

$\qquad\qquad\qquad$ HIGH DEMAND $\qquad\qquad\qquad\qquad$ LOW DEMAND

$\quad$ = $\quad$ £16,400 × 2.795

$\quad$ = $\quad$ £45,838

It seems clear that Marco should expand if demand is strong in the first year. We will thus discard 'No expansion' as being less attractive. But we still have to decide whether starting small and expanding has a higher NPV than starting large. The larger store has higher overheads that it has to cover so its payoff will be lower if demand is poor. On the other hand it will have higher sales if demand turns out to be good.

$\quad$ The expected payoffs for the large shop are as follows:

In Year One

$\quad$ = $\quad$ (£25,000 per year × 60% probability) + (–£15,000 × 40% probability)

$\qquad\qquad\qquad$ HIGH DEMAND $\qquad\qquad\qquad\qquad$ LOW DEMAND

$\quad$ = $\quad$ £9,000 × 0.901 discount factor

$\quad$ = $\quad$ £8,109

In Years Two to Five

$\quad$ = $\quad$ 60% × ((£40,000 per year × 80% probability) + (£0 × 20% probability))

$\qquad\quad$ + 40% × ((£40,000 per year × 30% probability) + (£0 × 70% probability))

$\quad$ = $\quad$ £24,000 × 2.795

$\quad$ = $\quad$ £67,080 Present Value in Year One

$\quad$ = $\quad$ £60,439 Present Value in Year Zero

The Net Present Value is

$\quad$ = $\quad$ (£50,000) + £8,109 + £60,439

$\quad$ = $\quad$ £18,548

The expected payoffs for the small shop are as follows:

In Year One

$\quad$ = $\quad$ (£12,500 per year × 60% probability) + (–£5,000 × 40% probability)

$\qquad\qquad\qquad$ HIGH DEMAND $\qquad\qquad\qquad\qquad$ LOW DEMAND

$$= \quad £5,500 \times 0.901$$
$$= \quad £4,956$$

In Years Two to Five

$$= \quad 60\% \times £69,117$$
$$+ \, 40\% \times 2.795 \times ((£20,000 \text{ per year} \times 30\%) + (£2,000 \times 70\%))$$
$$= \quad £49,743 \text{ Present Value in Year One}$$
$$= \quad £44,818 \text{ Present Value in Year Zero}$$

The Net Present Value is

$$= \quad (£30,000) + £4,956 + £44,818$$
$$= \quad £19,774$$

It would seem that it is a marginally more attractive investment to start with a small shop and expand if the demand is strong.

Limitations of decision trees

The main limitation of decision trees is that they have a tendency to get very complicated, very quickly. It is important at the outset to decide what the main decisions are and not to get sidetracked into devising more and more branches of possible outcomes which will add a lot of detail but which may not be very helpful.

Decision trees and management options

Decision analysis is particularly useful when comparing two or more alternative courses of action. It not only looks at the ENPVs of each investment, it also looks at the flexibility of each investment option and puts a *value* on that flexibility.

The option to expand a project

One of the most important options is the option to expand if the investment is going well. In the previous example, this option to expand was included in our analysis. What would the Net Present Value of the small shop option have been if this option had not been included?

The expected payoffs for the small shop if Marco does not expand are as follows:

In Year One

    = £4,956 (see earlier for calculation)

In Years Two to Five

    = 60% × ((£20,000 per year × 80% probability) + (£2,000 × 20% probability))
       + 40% ((£20,000 per year × 30% probability) + (£2,000 × 70% probability))
    = £12,800 × 2.795
    = £35,776 Present Value in Year One
    = £32,234 Present Value in Year Zero

The Net Present Value would have been
    = (£30,000) + £4,956 + £32,234
    = £7,190

Thus we can say that the option to expand had a value of £19,774 minus £7,190, or £12,585.

Option to abandon a project

However, what we did not discuss is what Marco Poloni would do if the demand did not develop. Just as the investment project places an implicit value on the ability to expand, so there is also an implicit value if the investment project can be contracted or abandoned if, for example, demand does not materialise. Sometimes this can be quite easy to do, for example, if the investment does not lock the company into long-term supplier or customer contracts, if the assets are fixed (plant, property and equipment) rather than intangible assets, such as highly specific research, and if there is a ready market for those assets. It is important to assess how easy it would be to walk away from the investment when analysing a project.

To assess the implicit value of abandonment, we will return to our delicatessen entrepreneur. We can reformulate the decision tree as in Figure 5.4 to include a decision to sell assets of the shop if the demand does not develop after one year. Let us assume, for simplicity's sake, that he can sell the assets of the large shop for £50,000 but he can only realise £27,000 for the assets of the small shop.

When we do this, the ENPV changes for both original options. The small shop NPV is now £22,051 whilst the large shop NPV is £24,480, an increase of £2,277 and £5,932 respectively. When we include the option to abandon the investment, the larger store has the greater NPV.

Can decision analysis replace NPV and other appraisal methods?

Some supporters of decision analysis have suggested that building decision trees and simulation models which map all the possible alternative scenarios for the investment project makes the Net Present Value method redundant. Certainly the discipline of building a decision tree leads to a deeper understanding of the proposed investment. But it will not help you answer the question – should this investment project be accepted or not?

The *risk* of an investment project is the likelihood that expected performance is different from actual performance. No decision tree, however complex, can map every possible outcome. It will always underestimate the worst and the best possible outcomes because of managers' ability to change the course of the investment *once it has begun*. But by giving a range of NPVs and assigning expected possibilities, it lulls the manager into a false sense of confidence in the 'results'.

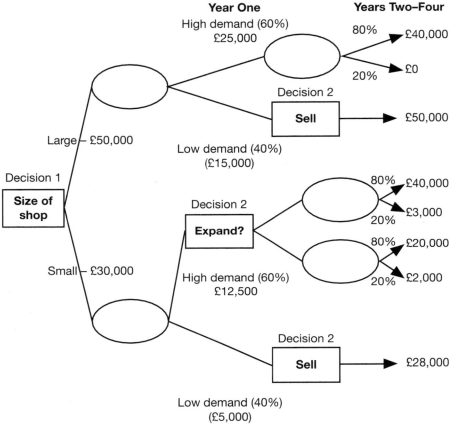

Figure 5.4   Delicious Deli – option to abandon

How to reduce uncertainty

Of course, *identifying* the main areas of uncertainty is only half of the problem. The other half is trying to find ways of *reducing* that uncertainty. Usually the process of detailed analysis will highlight where you have to do some further analysis, or where the company should consider market research or further testing. Some of the possible approaches are outlined below.

Market research

Investing in market research or in test marketing gives managers a highly valuable option to expand or to abandon a project.

Example

Compare two different approaches to the same investment project. The proposed investment is a product introduction into a new market. The initial investment of £1 million entails setting up assembly facilities and advanced marketing costs. Once production has begun, there are some incremental production and transportation costs but assuming the strong demand forecasted, the NPV will be £5 million. The project team believe that there is an 80 per cent chance that demand will be as forecasted. If the product does not take off, the NPV will be (£3 million). The project leader reviewing the investment decides to conduct some market research to find out whether the consumers in the new market are interested in buying this product given that cultural differences may translate into a lack of demand. The market research will cost £80,000 and has a 90 per cent chance of being correct. The two tables below show the ENPVs.

Option A: No market research			
Outcome	Probability	PV (in 000s)	NPV (in 000s)
Success	80%	£5,000	£4,000
Failure	20%	(£3,000)	(£600)
ENPV			£3,400 (£3.4 million)

Option B: Conduct a market research survey					
Outcome	Probability	Correct	Probability	PV (000s)	NPV (000s)
Success	80%	Yes	90%	£5,000	£3,600
	80%	No	10%	−£300	−£240
Failure	20%	Yes	90%	£0	£0
	20%	No	10%	−£5,000*	−£100
ENPV					£3,260 (£3.26 million)

* this represents the lost opportunity to invest in a successful project.

The £80,000 market research has led to a change in valuation of the investment project of £240,000, albeit in a downwards direction. This could be said to be the value of the research.

Reducing the variability of your cashflows

Through analysis you should be able to work out which components of the investment proposal are the drivers of the Net Present Value. Armed with this information you may be able to reconfigure the investment so that the likelihood of change in these components is reduced. For example, if a change in the exchange rate could increase operating costs to such an extent that the investment is no longer viable, are there ways that you can hedge this risk, either through a financial hedge, or through the negotiation of fixed contracts? Other contracts with suppliers for fixed-price supplies for a set period can further eliminate an area of uncertainty. Negotiating a supply contract with customers may mean that you do not gain the highest price possible in the market place but it will ensure a minimum sales volume so that the sales risk is reduced.

Altering the scale of your operation

Earlier on we discussed the value of the option to expand. By starting small and expanding when you see that there is a market demand for your product, or that your operating costs are acceptable, you can reduce your risk. Of course, this assumes that the investment is configured in such a way that expansion is possible relatively quickly.

More effective monitoring

Finally identifying the key drivers of positive cashflow will ensure that ongoing monitoring of the investment's costs and resulting cash inflows will be focused on the critical variables.

Flow chart summary

Figure 5.5 reminds you of the main questions to ask when considering how to forecast cashflows.

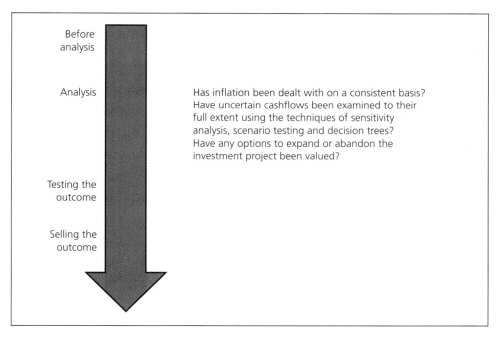

Figure 5.5   Flow diagram for investment appraisal

CHECKLIST OF PRACTICAL TIPS

1 Be consistent in your use of inflation – use nominal cashflows with a nominal cost of capital and real cashflows with a real cost of capital.

2 Think broadly about all the possible outcomes of the investment project:

- What are the main macro-economic variables that could affect your cashflows?

- What are the main scenarios for which you should forecast different sets of cashflows, such as varying levels of demand or varying operating unit costs?

- Are there ways of building flexibility into the investment project such as the ability to expand from a small base, or the ability to contract or abandon the investment if market or operating conditions do not favour it?

3 If forecasts are coming from different members of a project team or if you are consulting different departments for forecasts, make sure that all parties are using the same base assumptions about the macro-economic environment such as inflation, exchange rates and so forth.

4 Think broadly and don't get bogged down in detail! Concentrate on the important links rather than expanding the detail of the simulation or the branches of the decision tree. It will save you headaches and will make selling your recommendation much easier.

5 Having conducted some analysis, try to reduce the risk by conducting market research or product testing; hedging the main components or using fixed contracts to decrease uncertainty.

You will get the most from this chapter if you read the outline of the case and decide how you would set out the investment appraisal – which issues you would consider; which cashflows are relevant; how to deal with tax; how to deal with inflation, and so on.

CHAPTER SIX

Case studies

- How to get the most out of these case studies

- Case study 6.1: Diversifying into an overseas market

- Case study 6.2: Evaluating a cost-saving investment in a food manufacturing company

- Case study 6.3: Choosing between investment projects when there is a limited budget

- Case study 6.4: Expansion into a new product area for a manufacturing company

- Case study 6.5: Evaluating the centralisation of a customer service department

- Case study 6.6: Deciding when to replace a piece of equipment

- Case study 6.7: Lease or buy decision for a voice mail

How to get the most out of these case studies

Each of the case studies outlined in this chapter involves several issues that we have discussed in the book so far.

You will get the most from this chapter if you read the outline of the case and decide how you would set out the investment appraisal – which issues you would consider; which cashflows are relevant; how to deal with tax; how to deal with inflation, and so. Jot down some cashflows and work out an NPV. All the figures are straightforward and all that is needed is a computer or a sheet of paper, the PV factors in the appendices and a calculator.

Having developed your own method, look at the way I approached the appraisal and note any areas where you differed. Sometimes, there is more than one way to analyse the investment and, in such cases, I give an indication of alternatives methods that are equally valid.

CASE STUDY 6.1   **Diversifying into an overseas market**

Key issues

- What is the investment life?
- What are the relevant cashflows to include in the analysis?
- The use of Expected Net Present Value analysis.

Case outline

Tenito Ltd is a clothing manufacturer producing a successful line of leisure and sports clothing under the brand name 'Monster Joe's'. They operate in a low cost country in the developing world and are considering whether to expand into the European market, initially through Switzerland and Germany. The sales director and two colleagues have just spent the equivalent of £20,000 on a research trip to Europe. They interviewed clothing wholesalers in three markets and purchased some secondary market research.

If they sell in Europe, they expect to be able to set a higher price for their clothing. For example, a shirt that would retail in their home market for £12 would be sold for £20 in Switzerland. They have found an agent who will sell their range to stores for a commission of 20 per cent of sales. Though they talked to a number of people, they are still not sure of the demand for their product. Their primary concerns are whether the finish on their clothing articles will meet the very high quality standards of Swiss and German consumers, and whether the agent that they have appointed will be able to deliver the target sales that he has proposed.

Realistically they believe that they have a 30 per cent chance of selling between £225,000 and £275,000 in the first year with an average of £250,000; a 50 per cent chance of selling between £175,000 and £225,000 (i.e. an average of £200,000) and a 20 per cent chance of selling only £125,000 to £175,000 (i.e. an average of £150,000) of goods. Furthermore they are uncertain as to how fast the agent will be able to grow the sales. He has been given exclusive sales rights for three years and he has projected sales growth of 25 per cent for Year 2 and 15 per cent growth for Year 3 and 10 per cent growth after that. However Tenito believe that this may be too optimistic and have decided that there is a 30 per cent chance that growth will be lower – only 15 per cent for Year 2, 10 per cent for Year 3 and 5 per cent growth after that.

Tenito's nominal after tax cost of capital is 15 per cent for this investment and inflation is currently running at 8 per cent. The tax rate is 40 per cent. The forecast for initial set up costs is as follows:

Market research	£50,000 (£20,000 spent to date)
Product design for the European market	£40,000
Alteration of existing equipment	£30,000

The existing plant can be utilised for five years but a major investment in a new plant will be needed in Year Six. Tenito's costs will be approximately 60 per cent of sales excluding the commission payable to the European agent. For the sake of simplicity, we will assume that this ratio remains constant.

Should Tenito expand into the European market?

How to analyse this case

There are many issues to consider in this case study and it is useful to decide at the outset in what order to tackle them. I propose to look at the appraisal in the following manner.

- What is the time horizon for this investment project?
- Which costs and benefits are relevant to the investment?
- What is the Expected NPV of the Swiss expansion?

What is the time horizon for this investment project?

As with any expansion/diversification investment project, there is no clear end to the investment. If the expansion goes successfully, Tenito may be supplying the European market for decades. However, we have not yet established how we can value the later years of an investment project that will go on indefinitely. This will be reviewed in Chapter 9. Until that time, we will take the investment to have a life of five years which is the same period as the existing plant. (Furthermore, with a high discount rate, the contribution of cashflows after five years becomes very small. The major determinants will be the cashflows in the first few years.)

Which costs and benefits are relevant to the investment?

The relevant cashflows to be included in the investment appraisal are as follows:

- All set-up costs from now on – not including the £20,000 already spent.
- Taxes when they are paid. (The cost of capital is a nominal after tax rate.)

As the growth of the sales and costs will not mirror the current inflation rate, it is appropriate to measure the costs in nominal rather than real terms.

What is the Expected NPV of the Swiss expansion?

Given that there are a range of possible cashflows depending on the demand for Tenito's goods and the growth of sales, let us first establish the cashflows for each scenario. There are six possible scenarios, one for each of the three demand levels at both growth levels.

The NPV for each scenario was calculated using a simple computer model.

The cash outlay remained the same at (£100,000) in Year 0 which encompassed:

- £40,000 design costs
- £30,000 market research costs
- £30,000 adaptation costs.

INVESTMENT APPRAISAL FOR NON-FINANCIAL MANAGERS

High demand with high growth (HH) Probability: 30 per cent × 70% = 21%					
Cashflows in (000s):					
Year	Year 1	Year 2	Year 3	Year 4	Year 5
Sales	£250,000	£312,500	£359,375	£395,313	£434,844
Net sales	£200,000	£250,000	£287,500	£316,250	£347,875
Costs	£150,000	£187,500	£215,625	£237,188	£260,906
Tax*	−£40,000	£20,000	£25,000	£28,750	£31,625*
Cashflows	£90,000	£40,500	£46,875	£50,313	£55,344
PV factor	0.870	0.756	0.658	0.572	0.497
PV	£78,300	£32,130	£30,844	£28,799	£27,506

* there was also a tax payment due on Year Five sales in Year Six of £34,788 which has a present value of £15,028.

The resulting NPV was £82,530.

The same process was repeated for each of the scenarios and the resulting NPV shown below.

	Probability	NPV
High demand with low growth	30% × 30% = 9%	£66,056
Moderate demand with high growth	50% × 70% = 35%	£52,984
Moderate demand with low growth	50% × 30% = 15%	£39,804
Low demand with high growth	20% × 70% = 14%	−£23,438
Low demand with low growth	20% 2 30% = 6%	−£13,553

When the NPV for each scenario was multiplied by the probabilities, the Expected NPV, the weighted average of the six scenario NPVs, was £51,886.

Other issues

- There are a range of possible outcomes and Tenito may want to conduct some test marketing to try to narrow down the possible outcomes.
- Are there any opportunity costs involved?

CASE STUDY 6.2   Evaluating a cost-saving investment in a food manufacturing company

Key issues

- The impact of capital allowances and tax implications.
- Changing salvage values.
- How to evaluate uncertain cashflows.

Case outline

Country Foods Ltd is a manufacturer of cook-chill foods – premium priced convenience foods prepared to taste like home-made 'country' food. They have grown quite rapidly in the last few years and are now considering whether to redesign part of their plant to allow for a larger refrigeration unit to be located between the food preparation area and the delivery yard. The initial capital cost will be £30,000 for the refrigeration unit itself and £10,000 for the construction work and installation. They believe that this will lead to cost savings for a number of reasons: the unit will be sited nearer to the food preparation area and so will decrease production time, it has a more efficient cooling system and so requires less power to run than the two smaller units; it will allow for mechanised handling onto the refrigerated lorries thus reducing the loading time.

The company will be eligible for capital allowances of 25 per cent per year on a reducing balance basis which should lead to tax savings in Year Two onwards as the company is currently making a profit. However, there is some uncertainty as to the exact level of cost savings that will be achieved each year. The operations manager of Country Foods has estimated that fuel savings will equate to £4,000 per year and that productivity savings are worth another £5,000. He believes that these will go up in direct proportion with production cost increases, though he accepts that some of the savings may not materialise. Country Foods have forecast that the factory will be too small after six years and the company will need to move to a larger site. The unit would have a salvage value of £4,000 realisable at the end of Year Six.

▶

However, there is a possibility that Country Foods will have to move to a new site after five years, due to other space constraints. In this scenario, the salvage price of the refrigeration unit would be higher at £7,000.

Country Foods has estimated that its *real* opportunity cost of capital after tax is 7 per cent and it believes that inflation will be 4.7 per cent on average for the investment period but the production costs are forecast to increase at a slightly higher rate of 5 per cent per year. The tax rate is forecast to remain at 33 per cent.

Should Country Foods invest in a new refrigeration unit?

How to analyse this case

It is worthwhile first to consider the basic appraisal and then the uncertainty involved in some of the cashflow forecasts. Given that the cashflows are not increasing in line with inflation, we must forecast the cost savings in nominal terms and convert the real discount rate into a nominal discount rate, which is done as follows:

Nominal after-tax discount rate $= (1 + \text{Real discount rate} \times 1 + \text{Inflation rate}) - 1$

$$= (1.07) \times (1.047) - 1$$

$$= 12\%$$

The basic Net Present Value

The cashflows converted into present values are given below.

Year	Cashflows	Capital allowances	Tax saved	Net cash flows	PV factors at 12%	PV
0	(£40,000)			(£40,000)	1.000	(£40,000)
1	£9,000	£7,500*		£9,000	0.893	£8,037
2	£9,450	£5,625	£2,475	£11,295	0.797	£9,504
3	£9,923	£4,219	£1,856	£11,779	0.712	£8,386
4	£10,419	£3,164	£1,392	£11,811	0.636	£7,512
5	£10,940	£2,373	£1,044	£11,984	0.567	£6,795
6	£15,487†	£3,119**	£783	£16,270	0.507	£8,249
7			£1,029	£1,029	0.452	£465
NPV						£8,948

*   only the direct refrigeration unit can be offset against tax not the installation costs.

**   the capital allowances after five years amount to £22,881 leaving a book value of £7,119. However, the salvage value, when it is sold in Year Six, is only £4,000. Thus the Inland Revenue should give an additional capital allowance of £7,119 – £4,000 = £3,119 in Year Six.

†   cash savings plus £4,000 salvage value.

▶

Dealing with uncertainty

This is the more optimistic scenario. If the company has to change location after five years the investment's life will be cut short. Though the company will be able to sell the unit for a higher price, this will only partially offset the cost savings that could still have been realised and the NPV will be reduced to £4,620.

Year	Cashflows	Capital allowances	Tax saved	Net cash flows	PV factors at 12%	PV
0	(£40,000)			(£40,000)	1.000	(£40,000)
1	£9,000	£7,500		£9,000	0.893	£8,037
2	£9,450	£5,625	£2,475	£11,295	0.797	£9,504
3	£9,923	£4,219	£1,856	£11,779	0.712	£8,386
4	£10,419	£3,164	£1,392	£11,811	0.636	£7,512
5	£17,940	£2,492*	£1,044	£11,984	0.567	£10,764
6			£822	£822	0.507	£417
NPV						£4,620

* the capital allowances after four years amount to £20,508 leaving a book value of £9,492. However, the salvage value when it is sold in Year Five is £7,000. Thus the Inland Revenue should give an additional capital allowance of £9,492 – £7,000 = £2,492.

What about the other area of uncertainty? The possibility that the cost savings may not be as great as Country Foods has forecasted? Given that the operations manager has no clear idea of how low the cost savings could be, the best way to tackle this is to turn the question around and ask how small would the cost savings have to be before this investment gives a negative NPV?

This is much easier to calculate on a computer than using the PV tables as the PV tables will require much trial and error. Using a simple computer model, you will find out that if cost savings were actually only £7,050 in the first year, the investment would provide a small negative NPV. Any cost savings above this will make the refrigeration unit an attractive investment. Of course when we look at the four-year investment life scenario, any cost savings amounting to less than £7,700 would result in a negative NPV for the investment project.

Next steps

- The operations manager must now decide whether this is likely, and try to assess the probability that the factory site will be moved after only five years as this seems to be the most critical factor determining the attractiveness of this investment.

- Can he be more precise about the timing of the capital investment?

- He should also look more closely at some of the other inputs into the cashflows such as the rate of production cost increases.

- He should also consider what would happen to Country Foods if they did not change their refrigeration unit. Will their existing unit last for another five years? Is this actually a replacement investment rather than a cost-saving investment?

Choosing between investment projects when there is a limited budget

Key issues

- Which investment appraisal method to use.
- Breaking down artificial barriers in capital budgets.

Case outline

Tellymore Ltd is a medium-sized chain of video rental stores. It has been growing reasonably in the last couple of years and has now formalised its capital expenditure programme into a yearly capital budget. Each store manager puts forward investments which are reviewed by the senior management team. For the current year they have set a capital budget of £180,000. Furthermore, they have divided this budget into the following categories with a budget limit attached to each: sales expansion investments (£110,000); cost reduction investments (£50,000); and other investments (£20,000).

It is now budget time and they have sifted through numerous investment proposals and held a series of presentations with store managers. They are now left with a shortlist of projects, all of which are forecast to achieve positive NPVs when their cashflows are discounted at the opportunity cost of capital of 15 per cent. But Tellymore cannot afford to invest money in all of them as the combined required investment is £282,000, exceeding the capital budget by over £100,000. The seven projects are outlined together with their initial cash outflow and expected cash inflows.

Which investment projects should Tellymore accept and what would be their combined NPV?

	Capital outlay	PV of annual cashflows at 15%
Project A – Expansion investment	£110,000	£125,000
Project B – Expansion investment	£45,000	£53,000
Project C – Expansion investment	£25,000	£37,000
This investment can be replicated once.		
Project D – Cost-saving investment	£6,000	£9,000
This investment can be replicated once.		
Project E – Cost-saving investment	£60,000	£74,000
This investment is divisible by half.		
Project F – Cost-saving investment	£20,000	£28,000
This investment can be replicated once.		
Project G – Other	£16,000	£18,000

How to analyse this case

What is the best appraisal method to use?

As we saw in Chapter 3, when a company is under a budget constraint, taking the investment projects with the highest NPVs does not necessarily produce the greatest return. By considering the actual monetary return of an investment, the NPV method naturally tends to favour larger projects over smaller ones. When money is limited, the NPV method may not give sufficient flexibility. The Profitability Index focuses on the best return for the company's capital outlay.

Let us first set out the Net Present Values and the Profitability Index for each investment.

	Capital outlay	Net Present Value	Profitability Index
Project A	£110,000	£15,000	1.14
Project B	£45,000	£8,000	1.18
Project C	£25,000	£12,000	1.48
Project D	£6,000	£3,000	1.50
Project E	£62,000	£14,000	1.23
Project F	£20,000	£8,000	1.40
Project G	£16,000	£2,000	1.13

Under the constraints given in the capital budget (that is the division of the budget into three areas: sales expansion, cost saving and other investments), if the projects are ranked according to their Net Present Value, only Projects A, F and G would be taken. The total Net Present Value forecast would be £25,000 but only £146,000 out of the potential budget of £180,000 would have been allocated due to the size of the investment projects chosen and the budget limits for each of the three types of investment. If the projects were ranked by Profitability Index, a completely different set of projects would be chosen: Projects D, C, B, F and G with a total Net Present Value forecast of £33,000 but with even less of the potential budget of £180,000 allocated, only £112,000. Obviously neither of these solutions provides the best possible result.

> By considering the actual monetary return of an investment, the NPV method naturally tends to favour larger projects over smaller ones. When money is limited, the NPV method may not give sufficient flexibility.

The next thing to check is whether any of the investment projects are divisible or replicable, that is to say, whether they can be reconfigured to be either larger or smaller investments than currently indicated in the formal capital budget. A glance at the proposal list indicates that Projects A, B and G are neither divisible nor replicable, but Project E is divisible into a smaller investment requiring only £30,000 in capital outlay. Projects C, D and F can be replicable, but only to twice the original investment size. What are the implications for our investment project allocation?

If projects can be replicated, when we rank the projects accordingly to their Profitability Indices, Projects D, D, C, C, B, F, E and G are chosen and yield a Net Present Value of £55,000 with most of the allocation spent, £173,000 of the £180,000 available.

Breaking down artificial barriers

However, the imposition of categories within the capital budget has meant that the optimum mix of projects is still not obtained. There is only one investment in the other category and so that is selected even though its Profitability Index and NPV surplus are lower and smaller than other investments. By removing this constraint, the overall NPV can be increased from £55,000 to £61,000 by doubling the size of Project F rather than taking Project G.

Next steps – other issues to consider

- What is the possible impact on future projects? The timing of the net cashflows needs to be considered. Certain investments may be releasing sufficient cashflow at early stages to allow Tellymore to take subsequent projects in the following year.

- Some investment projects may require a second year of financing in order to get the project off the ground. In this case, the Profitability Index will not necessarily give the optimal mix of projects. Tellymore would need to use Linear Programming. LP is particularly useful when you have a number of projects to evaluate and when there is more than one constraint.

- Is Tellymore's capital budget completely fixed or is there scope to argue for the capital budget to be increased on a one-off basis? Even if the company has a hard ceiling on investment, artificial barriers such as breaking the budget up by store or by investment type may lead to sub-optimal decisions. Try to remove such barriers as far as possible.

CASE STUDY 6.4   **Expansion into a new product area for a manufacturing company**

Key issues

- Use of decision trees.
- The value of the option to expand/abandon.

Case outline

Auton Ltd is a company which specialises in manufacturing computerised and robotic tools for agricultural and garden use. It has been working on developing an automated hedge cutter for garden use and is evaluating whether to develop this product on a commercial basis. It estimates that it will take a further £50,000 to complete the research and between £100,000 and £250,000 to set up a plant with capacity of either 50,000 or 100,000 units per year to produce the product. But Auton is unsure as to what the demand will be for this product. Early focus groups have shown mixed results with some gardeners reacting enthusiastically to the product concept whilst other are mistrustful – they are concerned that the machine could go berserk and eat up their prized hedge. (The researchers believe that there is a 5 per cent possibility that this could happen!) So Auton would like to look at two alternatives – one is to go ahead with production capacity for 100,000 units per year. The other option is to build a smaller production unit which only has the capacity for 50,000 units per year but with an option to expand to 100,000 units after a year if the product takes off. The additional cost of adding the capacity will be £150,000.

Auton's after-tax nominal cost of capital is 14 per cent. The probabilities and after-tax payoffs are given in Figure 6.1. If demand does not materialise, Auton can sell some of the assets of the investment, for £240,000 in the case of the large capacity factory, and £120,000 for the small capacity factory.

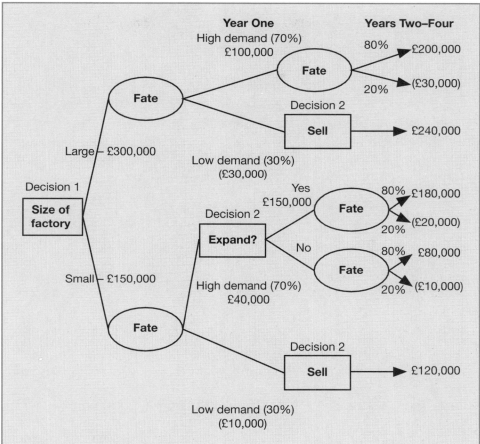

Figure 6.1   A decision tree

How to analyse this case

The most appropriate way to analyse this case is to look at the information given in the form of a decision tree. In order to decide what capacity factory Auton should build, we work back from the second decision. If demand is strong, Auton has the option to expand the production capacity up to 100,000 units.

Now let's imagine we are at the end of Year One which has been a successful year for Auton. If they expand, the expected payoff per year will be:

=   (£180,000 per year × 80% probability) + (− £20,000 × 20% probability)

HIGH DEMAND   LOW DEMAND

=   £140,000

Now we have to convert this back to present values in Year One, so we take the cumulative PV factor for five years at 14 per cent and take away the PV factor for the first year (0.877) which leaves us with 2.556. We also have to account for the additional capital outlay of £150,000.

=   (£140,000 × 2.795) − £150,000

=   £207,840

What is the payoff if they decide *not* to expand?

=   (£80,000 per year × 80% probability) + (−£10,000 × 20% probability)

HIGH DEMAND   LOW DEMAND

Converted back to its Present Value in Year One:

=   £62,000 × 2.556

=   £158,472

Thus it seems clear that Auton should expand if demand is strong in the first year. We will therefore discard 'No expansion' as being less attractive. But we still have to decide between building the large capacity factory or the small capacity factory in Year Zero.

The expected payoffs for the large capacity factory are as follows:

In Year One

=   (£100,000 per year × 70% probability) + (− £30,000 × 30% probability)

HIGH DEMAND   LOW DEMAND

=   £61,000 × 0.877 discount factor

=   £53,497

In Years Two to Five

=   70% × ((£200,000 per year × 80% probability) + (−£30,000 × 20% probability)) + 30% × (£240,000)

=   (£107,800 × 2.556) + (£80,000)

=   £355,536 Present Value in Year One

=   £311,806 Present Value in Year Zero

The Net Present Value is

= (£300,000) + £53,497 + £311,806

= £65,303

The expected payoffs for the small capacity factory are as follows:

In Year One

= (£40,000 per year × 70% probability) + (− £10,000 × 30% probability)
                    HIGH DEMAND   LOW DEMAND

= £25,000 × 0.877

= £21,925

In Years Two to Five

= 70% × £207,840 + 30% × £120,000

= £181,488 Present Value in Year One

= £159,165 Present Value in Year Zero

The Net Present Value is

= (£150,000) + £21,925 + £159,165

= £31,090

The larger capacity factory has a higher NPV and so should be chosen.

Next steps

■ Consider an investment in some test marketing to ensure that the probabilities are the most likely forecasts.

■ Should Auton be considering a third alternative, a larger factory capacity for perhaps 150,000 units?

CASE STUDY 6.5 — Evaluating the centralisation of a customer service department

Key issues

- What are the relevant costs and benefits to include in the analysis?
- Which costs and benefits can be converted into monetary values?

Case outline

A car rental company is considering whether or not to invest in centralising their customer service departments. Currently they have ten sites across the country and they are considering the costs and benefits of combining these sites into one unit. The major tangible and intangible costs and benefits are given in Figure 6.2 below.

	Tangible	Intangible

Costs	Relocation*
	Building and
	  telephone costs*
	Freephone system
		Disruption while
		  moving*
		Reduction in
		  personal service

Benefits	Cost savings
	  – space, overheads
	  and personnel
		Improved service
		Staff morale
		Key accounts service
		  introduced

* one-off costs

Figure 6.2   The costs and benefits of centralisation

There is an initial investment in relocation (the costs of moving, the cost of relocation packages to those employees who are moving; the redundancy packages for those employees who have taken redundancy); in building the new department and the investment in new telephone and computer equipment. There is also an intangible cost of disruption to the customer service department while the relocation is taking place. Once the new site has been developed there are some ongoing tangible costs such as the Freephone system needed for customers so that they do not have to pay for a long distance call but also some tangible benefits in terms of lower overheads and fewer employees required to perform the same (or better) service. There is also an opportunity benefit in that the space in the regional offices that is now free can be used by those offices to expand and they do not need to relocate to larger offices.

The intangible costs and benefits are difficult to assess. On the one hand, staff morale initially plummets as they have to relocate with all the psychological problems that this entails and they lose some of their colleagues who do not wish to relocate. However, in the medium to longer term the creation of a strong customer service 'team' and the resulting increased morale could compensate for this. On the benefit side, the new computer equipment leads to an improved service with a faster pick-up time (under three rings in 80 per cent of cases) and to faster response to customer queries due to the computer link-up. The centralised unit can justify the existence of dedicated key accounts personnel to deal with their large corporate accounts. This is partly offset by a reduction in the regional, more personal, service offered before. These intangible customer service benefits are converted into assumptions about improved sales performance with an increase in sales of 2 per cent for key account sales and 0.5 per cent for general sales.

Other information

- The company sales are currently £200 million. Of these £80 million come from key accounts and the rest from general sales. The net profit margin is 10 per cent.
- The tangible relocation costs are £800,000.
- One-off disruption will lead to loss of productivity which is equated to 1 per cent of sales for the three months surrounding the relocation.
- Annual additional costs are £50,000 for the Freephone telephone system and the maintenance of the centralised computer system.
- Annual cost savings after tax are forecast to be £150,000.
- Inflation is currently 3 per cent but the net annual cashflows are forecast to increase at 2 per cent.

- The company has a head office site which has some additional space. The allocated cost of the space is £25 per square metre per year and the customer service unit will require 400 square metres of space.
- The nominal after-tax cost of capital is 15 per cent.
- The project's life is six years.

How to analyse this case

Let us first look at the intangible costs and benefits. Are there any qualitative benefits that can be given a monetary value through the use of some conservative assumptions? The table below outlines the main cash costs and benefits.

Components	Tangible	Intangible	Total
One-off	(£800,000)	1% loss of business for 3 months = £50,000 lost profit	(£850,000)
Annual cash outflow	(£50,000)		(£50,000)
Annual cash inflow	£150,000		£150,000
Revenue increase p.a.		2% of key accounts	£160,000
		0.5% increase in non-	
		key accounts	£60,000

Let us look at the NPV taking only the tangible costs and benefits. Each year the net cashflow is £100,000. The project life is estimated to be six years with a growth of 2 per cent in the net cash cashflow each year. The nominal after-tax discount rate is taken as 15 per cent. The NPV is taken to be an annuity.

Present Value = £100,000 times six-year annuity factor of 3.998
for 15% – 2% = 13%)
= £399,800
NPV = £399,800 – £800,000 = (£400,200)

If we include all the intangible costs and benefits under the assumption given above the picture looks very different.

Annual cashflows are £320,000 × 3.998

thus the PV is £1,279,360 approx. £1,280,000

NPV = £1,280,000 − £850,000

    = £430,000

I would propose that you take the middle ground. Take the increase in key accounts sales at 1 per cent rather than 2 per cent as that is a clear-cut benefit of the centralisation process. This results in an NPV of £110,000:

(£240,000 × 3.998) − £850,000 = £110,000

Next steps

What about using NPV analysis to consider the qualitative benefits which cannot be converted into cash values?

An alternative approach is to turn the question around and ask what level of sales improvement would be required to justify this centralisation investment? The PV of the net annual cashflows must be at least £850,000 which equates to approximately £212,500 in annual cashflows for six years. The tangible cashflows are £100,000 and so sales increases net of costs (free cashflow) must account for £112,500.

When we compare this to the current sales, £1.125 million in sales equates to 0.56 per cent of sales. It is up to the senior management to decide whether this is realistic to expect.

How to sell this investment proposal

- Be conservative with your assumptions about key account sales.

- Focus on tangible costs and benefits as far as possible.

- Look at the minimum sales increase that would render the investment attractive (i.e. a positive NPV).

Key issues

- Comparing investments across similar time horizons.
- The changing salvage value of old machinery.
- The impact of inflation on differential running costs.
- Capital allowances on the new machine and tax relief on maintenance costs.
- Life-Cycle Costing.

Case outline

Boronic Ltd is a contract tunnelling company. It regularly has to consider the issue of when it should replace its various tunnel boring machinery. In most cases it is a question of when to replace each machine but the finance director also believes that the company should not only consider each machine on its own merits but develop a comprehensive replacement policy for some of their frequently replaced machinery.

Part I

The immediate investment decision is whether to replace one of the tunnel boring machines. The existing machine has annual running costs of £40,000 including regular maintenance. It is forecast that these costs are increasing at 20 per cent in nominal terms. Its salvage value is £80,000 and decreasing in value rapidly with age at 20 per cent per annum. Its remaining economic life is estimated at three years. The alternative is to buy a new machine costing £450,000 with an estimated economic life of ten years. The running costs of this machine would be considerably less at £20,000 per year growing at 5 per cent per annum for five years, 10 per cent for three years and 20 per cent for the last two years. The new machine will enable Boronic Ltd to utilise the appropriate capital allowance (25 per cent reducing balance), with a two-year time lag. Their nominal after-tax cost of capital is 16 per cent.

Should Boronic Ltd replace the old tunnel borer?

How to analyse this case

With all investment appraisals involving the timing of replacements you have to compare the alternatives across the same time period. This can be done either by taking the lowest common denominator in terms of years or by calculating the Equivalent Annual Cashflows.

Here we must convert the different lifespans of the two machines into equivalent annual cashflows. We will accept the course of action which results in the lowest Present Value cost, as there are no varying sales implications for the company. Boronic's objective is to choose the machine with the lowest equivalent annual cost. To do this we calculate the equivalent annuity that would be payable on the cashflows invested.

If we assume that all costs will increase at the same rate we can just calculate the EAC of the new machine compared to the EAC of the opportunity cost of *not* selling the old machine and adding the running costs to achieve the total annual costs. But this would be too much of a simplification. Costs do increase and not in line with the inflation rate. Furthermore, we need to include the increasing tax savings for the old machine as those maintenance costs increase and the tax shield created by the capital allowances available on the new machine.

First let us calculate the NPV on both investments. There is a tax delay of one year in both cases.

Existing machine:	Year 0	1	2	3	4
Resale value after tax	£80,000				
Lost opportunity cost*	(£80,000)				
Annual running costs		(£40,000)	(£48,000)	(£57,600)	
Costs after tax		(£26,800)	(£34,800)	(£41,760)	£19,008
Net Present Value	(£164,352)				
Cumulative factor for 3 yrs	2.798				
Equivalent annual cost**	(£58,739)				

▶

Buy a replacement machine:
The same process is followed for the new machine. The Net Present Value for the new machine including the running costs after tax, the tax savings from the capital allowances and the capital outlay, is forecast and cashflows are derived. The cashflows are spread out over 11 years given the tax delays. The NPV and EAC are as follows:

Net Present Value	(£377,058)
Cumulative factor for 11 years	5.029
Equivalent annual cost**	(£74,977)

* the opportunity cost could be calculated as a lost opportunity each year – by taking the salvage value for each year from the salvage value that was achievable in the previous year. This difference times the opportunity of capital of 16 per cent is the annual lost opportunity. ** the annual equivalent cost takes the NPV and divides this by the annuity factor for 16 per cent for the life of each investment.

Part II

The operations manager of Boronic Ltd also wants to develop a replacement strategy which minimises the lifetime costs of some of his smaller digging machines. These machines are subject to a high degree of wear and tear and thus their economic life is much shorter, only four years. The real cashflows are given below and the real after-tax cost of capital is 13 per cent.

The salvage value of the machines decreases with age:

Purchase price	£20,000

Salvage value after:

1 year	£15,000
2 years	£11,000
3 years	£7,500
4 years	£4,500

In contrast, the running and maintenance costs go up with age:

1 year	£5,000
2 years	£5,500
3 years	£7,500
4 years	£10,000

For the sake of simplicity, we will assume that the various tax implications have already been included in these costs.

Solution

For this part, let us consider the NPV implications over the lowest common time period which is 12 years. Only over a 12-year time horizon can the different costs of replacing the machines every one, two, three or four years be compared. The cashflow and NPV for a one-year replacement strategy are given below.

Year	Cost	Salvage value	Running costs	Cashflow	PV factors at 13%	PV
0	(£20,000)			(£20,000)	1.000	(£20,000)
Years 1 to 11	(£20,000)	£15,000	(£5,000)	(£10,000)	5.687	(£56,870)
12		£15,000	(£5,000)	£10,000	0.231	£2,310
NPV						(£74,560)

The NPV of replacing the digger every year for 12 years is £74,560.

Let us now compare the cost of buying diggers and keeping them for two years before selling them.

▶

Year	Cost	Salvage value	Running costs	Cashflow	PV factors at 13%	PV
0	(£20,000)			(£20,000)	1.000	(£20,000)
1			(£5,000)	(£5,000)	0.885	(£4,425)
2	(£20,000)	£11,000	(£5,500)	(£14,500)	0.783	(£11,354)
3			(£5,000)	(£5,000)	0.693	(£3,465)
4	(£20,000)	£11,000	(£5,500)	(£14,500)	0.613	(£8,889)
5			(£5,000)	(£5,000)	0.543	(£2,715)
6	(£20,000)	£11,000	(£5,500)	(£14,500)	0.480	(£6,960)
7			(£5,000)	(£5,000)	0.425	(£2,125)
8	(£20,000)	£11,000	(£5,500)	(£14,500)	0.376	(£5,452)
9			(£5,000)	(£5,000)	0.333	(£1,665)
10	(£20,000)	£11,000	(£5,500)	(£14,500)	0.295	(£4,278)
11			(£5,000)	(£5,000)	0.261	(£1,305)
12		£11,000	(£5,500)	£5,500	0.231	(£1,271)
NPV						(£71,361)

This process can be repeated for the three-year and four-year replacement policies. The NPV values are £72,988 and £74,986 respectively. So it would seem that replacing their diggers every two years would be the most cost-effective policy for Boronic.

CASE STUDY 6.7 Lease or buy decision for a voice mail system

Key issues

- The value of the option to abandon.
- Taxation implications.
- The timing of the purchase and the timing of the lease payments.

Case outline

Fink and Boardman Associates are a firm of management consultants. It is June 1999 and they have decided to invest in a voice mail system which will allow messages to be left on each consultant's telephone. This will greatly improve communication not only within their offices but also with clients who are trying to get hold of them. There are two main alternatives: they can buy a system outright from one of the suppliers or they can lease a system for a set contract period.

They have estimated that there are measurable cost savings in terms of administration (secretarial and typing) of £5,000 per year. Project meeting details and divisional messages can be left by telephone rather than circulars going round. Furthermore, there is the intangible but highly important improvement in client service (knowing that their message has got through quickly and *correctly* to their consultant) and savings in time not spent going to people's desks to leave messages.

They have already decided to make the investment but they are undecided as to whether they should buy the system outright or lease it. The cost of buying the most effective system is £30,000. They will be eligible for capital allowances each year (i.e. a 25 per cent annual allowance on a reducing balance basis). They believe that it will have a life of five years before they would wish to purchase a new system. It would then have no value to them. In addition they would take up a yearly service and maintenance contract with the supplier costing £2,000 in the first year and increasing in line with inflation which is currently running at 5 per cent. This would be an annual advance payment. It is also tax deductible.

The leasing alternative would cost £12,000 per year to be paid in advance in twice yearly instalments of £6,000. This would include service and maintenance.

▶

The contract would be for three years with an option to renew the contract after two years – the annual cost would then be reduced to £6,000.

The company has calculated that their after-tax nominal opportunity cost of capital or discount rate is 12 per cent. They are paying tax at the 33 per cent corporate tax rate.

Should they buy or lease the system?

How to analyse this case

This is a financing decision and not an investment decision. Fink and Boardman have already decided that the cost savings and value of increased communication with clients are worth the investment to them. Thus all we are trying to establish is which proposal has the lowest PV cost.

The Net Present Value of buying the system will be as follows.

Year	Costs	Capital allowances	Tax saved	Net cash flows	PV factors at 12%	PV
0	(£32,000)			(£32,000)	1.000	(£32,000)
1	(£2,100)	£7,500		(£2,100)	0.893	(£1,875)
2	(£2,205)	£5,625	£2,970*	£765	0.797	£610
3	(£2,315)	£4,219	£2,549	£234	0.712	£167
4	(£2,431)	£3,164	£2,120	(£311)	0.636	(£198)
5		£9,492†	£1,808	£1,808	0.567	£1,025
6			£3,935	£3,935	0.507	£1,995
NPV						(£30,277)

* the annual maintenance contract is tax deductible and so it has been included in the tax savings given.

† the remaining book value is £9,492 and this is included as the capital allowance for that year.

The Net Present Value of leasing the system will be as follows.

Year	Costs	Tax saved	Net cash flows	PV factors at 12%	PV
0	(£12,000)		(£12,000)	1.000	(£12,000)
1	(£12,000)	£3,960	(£8,040)	0.893	(£7,180)
2	(£12,000)	£3,960	(£8,040)	0.797	(£6,408)
3	(£6,000)	£3,960	(£2,040)	0.712	(£1,452)
4	(£6,000)	£1,980	(£4,020)	0.636	(£2,557)
5		£1,980	£1,980	0.567	£1,123
NPV					(£28,474)

However, we have not yet included the timing implications. The lease payments occur on a bi-annual basis and are set cash outflows. It would thus be more appropriate to look at the leasing option on a twice yearly rather than a yearly basis. I shall continue to assume a delay in tax savings of 12 months. The discount factor will be a 6 per cent factor (12 per cent divided by two).

Year	Costs	Tax saved	Net cash flows	PV factors at 6%	PV
0	(£6,000)		(£6,000)	1.000	(£6,000)
1	(£6,000)		(£6,000)	0.943	(£5,658)
2	(£6,000)	£1,980	(£4,020)	0.890	(£3,578)
3	(£6,000)	£3,960	(£2,040)	0.840	(£1,714)
4	(£6,000)		(£6,000)	0.792	(£4,752)
5	(£6,000)	£3,960	(£2,040)	0.747	(£1,524)
6	(£3,000)		(£3,000)	0.705	(£2,115)
7	(£3,000)	£2,970	(£30)	0.665	(£20)
8	(£3,000)		(£3,000)	0.627	(£1,881)
9	(£3,000)	£1,980	(£1,020)	0.592	(£604)
10				0.558	£0
11		£990	£990	0.527	£522
NPV					(£27,323)

As Fink and Boardman would only have to pay £6,000 in advance rather than £12,000, the leasing option looks even more attractive when we compute the Present Value of the cashflows for six-month intervals rather than one year.

The value of abandonment

The final issue that we have yet to consider and include in our cashflow forecasts is the implicit value of abandonment that is available with the leasing option. If Fink and Boardman decide that the cost savings and customer service benefits are not that substantial, they may decide not to renew the contract after three years. If this is the case, then the Present Value of the leasing option in terms of cost is reduced to £21,246 (don't forget the delayed tax savings).

CHECKLIST OF PRACTICAL TIPS

- Always consider all possible alternatives.
- Remember the value of flexibility – the option to back out of a contract can be valuable.
- Consider the most appropriate time-frame for your cashflows. In most cases, yearly cashflows are most appropriate but in the case of lease payments, monthly cashflows are more relevant and can change the Present Value considerably.

This chapter goes into the theory behind the practice, and will give you a deeper understanding of how to evaluate the risk of differing investment projects and the impact of gearing on the cost of capital.

CHAPTER SEVEN

Risk and uncertainty – introducing some theory

- Why the theory is important

- Risk and uncertainty

- Sources of capital

- The cost of equity

- The Capital Asset Pricing Model (CAPM)

- The cost of borrowing

- Simplified version of the Weighted Average Cost of Capital (WACC)

- Introducing Modigliani and Miller

- Reasons why the WACC does change

- Tax implications of borrowing

- Costs of financial distress including bankruptcy

- A new Weighted Average Cost of Capital

- Other methods for calculating the cost of equity

CHECKLIST OF KEY POINTS

1 The purpose of this chapter is to provide some theory to support the ideas introduced in the following chapter, Chapter 8, when we look at how to estimate the opportunity cost of capital for an investment project.

2 Risk and uncertainty can be used synonymously. One way to look at risk is to say the more possible outcomes there are, the riskier the investment. A certain pound in the future is worth more than an uncertain pound in the future. Thus the greater the risk or uncertainty surrounding future cashflows, the higher the opportunity cost of capital should be to compensate.

3 The opportunity cost of capital *for a company* is found by calculating the weighted average cost of the different sources of capital; the cost of equity; and the cost of debt.

4 The cost of equity for a company is derived from the Capital Asset Pricing Model. It is computed from the risk-free rate of government bonds, the market premium for an efficient portfolio of shares and a specific company beta factor that compares the co-variance of the stock's risk profile with the risk profile of the market portfolio as a whole. The risk in question is not the unique risk of the company, but its exposure to market risk.

5 The cost of borrowing or debt is the average market rate of interest for the company. It is usually determined through a comparison with other investment opportunities of similar perceived risk.

6 A mix of debt and equity can lower the weighted average cost of capital initially because of the tax relief gained on interest payments. As gearing rises to high levels, this benefit is gradually offset by the risk of bankruptcy which increases both the costs of equity and debt.

7 This Weighted Average Cost of Capital is the required cost of capital for the company. It can be used as the discount rate when valuing the company; however, ideally it should not be used as the cost of capital for a particular investment *unless* the investment has exactly the same risk profile as the company and exactly the same financing. Chapter 8 examines how to adjust the cost of capital so that it reflects the specific risks of the investment itself.

Why the theory is important

Chapter 8 reviews the main methods used to determine the opportunity cost of capital for investment projects. We will look at how to calculate the opportunity cost of capital *for a specific investment*. This draws on the theory of how to calculate the opportunity cost of capital for a company. We will focus on the practical aspects of applying that knowledge to assessing an investment's cost of capital.

However, if you are going to be assessing the required cost of capital for a range of projects, this chapter goes into the theory behind the practice, and will give you a deeper understanding of how to evaluate the risk of differing investment projects and the impact of gearing on the cost of capital.

Risk and uncertainty

Firstly, what is risk exactly? The risk of an investment is associated with uncertainty – it is the chance that expected outcomes for tomorrow are not fulfilled – that something else happens instead. One way of looking at risk is to say that risk occurs when 'more things can happen than will happen'.

Any appraisal process must be able to compare cash inflows resulting from an investment with cash outflows in today's money. It must also take risk and uncertainty into account and be able to deal with risk in as objective a fashion as possible. Just as a pound today is worth more to a company than a pound tomorrow so a *certain* pound tomorrow is worth more than an *uncertain* pound tomorrow. The mechanism for comparing the future cashflows with today's cashflows lies in the discount rate. The further into the future that the cashflows occur, the greater the discount factor. Similarly, the lower the likelihood of receiving a pound tomorrow, the greater the discount factor.

So far we have assumed that the company has already calculated the discount rate to be used to evaluate the proposed investment. Now it is time to look in detail at how a company should compute the discount rate. The opportunity cost of capital *for a company* is found by calculating the weighted average cost of the different sources of capital; the cost of equity and the cost of debt.

> Firstly, what is risk exactly? The risk of an investment is associated with uncertainty – it is the chance that expected outcomes for tomorrow are not fulfilled – that something else happens instead. One way of looking at risk occurs when 'more things can happen than will happen'.

Sources of capital

There are two main sources of capital for a company: shareholders; and lenders, usually financial institutions. Shareholders are the owners of the company. If additional funds are needed, for new investments for example, they can be gained from shareholders either through a new rights issue or through retaining some of the profits of the company rather than returning all profits to shareholders in the form of dividends. This latter source of funds is useful because the company does not incur the costs associated with a rights issue.

Company gearing

The gearing of a company refers to the sourcing of funds – the mix between shareholders' equity and loans. (The shareholders' equity is the initial share capital and any retained profits.) If a company has 30 per cent gearing, 30 per cent of its capital is loan capital, the remainder is shareholders' equity. A company that has less than 10 to 15 per cent gearing is considered to have low gearing whereas a company with 50 per cent gearing is usually considered to be highly geared. The level of gearing often varies from industry to industry. For example, the pharmaceutical industry historically has had few companies with even moderate gearing. Companies with low gearing are reducing the risk of default on loan or interest payments (which can be marked at times of high interest rates such as the early 1990s), or the risk that dividends are reduced in times of recession because of the prior claims of interest payments. However, they are also losing the opportunity to reduce their cost of capital. This issue is explored later in the chapter.

The cost of equity

Shareholders' equity is the risk capital of the company. There are no set interest payments or a set loan repayment schedule to follow. Thus the cost of equity is simply the *expected return* that shareholders will earn on their money. This is the rate of return they expect in the form of dividends or an increase in the share price.

There are three common ways of looking at the cost of equity. The first method, the Capital Asset Pricing Model, is the one which I will concentrate on as it is the only one of the three that incorporates a *risk analysis* in its methods, i.e. it is the only one which assumes that the cost of equity changes, that is the required return for shareholders, as the perceived risk of the investment changes. (The other two methods are given in a note at the end of this chapter. They are both only relevant if the company is listed on the stock market. They assume that the risk of an investment is already captured in the current share price and this may be a very unrealistic assumption to make.)

The Capital Asset Pricing Model (CAPM)

The Capital Asset Pricing Model, the CAPM for short, relates the return on equity directly to the risk involved for the shareholder. The expected risk premium from any investment should be directly related to its market risk. Despite its long-winded name, it is an extremely flexible and empirically sound model so it is worth spending some time looking at its components. The CAPM divides the cost of equity into two components: the near risk-free return available on investing in government bonds and an additional risk premium for investing in a particular share. This risk premium in turn comprises the average return on the overall market portfolio and the beta factor (or risk) of the particular company. Putting this all together the CAPM assesses the cost of equity as the following:

$$\text{Cost of equity} = R_f + B\,(R_m - R_f)$$

where　R_f　= the risk-free rate
　　　　R_m　= the average market return
　　　　B　　= beta of the investment or company in question

As the beta, or risk, of the investment increases, so does the expected return on the investment (see Figure 7.1). Let's look at each of these three components in turn.

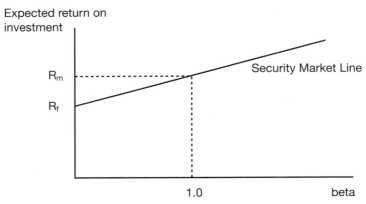

Figure 7.1 The Security Market Line

Risk-free return

The 'risk-free' return is the return available on three-month treasury bonds. Government bonds represent as safe an investment as is available. There is no risk of default. The only risk is the risk of inflation. The average *nominal* risk-free return, for the last 50 years, has been between 4 and 5 per cent whilst the average *real* risk-free return has historically been under 1 per cent. To find out the current nominal risk-free return available, look in the newspapers for the current return on three-month treasury bonds.

Market portfolio return

The average return from the market is composed of the risk-free return and a premium for the market risk. By investing in corporate stocks and shares the investor is taking on an additional risk, *the risk of default.* Furthermore, they are now owners of the company and they share directly in the risks of that company. A study completed by Ibbotson in 1986 showed that the average risk premium for investing in the market portfolio rather than government bonds was 8.4 per cent (measured over the period 1926 to 1985).

Market risk and unique risk

The CAPM makes a distinction between *unique risk or unsystematic risk*, the risk that can be diversified away by holding a portfolio of shares, and *market risk or systematic risk*, the overall market risk.

Unique risks are those that are unique to a particular company or a particular investment. Resulting downward movement in the performance of one company can be offset by an upward movement in another and so much of this unsystematic risk can be eliminated through diversification on the part of shareholders when they hold a portfolio of shares. Similarly, when companies invest in a range of different investment projects they are diversifying the unique risks associated with each investment project.

Market risk or systematic risk, however, cannot be avoided. It relates to economic trends which affect the whole market, hence its name. The degree to which an individual company is affected by a downturn in the market is the true indication of the commercial risk of that company. The same is true for individual investment projects. If a project is highly susceptible to market changes, it has a high market risk.

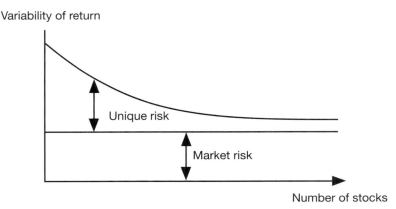

Figure 7.2   Market risk and unique risk

Figure. 7.2 demonstrates how risk, that is, the variability of possible returns, declines as shareholders hold a portfolio of stocks. As the number of shares held increases, so the portfolio's risk decreases. But the element of overall risk that is decreasing is the unsystematic risk, unique to the one share, not the systematic market risk. (This diversification is of marginal additional benefit once a portfolio of about 15 stocks is held.)

The beta factor

The market premium gives an indication of the additional risk that is borne, and rewarded, by the market as a whole. But it still does not tell us what the risk premium

Thus the beta factor measures an investment's marginal contribution to the risk of the market portfolio. It measures how sensitive the investment project is to market movements. If the beta is more than one, it is more sensitive to the market or systematic risk than the average investment.

for investing in a *particular company*, or a *particular* investment project is. It just gives the average risk premium for the market. The third required component is called the beta factor. The beta factor is the correlation co-efficient between the returns on a market portfolio of investments and the returns on a particular share or, more specifically, a particular investment. Thus the beta factor measures an investment's marginal contribution to the risk of the market portfolio. It measures how sensitive the investment project is to market movements. If the beta is more than one, it is more sensitive to the market or systematic risk than the average investment. If it is one, then it has the same risk profile as the market as a whole, the average risk profile. If it is less than one, it is not as sensitive to market risk as the average investment. In recent studies it has been shown that most companies have betas of close to one but, within these companies, some of the investments will have betas greater than one and some less than one.

Example

Bergis Company is an all-equity financed company. They are evaluating a new investment project. The current nominal risk-free return on government bonds is 4.2 per cent, the average market premium for risk is 8.4 per cent and the beta factor for the investment project is calculated to be 0.90. What is the cost of capital for the investment project?

Putting the information into the CAPM, it yields a cost of capital of:

Cost of capital = 4.2% + 0.90 (8.4%)

= 11.7%

The cost of borrowing
New loans

The cost of borrowing (also known as the cost of debt), will be the required rate of return needed by the financial institutions or lenders on *new* loans. It will be derived by looking at the returns of alternative investments of similar perceived risk that the financial institutions can invest in. Furthermore, it will depend on the size of the loan as well as the availability of other attractive alternatives at that time.

Existing loans

If the company already has loans or debentures, an alternative way must be found to assess the cost of their existing debt. The method used will depend on whether the loans are redeemable or not.

Redeemable loans

With a redeemable loan, the financial institutions or other lenders obtain an annual return through interest payments as well as the capital when the loan is repaid. The cost of this debt can be seen as the Internal Rate of Return and can be calculated in exactly the same way as the method used in Chapter 2. The cash inflows and outflows are fed into a calculator or computer, together with the interest payments, and the IRR is calculated.

Example

Lever Company has a redeemable 12 per cent loan. An investor today is prepared to pay £95 per nominal value of £100 repayable in five years' time at par. The investor therefore is willing to pay £95 today for the right to receive £12 per year for five years and £100 in five years' time. The cashflows are as follows.

Year	Cashflow	Year	Cashflow
0	−£95	3	£12
1	£12	4	£12
2	£12	5	£112

The IRR for this redeemable loan is 13.4 per cent, which equates to the cost of the debt.

Irredeemable loans

If the fixed rate on irredeemable loans is less than the current going rate for new loans, the loans will have a market value less than their par value. The interest yield at the *current market price* should equate to the market rate of interest on similar loans.

Example

An irredeemable 10 per cent loan is currently quoted at £80 per £100 nominal value, i.e. an investor is willing to pay £80 to receive a stream of interest payments of £10 per year in perpetuity. The cost of the loan is therefore:

$$\text{Market rate} = \frac{\text{Nominal value}}{\text{Market value}} \times \text{Old interest rate}$$

$$= \frac{£100}{£80} \times 10\% = 12.5 \text{ per cent}$$

Nominal and the real cost of debt

The real cost of the loan will be less than the nominal cost as investors are not compensated for the real drop in the value of their capital. Thus, if the nominal cost of a loan was 12 per cent and inflation was 4 per cent, the real cost of the loan can be calculated using the formula introduced in Chapter 5.

$$\text{Real cost of debt} = \frac{\text{Nominal cost of debt}}{\text{Inflation rate}}$$

$$\frac{1.12}{1.04} = 1.077 = 7.7\%$$

Simplified version of the Weighted Average Cost of Capital (WACC)

In this simplified case, we will assume away the impact of taxation (in the best tradition of all economists!)

Having looked at the cost of equity and the cost of borrowing we should be able to state the cost of capital for a company as a whole. Obviously if the company is all-equity financed, the cost of equity will be the cost of capital. In cases of geared companies, the Weighted Average Cost of Capital can be stated as:

> WACC (r_A) = (Cost of equity 2 % equity) + (Cost of debt 2 % debt)

If a company has a gearing ratio of 30 per cent, a cost of equity computed to be 18 per cent and a cost of debt of 9 per cent, its WACC will be:

WACC = (18% × 70%) + (9% × 30%) = 15.3%

This is the discount rate that can be used to evaluate the company's new investments, *provided that they have the same risk profile as the company as a whole and provided that they used the same combination of debt and equity to finance the proposed investments, or are financed by company reserves.* How realistic these two assumptions are will be reviewed later on.

Introducing Modigliani and Miller

Looking at the simplified WACC, one would be tempted to increase a company's gearing up to the maximum possible. *If the cost of equity doesn't change*, then by increasing the ratio of debt to equity, a company can lower its WACC until it has 100 per cent debt and the WACC equals the r_D, the cost of debt. This can be seen by plotting the cost of equity and lower cost of debt and the WACC as gearing increases.

This logical conclusion is unattainable because at 100 per cent debt, the company is technically owned by the lenders and thus the lenders become the shareholders (see Figure 7.3).

Rates of return

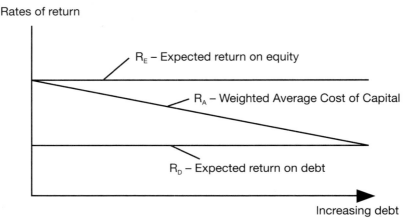

R_E – Expected return on equity

R_A – Weighted Average Cost of Capital

R_D – Expected return on debt

Increasing debt

Figure 7.3   The weighted cost of capital

However, Modigliani and Miller stated the opposite viewpoint in their infamous Proposition One:

> 'The market value of any firm is independent of its capital structure.'

A company cannot change the value of its shares through gearing. If that is the case, and if operating income does not change as the financing changes, then the cost of capital for a firm as a whole does not change even if debt financing is introduced. The reason Modigliani and Miller believed that this was the case is that the cost of equity *does* change, as the ratio of debt to equity changes. It increases and directly offsets the lower cost of debt. As a company takes on more debt, the risk for the shareholders increases and, as we have seen, as the risk increases, so the *required* rate of return increases to reward them for this greater risk. The increased expected rate of return for shareholders is exactly offset by the increased risk attached to the shares. According to Modigliani and Miller, the shareholders would be no better or no worse off than before and thus the value of the company, as a whole, remains unchanged.

Why is the risk increasing? As equity is subordinate to interest repayments, if a company fails, there is a much greater likelihood that creditors will get back more of their money than the shareholders. Indeed the shareholders may get nothing. Modigliani and Miller formulated a second related proposition (Proposition Two):

> 'The expected rate of return on the common stock of a geared firm increases in proportion to the capital gearing ratio.'

The rate of increase depends on the spread between r_A, the expected return on the company's total assets and r_D, the expected return on the debt.

This proposition of Modigliani and Miller can be seen graphically if we plot the cost of equity, debt and the WACC against gearing, as in Figure 7.4.

As gearing increases, the cost of debt at first remains the same but at a high level of gearing, it begins to rise. At this stage, lenders begin to take on some of the risk of default that was incurred solely by the shareholders at lower gearing levels. The lenders begin to bear some of the *commercial risk* of the company. In contrast, the cost of equity rises steadily as gearing rises. Shareholders demand a higher return to offset their greater risk (though this increase slows down at higher levels as some of the commercial risk is shared with the lenders). The combined effect of this is that the WACC remains the same.

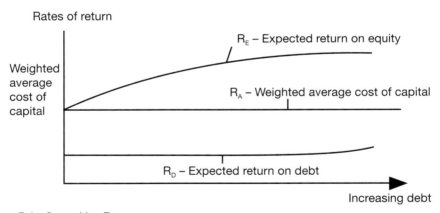

Figure 7.4   Proposition Two

Reasons why the WACC does change

These propositions of Modigliani and Miller are some of the most hotly debated issues in finance. An alternative view states that the Weighted Average Cost of Capital *does* change as gearing increases, and for several reasons. If you look at the last section, you will see that Modigliani and Miller's arguments were based on the assumption that operating income doesn't change if gearing is introduced. But this may not be the case, certainly when we consider post-tax income.

One factor that will help to reduce the WACC as gearing increases is the favourable tax implications of borrowing. A second factor works as a counter to this and increases the WACC when gearing levels become extremely high – this is the very real costs of bankruptcy if the company defaults on its payments and costs of financial distress if the company comes close to bankruptcy. For these reasons, it is thought by many that the WACC is actually U-shaped.

Initially the tax advantages, which allow a company to keep more of its operating profit, outweigh the less likely cost of bankruptcy and the WACC declines. However, as gearing increases, this situation is gradually reversed and the cost of equity rises sharply and with it, the WACC (see Figure 7.5). Let us look at both of these issues in turn.

Tax implications of borrowing

Probably the single most important reason why companies often borrow money rather than seek more money from shareholders is that the tax implications of borrowing money are favourable as they get tax relief on the interest. This can be clearly seen in the following example.

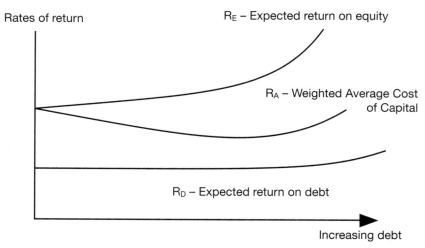

Figure 7.5   Adjusted Weighted Average Cost of Capital

Example

Two companies have exactly the same asset base and earn exactly the same profit, but one company has zero gearing, the other company has 50 per cent gearing and hence will get tax relief on its interest payments. The required return on equity is higher for the geared company at 20 per cent compared to 15 per cent. The loan requires 10 per cent interest per annum. A comparison of the WACC is shown below.

(£000s)	Company A	Company B
Balance sheet		
Shareholders' equity	5,000	2,500
Loans	–	2,500
Total	5,000	5,000
Profit and loss account		
Profit before interest and tax	1,500	1,500
Interest	–	250
Tax at 33%	500	413
Net profit	1,000	838
Return on shareholders' equity	20%	33.5%
Tax saved	–	87
Interest cost (net of tax)	–	163
Effective cost of debt	–	6.5%
WACC	15%	13.3%

The actual return on the investment has increased as the debt is introduced but so has the expected rate of return required by shareholders. However the WACC has decreased due in part to the favourable tax implications.

Tax shields

The tax saved can be looked at as a *tax shield*. We can calculate the value of these tax shields on any investments by discounting them back to today's currency. As the size of these tax shields depends only on the corporate tax rate, the Present Value should be calculated using the expected rate of return required by investors as the discount rate.

If this debt is going to be permanent then you can treat it as a perpetuity and use the perpetuity formula:

$$\frac{\text{PV of the tax shield}}{\text{(if a perpetuity)}} = \frac{\text{Annual tax saved}}{\text{Interest rate}} = \frac{\text{Tax rate} \times \text{Interest payment}}{\text{Interest rate}}$$

$$= \text{Tax rate} \times \text{Amount borrowed}$$

These tax shields can be viewed as an additional benefit that accrues to a company which is geared. The Present Value of these tax shields increases as gearing increases. Of course the tax shield will only be a perpetuity if the following conditions apply:

- The company is sustaining permanent debt and simply rolls over its outstanding loans.

- It always makes sufficient profit to be able to use its tax shield to the full.

If this is not the case, then the Present Value of the tax shield will be lower:

$$\text{PV of tax shield} = T*L$$

where $T*$ indicates a lower percentage than the corporate tax rate and L is the outstanding loan.

How big is the tax advantage?

Brearley and Myers have suggested that it is unlikely that companies can *always* gain the full tax advantage. If they could, then most companies would be geared to a reasonable degree and that is simply not the case when we look at the evidence. One of the reasons is that we have only considered corporation tax so far and not the effect of personal taxes. Interest is only taxed at the corporate level, but equity income is subject to corporation and personal taxes on dividends and on any capital gains. If the personal tax rate on dividends and capital gains is the same as the personal tax on interest payments, our conclusions will be unaffected.

However, the personal tax rate for equity can be less than the personal tax rate for interest. The effective personal tax on capital gains, given that this tax is only payable when the shares are sold, is often lower than the personal rate on interest payments (and dividends). In this case, the tax advantage of debt declines as the example below shows. If personal taxes on interest are high (for example, 40 per cent) and the capital gains tax is effectively zero, (when the shareholder does not sell his or her shares), the tax advantage can completely disappear.

Example

Interest	Income from debt	Income from equity
Income before tax	£100	£100
Corporate tax	£0	£33
Income after tax	£100	£67
Personal tax rates	40%	0%*
Income after all taxes	£60	£67

* there is no personal taxation as shares are retained in this example.

Brearley and Myers do not contend that this extreme scenario occurs often in reality but they suggest that there are a number of reasons why a company may not gain the full tax shield. To gain the full tax shield the following conditions *must apply and apply indefinitely:*

■ The company must be able to show a taxable profit every year to take full advantage of the tax shield.

■ If there is a chance that the company will make a loss, the expected tax shield goes down and thus the expected cost of borrowing increases. The greater the borrowing, the greater the likelihood that the company may make a loss and thus the expected cost of borrowing increases.

Costs of financial distress including bankruptcy

The costs of financial distress offset the tax benefits of gearing. This encompasses both the costs of bankruptcy which increase with gearing and the indirect costs such as conflicts of interest. The costs of bankruptcy may be the direct costs of court fees or the indirect costs of trying to manage a company in liquidation.

However even before bankruptcy occurs, as a company is nearing bankruptcy, there are other costs which arise out of the conflicts of interest between the managers, shareholders and lenders. The costs of financial distress are borne by the shareholders and thus they demand a higher return for the greater risk of incurring such costs. Shareholders have the option to default and in this case these costs are borne by the lenders. Therefore the lenders, if they perceive a risk of default, will demand a higher interest rate as gearing rises to compensate them for this risk.

A new Weighted Average Cost of Capital

It is time to reformulate the Weighted Average Cost of Capital to incorporate the tax implications of gearing. It can now be stated as the following:

WACC = (Cost of equity × % equity) + (Cost of debt (1 − tax rate) × % debt)

= (R^e 2 % equity) + (R^d [1− T*] 2 % debt)

where R^e = the required return on equity
R^d = the cost of borrowing
T* = the tax rate.

Please note that the WACC only includes the side effects of tax. It does not include other financing implications discussed.

Example

A company has a gearing ratio of 40 per cent which it is holding permanently, a cost of equity computed to be 20 per cent and a cost of debt of 12 per cent. It forecasts profits for the foreseeable future. The corporate tax rate is 33 per cent.

Its Weighted Average Cost of Capital is:

= (20% × 60%) + (12% × (1 − 33%) × 40%)
= 15.2%

PRACTICAL TIP

Essentially this has been a chapter on theory and so the need for practical tips is less apparent. There is only one practical tip. Read the theory, understand the theory but don't *use* all of the theory. *Keep it simple!*

CASE STUDY 7.1

Lever Ltd has decided that it must update its calculation of the company cost of capital. This exercise was last done by its company accountants three years ago and its trading circumstances have changed since then. It wants to use the company cost of capital as a starting point for managers who are conducting investment appraisals for new investment projects.

Lever's company accountants have amassed the following information.

Current risk-free rate on government bond	
Nominal:	3.8%
Real:	0.4%
Average market premium:	8.4%
Company equity beta:	1.2
Shareholders' equity	£200 million
Redeemable loans	£45 million
Current average cost of redeemable loans:	10%
Irredeemable loans	£30 million
Current yield on irredeemable loans:	12%
Tax rate:	33%
Status of debt:	Permanent

Calculate the Weighted Average Cost of Capital for Lever Ltd.

▶

Solution

First let us calculate the cost of equity, that is to say, the return required by shareholders to hold the stock. We can compute this using the CAPM:

$$= 3.8\% + 1.2\ (8.4\%)$$
$$= 13.88\%$$
approx. 13.9%

Next we need to assess the gearing of Lever Ltd. It has £200 million in shareholders' equity and £75 million in debt which equates to a gearing of 37.5 per cent.

The final component that we need is the cost of that debt. It comprises two types, redeemable and irredeemable debt and we calculate the weighted average cost of debt as follows:

$$= (10\% \times £45\ \text{million}) + (12\% \times £30\ \text{million})/£75\ \text{million}$$
$$= 10.8\%$$

Let us now put this all together in the Weighted Average Cost of Capital formula:

$$\text{WACC} = (13.9\% \times 62.5\%) + (10.8\% \times (1 - 33\%) \times 37.5\%)$$
$$= 11.4\%$$

The Weighted Average Cost of Capital is 11.4%.

Other methods for calculating the cost of equity
The earnings yield

Before the Capital Asset Pricing Model, a popular method for calculating the cost of equity was to see it as an earnings yield:

Earnings yield	=	$\dfrac{\text{Expected earnings per ordinary share}}{\text{Market price per share}}$

Taking a simple example, Berger Company's shares are currently trading at a price of £7 with outstanding shares of 5 million. Their expected profits after tax for the coming year are £6 million. The cost of equity is calculated as follows:

$$\text{Cost of equity} = \text{Earnings yield} = \frac{(£6,000,000/5,000,000)}{£7} = 17\%$$

The Dividend Growth model

An alternative method is to take the expected dividend for the next year and calculate the dividend yield (i.e. the expected dividend over the market price per share). The dividend yield is then added to the expected average growth in dividends to calculate the cost of equity.

$$\text{Cost of equity} = \frac{\text{Next year's dividend}}{\text{Market price per share}} + \frac{\% \text{ growth}}{\text{rate of dividends}}$$

Again taking Berger Company, they are planning to give a dividend of 70p next year and the historical average dividend growth has been 8 per cent.

$$\text{Cost of equity} = \frac{£0.70}{£7} + 8\% = 18\%$$

Both the Dividend Growth method and the Earnings Yield method are probably more appropriate for estimating the cost of retained earnings than the cost of equity as a whole. When the company is considering a new rights issue, the cost of the rights issue should be taken into account.

An investment project which is highly sensitive to market movements is said to have a high project risk.

CHAPTER EIGHT

Risk and uncertainty – what is the cost of capital of the investment?

- How to estimate the discount rate

- Part I – Assuming all-equity financing

- The traditional approach – the concept of a risk premium

- Part II – Introducing financing implications

- The Weighted Average Cost of Capital

- Adding in the financial implications

CHECKLIST OF KEY POINTS

1 The appropriate discount rate to apply to the forecasted cashflows in an investment appraisal is the opportunity cost of capital for that investment.

2 The opportunity cost of capital is the expected rate of return offered in the capital markets for investments of a similar risk profile. Thus it depends on the risk attached to the investment's cashflows.

3 In practice, the only risks of an investment project that investors are concerned with are the risks that cannot be diversified away, in other words, the overriding market risk. Investment risk is thus assessed by looking at the likely relationship of forecasted cashflows with overall market movements. An investment project which is highly sensitive to market movements is said to have high project risk.

How to estimate the discount rate

First calculate the opportunity cost of capital assuming the investment project is equity financed:

- If some of the investment's cashflows are safe and risk-free, these can be discounted at the nominal risk-free rate, that is to say the rate of borrowing.

- The cost of equity for an investment is the return required by shareholders. It can be derived from the Capital Asset Pricing Model and is calculated from adding together the risk-free rate on government bonds, the average market risk premium (for a portfolio of shares), and a specific investment project beta which compares the co-variance of the investment's risk profile with the risk profile of the market portfolio. It is this investment project beta which indicates the level of market risk that the investment project bears.

Next you must account for any financing implications. There are two ways of doing this:

- You can calculate the NPV of the investment assuming equity finance and then add the present value of any financing implications. There may be a tax shield. Other financing implications are the present value of a share issue or the value of any special financing arrangements.

- You can adjust the cost of capital to incorporate these financing effects.

Part I – Assuming all-equity financing

Before we look at how to correlate an investment's risk with its opportunity cost of capital, it is worth considering the essential maxim:

'The opportunity cost of capital depends on how it is to be used.'

The opportunity cost of capital is the expected rate of return that equates to the market interest rate for investments of a *similar risk profile*. All new investment proposals must earn at least this rate of return otherwise they will find it difficult to raise capital in the future. Once we have calculated this cost of capital, it can be used in your NPV model to establish the viability of new investment projects. However, if the investment is not all-equity financed, we have to add the present value of the financing effects (see Part II).

I shall examine two broad approaches, the first is what I shall call the 'traditional approach' and the second is based on a theory developed in the late 1960s and since put to much empirical testing, the Capital Asset Pricing Model.

The traditional approach – the concept of a risk premium

Many companies introduce the concept of discounting risky cashflows at different rates when they introduce variable risk premiums for different types of investments. They set different required rates of return, or hurdle rates, for their investment projects depending on the nature of the investment. This is usually in the form of a premium on what is considered the basic company cost of capital. In some cases they take the four broad categories of investment projects that we introduced in Chapter 1 and they assess the degree of risk generally associated with each type of investment. Thus a company may set up a decision rule which gives the following risk premiums:

> The opportunity cost of capital is the expected rate of return that equates to the market interest rate for investments of a *similar risk profile*. All new investment proposals must earn at least this rate of return otherwise they will find it difficult to raise capital in the future.

Safety and maintenance investments (financing decision) – no risk as it is simply a financing decision to choose the investment with the lowest cost = zero risk premium

Cost-saving investments – low risk = 3% risk premium

Expansion investments – moderate risk as taking existing products into new markets or new products into existing markets = 6% risk premium

Diversification investments – high risk as expanding with new products into new markets = 9% risk premium

Sometimes the decision rule will not be on the basis of what type of investment it is, but rather on a subjective measure of how risky the investment is. For example, all new investments in a company could be divided into high risk investments, with a risk premium of 9 per cent; moderate risk investments, with a risk premium of 6 per cent; low risk with a risk premium of 3 per cent; and finally those investments with zero risk which are discounted at the company cost of borrowing.

A critique

Though both these approaches recognise that risk will vary with specific investments, they are very subjective measurements and an arbitrary classification into one risk category rather than another might add another 3 per cent onto the discount rate. This can often be the difference between acceptance and rejection of an investment proposal and thus it is open to abuse. An investment project which has a negative NPV in the moderate risk category is reclassified into the low risk category in order to be accepted. A more objective measure is needed, even if the accuracy is not refined to the last decimal point.

There is also a further difficulty – the risk premium models add a premium to the basic cost of capital but the models give us no clues as to how to assess this cost of capital. Is it the risk-free interest rate to be found on government bonds? Is it the corporate cost of capital already calculated by the company's accountants? If it is the corporate cost of capital, some risk has already been assumed as logically not all investments can be riskier than the portfolio of current projects that comprise the company. This model really takes us nowhere.

However, an alternative approach, the Capital Asset Pricing Model, does provide useful answers to both of these problems, the subjectivity and the appropriate discount rates for different investments. It addresses the issue of how to calculate the cost of capital for different companies. This can then be used as a starting point to establish the cost of capital for a specific investment project.

Relating investment risk to the cost of capital

Shareholders' equity is the risk capital of the company. There are no set interest payments or a set loan repayment schedule to follow. Thus the *cost* of equity is simply the *expected return* that shareholders will earn on their money. This is the rate of return they expect in the form of dividends or an increase in the share price.

As discussed in Chapter 7, the CAPM divides the cost of equity into two components: the near risk-free return available on investing in government bonds and an additional risk premium for investing in a particular share or investment. This risk premium in turn comprises the average return on the overall market portfolio and the beta factor (or risk) of the particular investment. Putting this all together the CAPM assesses the cost of equity for an investment as the following:

$$\text{Cost of equity} = R_f + B\,(R_m - R_f)$$

where R_f =   the risk-free rate
            R_m =   the average market return
            B   =   beta of the investment

The beta

The unique risk attached to each share is diversified away when a portfolio of shares is held. Thus the risk attached to a well-diversified portfolio depends on the combined weighted *market risk* of the shares in that portfolio. The risk of a portfolio is measured by the variability of possible returns – the greater the variety of possible returns, the greater the risk. In statistical terms, risk is expressed in terms of standard deviation and variance. The sensitivity of a portfolio to market movements is usually called its *beta*. (The beta reflects the variability of possible returns compared to the variability of possible returns of the market. The variability of the market returns is called the movement of the market.)

Similarly, it is not the *individual* investment risk that should be considered when evaluating the risk of an investment project, but its *effect on the overall portfolio risk*. In the case of a company, the portfolio can be taken to be the sum of all the investment projects that the company is undertaking at any one time. Thus when looking at an investment project, we need to consider the co-variance between the market risk of the investment project and the risk of the existing portfolio of projects. If, when the value of the existing portfolio decreases by 20 per cent due to movement in the market, the value of the investment project decreases by more than 20 per cent, its risk is greater than the existing portfolio and its beta greater than the existing portfolio beta.

Hedging

Ideally a company should be seeking new investment projects which reduce its overall relationship with the systematic risk of the market. A new investment which has dramatically different risk characteristics will have a lower beta factor and require a low cost of capital. Of course these investments are easier to identify in theory than in practice!

Project betas

The simplest way of ascertaining your company beta is to ask one of your company accountants. If your company is sufficiently large you could also look up your company beta in one of the beta books such as the Merill Lynch beta book. Remember these betas will be equity betas. If you are working for a small company or if the investment project bears no relationship to the company, read this section on how to estimate the beta.

Sometimes an investment project will mirror the risk profile of the company as a whole, in which case taking the equity beta for the company as a whole would be appropriate. But as we've already seen, companies are rather like a portfolio of investment projects; some with low betas and others with high betas. Figure 8.1 indicates how the CAPM works to estimate the required return for each investment within a company.

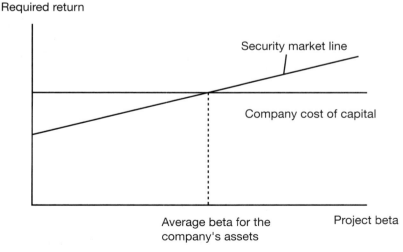

Figure 8.1   Project betas

The company cost of capital is the Weighted Average Cost of Capital for all the investments that comprise that company. If the investment is more risky than the risk of the company as a whole, the beta of the project will be higher than the company beta and consequently investors will require a higher rate of return to compensate them for the greater risk.

It is worth reminding ourselves at this point what the beta value relates to. It does not measure the unique or unsystematic risk associated with the project. As we have seen, this can be eliminated by diversification on the part of investors. The project beta relates to the co-variance of the project with *market risk, i.e. systematic risk.*

PRACTICAL TIPS: HOW TO CALCULATE THE PROJECT BETA

There are no hard and fast rules as to how to calculate the project betas but some tips can be given:

■ The more diversified the company, the less appropriate it is to use the company beta as an approximation.

■ If the company has several divisions which are in different industries, you should not take the company beta if the investment is within only one of these divisions. It would be more appropriate to look in a beta book and take the average industry beta for the investment.

■ If the investment is fairly specific, and the average industry beta does not reflect the risk of the investment, then you could use the following suggestions to help you adapt the average industry beta. First make sure that all possible outcomes of the investment are identified in the cashflows. All upside and downside scenarios should be captured in the expected cashflows.

Now review the pattern and nature of these cashflows.

Cyclicality

Is the pattern of cashflows very cyclical so that a downturn in the economy will affect the cashflows significantly? If so, this would suggest that the investment has a high exposure to market risk and is likely to have an investment beta greater than one. In an economic downturn, if the percentage drop in forecast cashflows is greater than the percentage drop in the whole market, then the investment beta will be greater than one. If it is identical, it will be exactly one and if the percentage drop is less than the market as a whole, the beta would be less than one.

Operating leverage

What is the ratio of fixed costs to variable costs? A high ratio of fixed assets to total assets is called high operating leverage and it is similar to financial leverage. The commitment to fixed production costs increases the risk of the investment and hence its beta. It increases the variability of the profits coming from the investment projects as fixed costs have to be paid before any profits can be made. (Similarly the commitment to interest payments on a loan increases the equity beta.) Generally the higher the fixed cost to variable cost ratio is, the higher the beta of the investment.

I'm afraid that there are no set answers as to how to assess the investment beta precisely. The above comments are designed to help you make a more informed estimate.

Discounting safe risk-free cashflows

Now I should probably put a spanner in the works. So far we have been implicitly assuming that the investment's cashflows are risky, i.e. uncertain and thus we have been trying to assess at what rate they should be discounted to obtain their present value. But *not all cashflows in your investment project are necessarily risky.* You must be careful not to discount your cashflows back at the cost of equity if a *large* number of those cashflows are risk-free. What sort of cashflows are risk-free? The most obvious example is when a company can claim capital allowances for investments made in plant and machinery. The tax savings, if the company is sure that it will make a profit every year, are safe nominal cashflows. Similarly, if you have leased a machine from a leasing company, those lease payments are safe, nominal cashflows assuming that you cannot cancel the contract – they are not going to increase or decrease. The same goes for any fixed contracts where the cash is set in nominal terms.

For all these cashflows, the correct approach is to discount them at the nominal after tax risk-free rate, the rate of bank borrowing.

However, if these are a small component of your annual cashflows, it is simpler to use just one discount rate, the opportunity cost of capital.

Discounting when using specific finance

Another case when the cost of capital for the company will not be the same for a new investment is when the finance for the investment is coming from a specific source which has indicated that this capital should be used in a particular way. This could be the case for government loans or EEC grants for example. In these cases, it is the cost of this finance which is used to assess the viability of the investment. Similarly, if a joint venture between two companies has been created for a new investment, the joint venture may be able to attract specific finance for that investment at a different cost of capital from its parents. This specific cost of capital should be used in the discounting process.

WHERE HAVE WE GOT TO SO FAR?

1 If we are evaluating an investment project with risk-free cashflows, then we must discount them at the risk-free rate (e.g. three-month treasury bonds).

2 If we are evaluating a project with an average market risk, we know we can evaluate it at the market risk premium, typically the risk-free rate prevailing at the time plus the average market risk premium of 8.4 per cent.

3 The CAPM also gives us a way of evaluating all other risk categories. The cost of capital will always be related to the risk of that share or that investment and that risk is expressed by the beta factor.

Part II – Introducing financing implications

Converting equity betas into asset betas

If your company is geared then the asset beta will not equal the equity beta. Once you have arrived at a satisfactory equity beta for the proposed investment, the final step is to convert this into an asset beta for the investment. If it is a mix of debt and equity, the asset beta will be lower than the equity beta because debt has a beta of zero (as there is no correlation between debt and market risk). The asset beta is a weighted average of the equity and debt betas:

> Asset beta = (Equity beta × % equity) + (Debt beta × % debt)
> or simply: (Equity beta × % equity)

Assuming an investment had an equity beta of 1.2 and was going to be financed by a combination of 30 per cent debt and 70 per cent retained earnings (equity), the asset beta would be as follows:

$$\text{Asset beta} = (1.2 \times 70\%) + (0 \times 30\%)$$
$$= 0.84$$

The Weighted Average Cost of Capital

The Weighted Average Cost of Capital assesses the costs of different sources of capital and weights them to produce a company cost of capital. It also takes into account the tax benefits of using debt to supplement shareholders' equity as interest payments are tax deductible whereas shareholders' dividends are taken after tax.

The formula used to calculate the WACC is as follows:

> WACC = (Cost of equity × % equity) + (Cost of debt [1 − tax rate] × % debt)

where the cost of equity is the expected rate of return on shareholders' equity and depends on the commercial risk and the level of gearing.

Implications for investment appraisal

How does this help us with our investment appraisal? Some companies use the company weighted cost of capital as the cost of capital for all new investment projects. However, it is only really appropriate to use the company weighted cost of capital as the discount rate if the following two conditions apply:

- The risk of the project is identical to the risk profile of the company as a whole.
- The project uses the same ratio of debt to equity as the company, i.e. the gearing ratio doesn't change if the company takes a particular investment.

This may or may not be the case. So let us look at how we can adapt what we have learnt so far to calculate an investment-specific discount rate. It is easier and more accurate to build up the cost of capital for the investment from what we know about the investment rather than make assumptions from the company as a whole.

> Now that we have established how to calculate the opportunity cost of capital for an equity financed investment project, we must consider the financing implications.

Adding in the financing implications

Now that we have established how to calculate the opportunity cost of capital for an equity financed investment project, we must consider the financing implications.

There are two methods of doing this – the additive approach and the Adjusted Present Value (APV) technique.

The additive approach

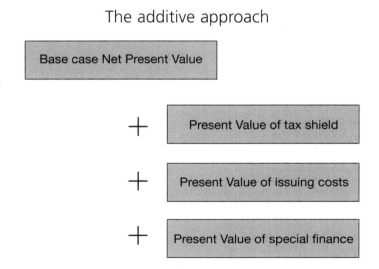

Figure 8.2 The additive approach

First calculate the NPV of the project under the assumption that it is financed solely by equity. Then add in the present values of the financing decisions. These could come from three sources:

- the tax benefits of the tax shield
- the issue costs of issuing new shares
- special financing opportunities.

The advantage of the additive approach is that you can see whether the base-case NPV looks promising but is negatively affected by the financing implications or indeed vice versa, the promising tax benefits are masking an unattractive investment proposal.

The tax benefits of the tax shield

If the investment has led to increased debt capacity, this has a value due to the value of the tax relief on interest payments, commonly known as a tax shield. This might be the case if the company maintains a fixed ratio of borrowing to its assets for example.

Example

A company is contemplating an investment of £600,000 and increasing its borrowings in line with this increase in its assets, by an additional £120,000. The corporate tax rate is 33 per cent. The investment has an economic life of five years and the debt will be paid off in equal instalments throughout the life of the investment.

Year	Debt at 12%	Interest	Tax saving at 12%	PV factor	PV
1	£120,000	£14,400			
2	£96,000	£11,520	£4,752	0.797	£3,787
3	£72,000	£8,640	£3,801	0.712	£2,706
4	£48,000	£5,760	£2,851	0.636	£1,813
5	£24,000	£2,880	£1,901	0.567	£1,078
6			£954	0.507	£484
PV of the tax shield					£9,871

Thus the debt leads to an additional present value of £9,871.

The issue costs of issuing new shares

If the company has to issue more shares specifically to take this investment that is an incidental cost of the investment and its present value should be added to the NPV of the underlying investment. The issue costs are those payments to underwriters, lawyers and so forth when issuing the shares.

Special financing opportunities

Earlier on, we discussed cases where specific finance was available for an investment project. If you are concerned that this specific financing opportunity might lead you to accept an investment which would otherwise have a negative NPV, you might like to calculate the NPV under normal financing and separate out the additional benefit that this cheaper financing gives. (For example, you might be concerned that this investment will lead the company into future investments in the same area which may not be eligible for attractive financing.)

Example

An investment has an initial cash outlay of £1.5 million and the present value of its cashflows, using the base-case cost of capital of 15 per cent is £1.4 million, resulting in a negative NPV of £100,000. The effect of special financing is to reduce the cost of capital to 12 per cent and thus the present value of its cashflows is £1.7 million, providing a positive NPV of £200,000. The present value of the financing implications is £1.7 million − £1.4 million = £300,000.

The Adjusted Present Value technique

An alternative approach is to adjust the opportunity cost of capital so that it incorporates the tax aspects of financing. Note this method is only appropriate if the only financing implication is the creation of a tax shield. In this case the new discount rate is called the *adjusted cost of capital* and denoted by r*. It is easier to compute the APV but it is not such a transparent process.

Unfortunately there is no universal formula for calculating r*. It depends on the nature of the debt borrowed. Two formulas have been derived to enable us to incorporate tax into an adjusted cost of capital.

Permanent debt

If the investment will be supporting a set amount of permanent debt, i.e. as one loan is repaid, a new loan for the same amount is taken out, and if the cashflows are reasonably consistent, then the tax shields can be taken as permanent and the following formula applies:

$$\text{Adjusted cost of capital} = r\,(1 - TL)$$

where
- r = opportunity cost of capital derived from the CAPM
- T = net tax saving as a percentage of interest payments
- L = the marginal contribution to the company's debt as a proportion of the investment's capital outlay.

Even if these conditions do not apply strictly, the margin of error is between 2 and 6 per cent which is reasonable considering the multitude of other areas which are open to errors being made, for example, cashflow forecasting!

Note: It is important to remember that a company may take out a new loan to finance an investment project but **that investment is not funded by 100 per cent debt**. A large part of the new loan is actually supported by the company's other assets. It is simply convenient to take out a new loan at this time. Thus it is the **contribution to the corporate debt capacity** that is the important variable.

Example

Mattison Ltd is considering the adjusted cost of capital to use for a proposed investment. They are paying tax at the full corporate rate of 33 per cent. An investment project requiring a capital outlay of £600,000 would allow Mattison to expand its borrowing capacity by £120,000 on a permanent basis. The company's opportunity cost of capital is 17 per cent.

$$\begin{aligned}
\text{The adjusted cost of capital} &= 17\% \times [1 - (33\% \times 20\%)] \\
&= 15.9 \text{ per cent}
\end{aligned}$$

Variable debt

A second approach can be taken if the company is adopting a policy of adjusting its investment debt according to the cashflows of the investment, i.e. it maintains a fixed proportion of debt to cashflows. Then the following formula can be used:

$$\text{Adjusted cost of capital} \quad = \quad r - Lr_D T \times \frac{(1 + r)}{(1 + r_D)}$$

where   r   =   opportunity cost of capital
           r_D =   cost of borrowing
           T   =   net tax saving as a percentage of interest payments
           L   =   the marginal contribution to the company's debt as a proportion of the investment's capital outlay.

This allows us to calculate the adjusted cost of capital for any investment regardless of its pattern of cashflows.

Example

Mattison is now considering how their adjusted cost of capital would change if they varied their debt as the cashflows from the investment changed. The cost of debt is 10 per cent.

The adjusted cost of capital   = $17\% - (20\% \times 10\% \times 33\%) \times \dfrac{(1 + 17\%)}{(1 + 10\%)}$

                    =   16.3%

Consistent treatment of inflation and taxation

If you are assessing the financing implications of having a tax shield for all or part of the investment's life, you must ensure that you are using *after-tax cashflows* in your calculations. Similarly, if you are using a nominal cost of capital or adjusted cost of capital, you must make sure that you have forecasted *nominal cashflows* and not real ones, i.e. you have adjusted your cashflows to take into account the variable effect of inflation on those cashflows. In all cases, remember: *consistency*!

Step-by-step guide to calculating the opportunity cost of capital

1 Forecast the investment project's incremental after tax cashflows.

2 Is there a specific source of finance which is unique to this investment? If so, discount the cashflows at the cost of that specific source of finance.

3 Are many of the cashflows risk-free?

- If a large number of the after tax cashflows are risk-free, discount them at the after tax risk-free rate.

4 Estimate an investment beta:

- How does the market risk of the investment project differ from the company as a whole?

- Can the company beta be used as an approximation?

- Is there an industry beta that is appropriate?

- Is the investment project more or less cyclical than the market as a whole?

- Does the investment project have a particularly high ratio of fixed assets or costs to overall assets or costs?

5 Estimate the opportunity cost of capital, *assuming the investment is equity funded*, using the CAPM

$$r = r^f + beta \ (r^m - r^f)$$

Then, if the investment is partially funded by debt:

6 Make sure that the beta in the formula represents the asset beta and not the equity beta of the investment. The equity beta of the investment will increase as gearing increases. If it is an equity beta use the following formula to convert it into an asset beta:

$$\text{Asset beta} \quad = \quad (\text{Equity beta} \times \% \text{ equity}) + (\text{Debt beta} \times \% \text{ debt})$$

7 Reformulate the opportunity cost of capital using the asset beta.

8 Add in the effects of financing. This can be done either by using the opportunity cost of capital to assess the NPV of the investment and then assess the present value of any tax shields and the present value of any issuing costs. These are then added to the base case to give the total NPV of the investment under these specific financing arrangements.

9 Alternatively, convert the opportunity cost of capital to an adjusted cost of capital using one of the two formulas below depending on your company's policy on gearing adjustments.

If the debt associated with the investment is at a permanent level:

$$\text{Adjusted cost of capital} \;=\; r\,(\,1 - TL)$$

where r = opportunity cost of capital
  T = net tax saving as a percentage of interest payments
  L = the marginal contribution to the company's debt as a proportion of the investment's capital outlay.

If the debt associated with the investment is at a constant ratio to the cashflows from the investment:

$$\text{Adjusted cost of capital} \;=\; \frac{r - Lr_D T \times (1+ r)}{(1 + r_D)}$$

where r_D = cost of debt.

Flow chart summary

Figure 8.3 identifies the main questions to be considered when calculating the opportunity cost of capital for a specific investment project.

CASE STUDY 8.1

Case 1:

What is the opportunity cost of capital in the following case?

The average government short-term bond rate has been 4.2 per cent for the last 30 years which equates to a real rate of 0.6 per cent. The market premium for the last 30 years has been 8.8 per cent. The current nominal short-term bond rate is 5.2 per cent and inflation is currently 4.8 per cent.

Champion Ltd is an all-equity financed company. Its equity (and asset beta) is 0.90. The particular investment project in question is thought to be more susceptible to market risk and thus the project beta is estimated to be 1.10.

Solution

The opportunity cost of capital can be found using the CAPM.

$$r = r^f + beta \,(r^m - r^f)$$
$$= 5.2\% + 1.10 \,(8.8\%)$$
$$= 14.88\% \text{ approx. } 14.9\%$$

Case 2:

What is the opportunity cost of capital and the adjusted cost of capital in the following case?

Imagine Champion Ltd is now partly funded through debt. Its current ratio of debt to total capital employed is 25 per cent (£2 million debt out of £8 million). Its project beta is 1.10. This investment project requires £500,000 in capital investment. The capital investment increases Champion's borrowing capacity by £125,000. The cost of debt is 10 per cent. The corporate tax rate is 33 per cent.

Solution

The asset beta is now

$$75\% \times 1.10 = 0.825$$

The opportunity cost of capital is thus

$$5.2\% + 0.825 \,(8.8\%) = 12.46\%$$

To get to the adjusted cost of capital, we use the second formula, given that the cashflows are not identical and that the debt will vary with the investment's value.

$$r^* = 12.46\% - [25\% \times 10\% \times 33\% \frac{(1 + 12.46\%)]}{(1 + 10\%)}$$

$$= 11.62\%$$

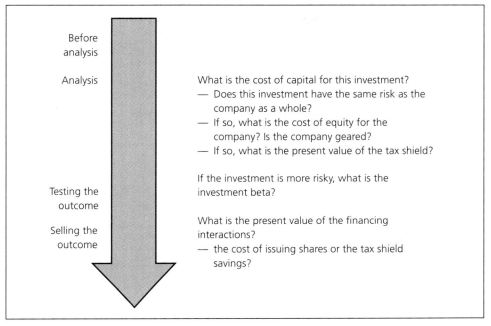

Figure 8.3   Adjusted Weighted Average Cost of Capital

CHECKLIST OF PRACTICAL TIPS

1 I have gone into some detail so that you have a full picture of the various complexities it is possible to investigate. If you start to feel you have lost your way, return to the checklist given above and follow the step-by-step process.

2 When assessing the cost of equity always conduct a reality check – generally if the cost of equity is less than the pre-tax cost of debt (borrowing) then something looks odd because of the greater risk that shareholders carry.

3 Another useful reality check is to look at the cost of alternative investments. If the cost of equity seems substantially different to the returns achievable on other shares of similar risk, then something looks odd. In these cases, check your calculations.

See Chapter 7 for a more detailed discussion on the cost of debt.

The phrase *terminal value* is used to define the residual value of a project after the initial years of its economic life.

CHAPTER NINE

Assessing the terminal value of an investment

- What is the terminal value of an investment project?

- The Perpetuity (or Annuity) method

- The Price/Earnings ratio method

- The Book Value method

- The Liquidation Value method

- Further considerations

CHECKLIST OF KEY POINTS

1 The terminal value of an investment is the residual value of that investment after its first few years of economic life. The size of the terminal value will depend on the ongoing viability of the investment. If it potentially has a long economic life, it will have a large terminal value compared to the present value of its early cashflows.

2 The ongoing viability of the investment, and the degree of conservatism that is required in the forecast, will be the two main factors determining which method is used to assess the terminal value.

3 There are four common methods used to calculate the terminal value: the Perpetuity method, the Price/Earnings (P/E) ratio method, the Book Value method and the Liquidation Value method. Each method defines the terminal value in a slightly different way.

4 The Perpetuity method and the P/E ratio method are the methods used when the investment is ongoing. The Perpetuity method assesses terminal value as the present value of an ongoing stream of cashflows in the future. The P/E ratio method considers the terminal value to be whatever the investment project could be sold for and the P/E ratio gives the best estimate of its market value.

5 The Book Value and the Liquidation Value methods are more conservative measures and are generally used to assess investments that are coming to the end of their economic lives.

What is the terminal value of an investment project?

The phrase *terminal value* is used to define the residual value of a project after the initial years of its economic life. In the chapters so far, we have often discussed expansion and diversification investment projects. Most investments of this type do not have a clear-cut end. Often, it will depend on whether the investment is successful or not. In the examples we have used to date, we have estimated a specific time horizon for an investment. However, in this chapter we examine how we can account for value after the first few years of the investment.

The Net Present Value calculation should be modified as follows. As well as assessing the NPV of the first few years of an investment's life, we should also add a terminal value that accounts for the residual value. If the investment project has a discrete end, there may not be a terminal value. If the investment is in plant or machinery, the terminal value may be simply the present value of the salvage price at the end of the investment. However, the residual or terminal value is often greater than this.

The calculation of an investment's terminal value is not without its complexities. You will have to decide after how many years the terminal value should be calculated and what method of valuation to use. The size of this residual value will vary considerably depending on whether it is an ongoing project or one which is being wound up and each method is appropriate under different circumstances.

For these reasons, it is worth spending some time considering the various methods as illustrated in Figure 9.1 and giving some practical pointers on when to use each method, at what stage the terminal value should be calculated and so on.

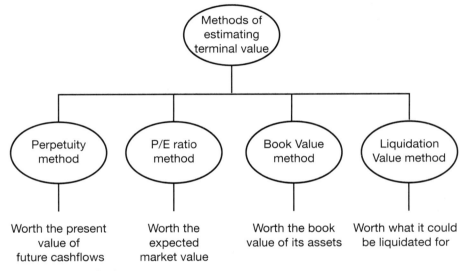

Figure 9.1   Terminal value

The Perpetuity (or Annuity) method

In Chapter 2 we looked at perpetuities and annuities in the context of the Net Present Value method and here we meet them again. If the investment has no foreseeable end, its terminal value can be viewed as a perpetuity. The company has invested a certain amount of money and it receives in return a regular cashflow that can carry on indefinitely. The terminal value is the present value of this perpetuity. If the investment is ongoing, for several years rather than indefinitely, the terminal value is like an annuity, and we have to compute the present value of this annuity.

When would the Perpetuity method be used?

As the terminal value of an investment is viewed as a perpetuity, it should only be used for investments that are ongoing and where the cashflows have settled down into a regular pattern showing approximately the same growth from year to year.

As the terminal value of an investment is viewed as a perpetuity, it should only be used for investments that are ongoing and where the cashflows have settled down into a regular pattern showing approximately the same growth from year to year (see Figure 9.2).

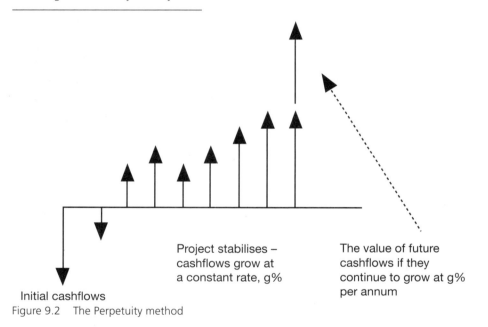

Project stabilises – cashflows grow at a constant rate, g%

The value of future cashflows if they continue to grow at g% per annum

Initial cashflows

Figure 9.2   The Perpetuity method

Examples of likely projects

■ The most obvious cases where the Perpetuity method is used is when a *company* is being valued, either because another company is seeking to acquire it or by analysts who are wishing to indicate its overall market worth and hence the value of its shares to investors. As companies can theoretically continue for ever, this is an appropriate occasion to use this method. But there are further conditions required which we will deal with in the next section.

- If a company was looking to buy established product lines from another company, they may wish to use the Perpetuity method to estimate the value of those products after the next five to ten years. Pharmaceutical companies often sell or swap product lines which are not in line with their therapeutic portfolios. Some of these products are in small niche markets where the likelihood of new products entering the market, and rendering them obsolete, is relatively small.

The most obvious cases where the Perpetuity method is used is when a *company* is being valued, either because another company is seeking to acquire it or by analysts who are wishing to indicate its overall market worth and hence the value of its shares to investors.

- Some companies may want to estimate the value of a *new* product line in this way if they believe that it may have a longer life than five or six years. This is probably only appropriate if the new product is trading on an existing and well-established brand name. Initially its sales will grow rapidly but later in the product's life-cycle the growth will probably slow down until its annual growth may be only marginal.

Conditions for the Perpetuity method

- The project's cashflows have settled down to a set pattern in the later years, i.e. years five, six and onwards.

- It is reasonable to expect that cashflow growth, rather than sales or profit growth, will continue at a set rate each year, if at all.

These two conditions will enable us to estimate the likely growth of cashflows in later years.

- The final condition is that this estimated growth must be significantly less than the discount rate. Otherwise the terminal value of the project will far exceed the value placed on earlier cashflows and this is rarely the case. Even if it was appropriate, it will be extremely difficult to sell such an investment project to senior management.

Terminal value estimated with the Perpetuity method

The Perpetuity method can be used to assess the terminal value of investments continuing indefinitely (a perpetuity) or investments continuing for a set period of years (an annuity). The former may be relatively infrequent but the latter variation is often useful.

Terminal value as a Perpetuity

Terminal value =	The value in Year N of cashflows in Years N+1 through to infinity
=	$\dfrac{(\text{Cashflow in Year N}) \times (1 + \text{Growth rate})}{(\text{Discount rate} - \text{Growth rate})}$

Example

Georgetown Company is evaluating whether to invest in a new lathe. They believe that the lathe will lead to productivity improvements and cost savings in the first four years. After the first four years, they will invest in a new lathe as precision tool technology improves. They will continue to use the existing lathe for less precise jobs as its low operating overheads mean that it is the most profitable equipment to use. They forecast that 10 per cent of their work will continue to require the original lathe and that the resulting cash inflow will grow at 2 per cent per year. They have calculated their opportunity cost of capital is 14 per cent.

Year	Cashflows	PV factor	Present value
0	−£100,000	1.000	−£100,000
1	£30,000	0.877	£26,310
2	£35,000	0.769	£26,915
3	£45,000	0.675	£30,375
4	£40,000	0.592	£23,680

Year 5 onwards £4,000 growing at 2% per annum

$$\text{Terminal value} \ = \ \frac{£4,000 \times (1 + 0.02)}{(0.14 - 0.02)} \ = \ £34,000$$

Net Present Value = £41,280

Terminal value as an annuity

As we have already indicated, there may be relatively few cases where the Perpetuity method is strictly appropriate, but the variant of this method, the Annuity method, which calculates the terminal value of an investment for a set time horizon, can often be appropriate. When estimating an annuity, we can use the cumulative PV tables.

Example

Ongoing Ltd is about to sell a product line to a fellow producer of premium widgets. The product line is still profitable but no longer fits into the overall portfolio of products and uses machinery that is not shared by other product lines. Glory-Widgets Ltd manufactures several related products and will therefore be able to share certain costs across a broader spectrum of machinery/personnel. Ongoing Ltd has calculated the next five years' cashflows. After five years, they see a steady growth of 1 per cent per annum for the following ten years. After the next ten years they do not believe that the product line will have any residual value. They have calculated that their opportunity cost of capital is 10 per cent.

Year	Cashflows	PV factor	Present value
1	£50,000	0.901	£45,050
2	£52,500	0.826	£43,365
3	£54,600	0.751	£41,005
4	£56,238	0.683	£38,411
5	£57,363	0.621	£35,622

Terminal value is £57,363 growing at 1 per cent per annum for ten years. Thus the PV factor table to be used is the 9 per cent column, that is to say (r − g), 10% − 1% growth.

The appropriate cumulative PV factor to take is not 6.418 (cumulative PV factor at 9 per cent for ten years) as this would indicate that this cashflow began in Year One and continued until Year Ten, not that it began in Year Six and continued until Year Fifteen.

We must take the cumulative PV factor for 9 per cent for 15 years and take away the cumulative PV factor for 9 per cent for five years:

$$8.061 - 3.890 = 4.171$$

Thus the terminal value is:

$$£57,363 \times 4.171 = £235,090$$

The total NPV for the sale is £438,543.

The Price/Earnings ratio method

Another way of estimating the terminal value of an investment is to ask – if I were to sell this investment project in the market place after five or ten years, what price could I expect? Thus the terminal value of the ongoing project is taken to be its market value. Financial analysts often use Price/Earnings ratios as a guide to the market value and this is exactly the approach that this method takes (see Figure 9.3).

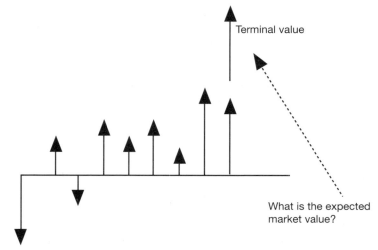

Figure 9.3   The P/E ratio method

When would the Price/Earnings ratio method be used?

The P/E ratio method would be used when it is not realistic to estimate the yearly cashflows far into the future or indeed the rate at which they will grow. The forecasts may be inaccurate or perhaps the cashflows are not likely to settle into a nice comfortable pattern that would allow us to use the Perpetuity method. In these cases you need to be able to use a method which recognises that the investment is ongoing but with an erratic stream of cashflows.

The investment has to be separable from the rest of the company as it is only really appropriate to use the P/E ratio method if the investment can be sold, for example, the case of a new product line with its own plant and equipment.

Examples of likely projects

A typical investment project may be a mining operation which will have an economic life of well over five or six years but where the cashflows are unlikely ever to settle into a set pattern given the cyclical nature of the mining industry and the variable price of the commodity being mined.

Conditions for the P/E ratio method

- There must be an industry P/E ratio that is appropriate for the investment.

- As with the Perpetuity method, the investment should be ongoing but, unlike the Perpetuity (Annuity) method, its economic life does not need to be known.

- The investment theoretically must be able to be sold as a separate entity. If an investment would never be sold, then this is a less appropriate method of valuation as it is not realisable.

Terminal value estimated with the P/E ratio method

An appropriate P/E value must be used. It should be a P/E ratio for the industry *at that stage in the industry's life-cycle*. As we are considering a time N years into the future, the P/E ratio may be slightly lower than it is today. The industry will have stabilised and may be in a mature phase of its life-cycle; growth may be slower, margins lower and so on.

Remember to use the P/E ratio that is based on the industry of the investment not the parent company (if that is different).

The formula for the P/E ratio method is very straightforward:

Terminal value	=	'Market' value in Year N
	=	Earnings after tax year N × the appropriate P/E ratio

Example

Magnum Ltd is considering an investment in some new machinery to produce some of its products. It wants to use this machinery for five years and after that time, it believes it can sell the machinery and the right to produce some of its smaller lines to a sub-contractor. The going P/E ratio in the industry at the moment is 12 but Magnum estimates that this will be more like 11 in five years' time. The after-tax profit in Year Five from those product lines is estimated to be £30,000.

Thus terminal value under this method would be:

$$= £30,000 \times 11 = £330,000$$

This is then discounted back to its present value alongside the net cashflows from Years One to Five.

The Book Value method

A third, but more conservative, approach to terminal value estimation is to ask how much the assets of the investment project would be worth after five or ten years. It seeks to estimate the balance sheet value of the tangible assets of the investment in the Year N and to use this as a proxy for the terminal value of the investment (see Figure 9.4). Thus an investment's terminal value is taken to be its adjusted book value (i.e. with all intangible assets removed from the book value).

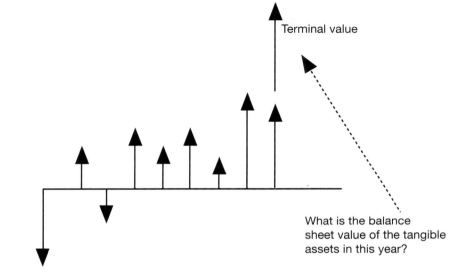

Terminal value

What is the balance
sheet value of the tangible
assets in this year?

Figure 9.4   Book Value method

When would the Book Value method be used?

This is a conservative measure of terminal value as it identifies *tangible assets* with the value of the whole investment. It is generally used as a reasonably accurate measure of the investment's terminal value if the investment is coming to an end. (Intangible assets are not considered given the subjective element in their valuation.)

It can be used as an alternative to the P/E ratio method if an investment is ongoing – for example, it could be appropriate for an industrial project if the investment was continuing but with extreme uncertainty as to its cashflow generation.

It is not an appropriate method to use if the investment is service-based as the book value of the tangible assets will bear no real relation to the value of that investment when most of the investment's assets are intangible, that is, goodwill, brand equity and so forth.

Examples of likely investment projects where the Book Value method would be an appropriate measure of terminal value would be plant and equipment-based investments which will be winding down over the next one to two years.

Conditions for the Book Value method

- The investment is either winding down or there is great uncertainty as to whether it will continue and what the annual cashflows will be.

- Intangible assets should not be a major part of the value of the investment.

Terminal value estimated with the Book Value method

The formula that is normally used in such cases is the following:

Terminal value	=	Book asset value in Year N
	=	Net property, plant and equipment plus current assets minus current liabilities

The Liquidation Value method

This is the most conservative measure of terminal value and so should be used only in very specific circumstances. We will not dwell in detail on it here. Suffice to say it defines an investment's terminal value as the liquidation value of the investment's assets in Year N (see Figure 9.5).

When would the Liquidation Value method be used?

By using this method to calculate terminal value, you are assuming that value tied up in the investment has to be realised in a speedy manner as in the case when a company has been liquidated and the receivers are trying to recover assets to pay at least some of the creditors. In reality there can be few occasions when you are reviewing an investment project 'on paper' that you need to assume this.

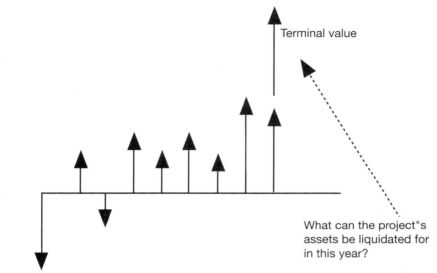

Terminal value

What can the project"s
assets be liquidated for
in this year?

Figure 9.5   Liquidation Value method

Terminal value estimated with the Liquidation Value method

Terminal value is taken to be the asset liquidation value. A common formula used is as follows:

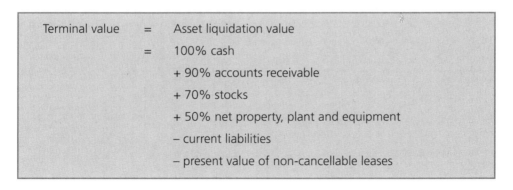

Terminal value	=	Asset liquidation value
	=	100% cash
		+ 90% accounts receivable
		+ 70% stocks
		+ 50% net property, plant and equipment
		− current liabilities
		− present value of non-cancellable leases

This is a good general formula but these percentages will vary by industry. For example, a very small percentage of stocks will be included in the perishable food industry whereas, in contrast, a precious metals dealer may get *over* 100 per cent of stock value.

Further considerations

We have reviewed the four main methods of evaluating terminal value and now two further issues must be addressed:

- When should you use the different methods?
- After what time period should you estimate the terminal value of an investment?

Which method should I use, and when?

By now you should be reasonably clear as to the main factors that affect the method to be used:

- Has the investment got a viable life in the future?
- Is the investment still growing?
- Are the cashflows erratic or easy to forecast?
- How conservative do I wish to be?
- What does the balance sheet look like?

The basic rule is that *the method chosen must fit the profile of the project.* Figure 9.6 outlines two of the main parameters, the degree of conservatism and whether the investment is ongoing.

If the investment is ongoing, for example, you are evaluating a new product line which could have many years of economic life, use either the Perpetuity method or the Price/Earnings ratio method. To use Book Value or Liquidation Value would be inappropriate as this would under estimate the value considerably.

Another factor is how conservative you want to be. The Liquidation Value method is the most conservative method to use, followed by the Book Value method. The Perpetuity method when a high growth rate is forecast, or the Price/Earnings ratio method when a high P/E is being taken, are the least conservative methods.

You may respond – I want to be neither conservative nor optimistic – I want to value the investment project correctly! However, there is a good case for erring on the conservative side when estimating terminal values and it is based on the need to 'sell' the investment to senior management. Most managers start to have less faith in cashflow forecasts once they are attributed to Years Six, Seven and onwards. If you propose an investment project that has a positive NPV due partly to a very high terminal value, senior management may reject the investment project as too 'risky' even if a smaller terminal value would still have resulted in a positive NPV.

If you have an investment that brings back sufficient value in its earlier years, be conservative with your terminal value. This does not mean choosing the Liquidation Value method as opposed to the Perpetuity method but rather taking a lower estimated growth rate for the Perpetuity formula (or taking a lower P/E ratio if you are using the P/E ratio method). You could then present what you consider to be the most appropriate value as an upside. However, you will not have jeopardised the acceptance of the whole project.

At what point should I estimate terminal value?

This will depend mainly on two factors: the estimated investment life and which method you are using to calculate the terminal value.

If the investment is going to finish naturally after a certain time, say four or five years, then estimate the cashflows for the economic life of the investment. Do not be swayed by the fact that your company normally only considers, say five years of cashflows. If there is a clear end to the investment in eight years, then calculate the stream of the cashflows for eight years.

If there is no clear end to the investment or if the investment life is likely to be more than ten years, it will depend on which method of estimation you are using. If you have decided to use the P/E ratio method, then it is better to restrict the number of individual cashflow estimates to about five. You do not have to wait until the cashflows have settled into a regular pattern in order to estimate the terminal value.

If you are using the Perpetuity method, estimate the yearly cashflows until they achieve a regular pattern and until the annual growth of those cashflows is relatively low compared to the cost of capital that is being used as the discount rate. This may take ten or more years. Though it may seem unrealistic to estimate yearly cashflows for ten years, it is preferable to estimating too high a terminal value. Let's expand on this. If you only estimate five years of cashflows and then try to use the Perpetuity formula to estimate the remaining terminal value, you may run into problems. The cashflows may not have settled into a regular pattern and, more worryingly, the cashflow growth could still be high. If you assume that level of growth is going to continue, you may over-inflate the value of the investment by estimating a large terminal value in relation to earlier cashflows. If you assume that the growth will slow down, you have no reasonable measure to say by how much – will it be 2 per cent or 3 per cent? This could make a significant difference to your terminal value.

Short cuts

If you are using the Perpetuity method, take the growth rate at the end of the estimation period and apply it to a terminal value which begins after Year Five or so. It is acceptable to do this because you are estimating a terminal value from Year Five to infinity. The fact that, say from Year Five to Year Ten there is higher cashflow growth is immaterial. It is the average growth from Year Ten onwards which is the main contributor to the overall NPV of the investment.

Flow chart summary

Figure 9.6 identifies the key questions to ask when considering which methods to use to assess an investment project's terminal value.

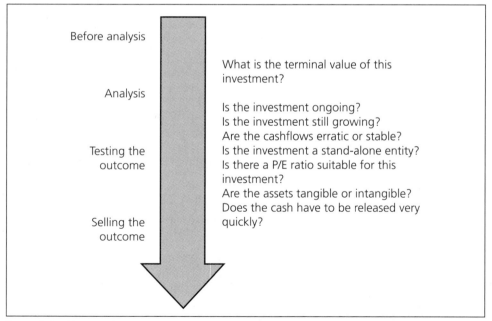

Before analysis

Analysis

Testing the outcome

Selling the outcome

What is the terminal value of this investment?

Is the investment ongoing?
Is the investment still growing?
Are the cashflows erratic or stable?
Is the investment a stand-alone entity?
Is there a P/E ratio suitable for this investment?
Are the assets tangible or intangible?
Does the cash have to be released very quickly?

Figure 9.6 Key questions

CASE STUDY 9.1

Robert Newman is considering which method of estimating terminal value is appropriate for the investment project that he is evaluating. It is for an expansion of his company's current product range. It involves capital investment in plant machinery and equipment as well as expenditure on marketing and sales. The new product lines will share some plant capacity with existing product lines. If the expansion is successful, there is no reason why the new product lines should not continue indefinitely. However, Robert believes that it is more realistic to expect that the economic life of the project will be between ten and twelve years. More than that he cannot say. Robert does not feel comfortable estimating the cashflows from the investment project for more than five years. These cashflow estimates are given below. The opportunity cost of capital is taken to be 15 per cent. The current P/E of the diversified company is 12 but the industry sector in which this investment project would take place has a P/E of 11. It is thought that this will decline to approximately 10 in five years' time.

Year	Profit	Expected cashflows*	PV factor	Expected PV
0	£0	(£1,000,000)	1.000	(£1,000,000)
1	£100,000	£250,000	0.870	£217,500
2	£150,000	£300,000	0.756	£226,800
3	£160,000	£312,000	0.658	£205,296
4	£165,000	£319,800	0.572	£182,926
5	£170,000	£326,196	0.497	£162,119

* these cashflows are the expected cashflows that Robert has computed using various scenarios combined with probability values.

Which method should Robert choose and what is the terminal value?

Suggestions

This is not a clear-cut case. As the investment project is ongoing it is most appropriate to assume that either the Perpetuity or the P/E ratio method should be used. The arguments for each method are as follows:

▶

▶

Why should Robert use the Perpetuity method?

- Cashflows are steady.

- The growth rate is reasonably low.

- The investment cannot be easily separated from the rest of the company as plant and equipment will be shared with existing product lines.

Why should Robert use the P/E ratio method?

- There is a clearly defined P/E value for the industry in which this investment takes place.

On balance, it is more appropriate to use the Perpetuity method given that this is not an investment that can easily be sold. However, in order not to over estimate the terminal value of this investment project, I would suggest that the economic life is taken to be ten years rather than twelve years.

> Cumulative PV factor of 13% (15% – 2%) for 10 years = 5.426
>
> Cumulative PV factor of 13% for 5 years   = 3.517
>
> Remaining cumulative PV factor   = 1.909
>
> 1.909 × £326,000 = £622,708

Thus the total NPV is (£1,000,000) + £994,641 + £622,708 = £617,349.

CHECKLIST OF PRACTICAL TIPS

- Be conservative with the Perpetuity method and the P/E ratio method. When looking at an investment's annual cashflow in eight to ten years' time, do not assume the most optimistic scenario. You run the risk of over estimating the NPV of an investment, with a high terminal value compared to the first few years of cashflows.

- Be consistent with tax when using the Perpetuity method – if you are using an after-tax discount rate, ensure that the cashflow in Year N is also after tax.

- Be consistent with your treatment of inflation when using the Perpetuity method – if you are using a nominal discount rate, ensure that you use a nominal growth rate, g per cent.

This chapter begins by looking at the capital budgeting environment in which many investment proposals need to be sold. It goes on to highlight some inadequacies of capital budgeting systems which must be negotiated not only by the investment 'champions' but also by the senior management who are deciding on which investments to accept. The chapter then tackles each of the critical steps one by one and rounds off with a brief overview of what should happen after an investment project is accepted.

CHAPTER TEN

How to sell an investment project with a positive NPV

- Part I – Checking it's the right decision
- Part II – Selling the investment proposal
- Part III – After your investment proposal is accepted

CHECKLIST OF KEY POINTS

1 Before submitting your proposal to senior management, make sure that you understand your company's capital budget environment, the process and all the biases. There are some common problems with budget systems which you can try to avoid. 'Soft ceilings' on investment may have been imposed in order to reduce the number of over-optimistic investment proposals; the remuneration systems or the corporate culture may lead to a short-term focus which jeopardises the chances of profitable, but longer-term, investments being accepted.

2 Think about where your positive NPV comes from. Is it exploiting an area of competitive advantage that will allow your company to earn above average profits? If so, how and when will your competitors react? Returns which are greater than the average competitive returns expected in a perfect market are sometimes called *economic rents*. A positive NPV is simply the present value of those economic rents.

3 Unfortunately, sometimes the positive NPV is not due to economic rents but rather to errors in the investment appraisal. This chapter outlines some of the possible errors that you may make in your appraisal. It may be that the cashflow forecasts are compiled from many sources and contain inconsistent assumptions about the economic environment or other assumptions. At other times the investment appraiser's enthusiasm for the proposed investment leads to over-optimism and insufficient attention is given to the possible negative outcomes.

4 When you are selling your proposal, think about your audience. What investment appraisal methods do they use and know? How open are they to new approaches? At such times a good dose of pragmatism in using terms that everyone is familiar with, and adapting to their requirements, will often bring the best results.

5 Support your case with sensitivity testing and other tools to examine uncertain cashflows so that all major outcomes have been explored. Keep such supporting analysis in the report appendices, unless this has revealed significant issues that need to be discussed at the meeting.

6 An investment is often followed by a post-audit. These are to be welcomed as they can give valuable insights into how the investment appraisal and forecasting methods can be improved. But there is a risk. It could lead to under estimation of the value of an investment, and perhaps rejection of 'risky' projects with potential high returns, if appraisers try to ensure that their investment's 'budgets' are always achieved.

Introduction

So you have now completed your investment appraisal and decided that this is an attractive investment. However, all is not yet over. You now need to convince others that your conclusions are correct. Figure 10.1 highlights the steps to be taken once the investment analysis is over. There are still a number of steps in the process to be followed if you are going to be in the optimum position to sell your investment proposal to its best advantage.

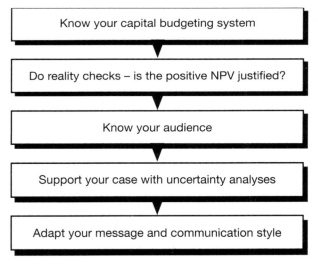

Figure 10.1 Critical steps

This chapter begins by looking at the capital budgeting environment in which many investment proposals need to be sold. It goes on to highlight some inadequacies of capital budgeting systems which must be negotiated not only by the investment 'champions' but also by the senior management who are deciding on which investments to accept. The chapter then tackles each of the critical steps one by one and rounds off with a brief overview of what should happen after an investment project is accepted.

Part I – Checking it's the right decision

A review of the capital budgeting environment

An overview of capital budgeting was given in Chapter 1 and is summarised in Figure 10.2 below. It is worth pointing out that in many companies the same basic process will be repeated throughout the company with investment projects being weeded out, for example, at factory level, divisional level or regional level. The list of projects which emerges through the screening process is then included in the capital budget which is compiled by the finance department. For large companies there may be several intermediate review stages before the investment proposal is finally accepted. Usually the size of the investment will determine at what level within the company it can be agreed and thus acted upon. Each manager will have a different discretionary budget limit that is within his or her control.

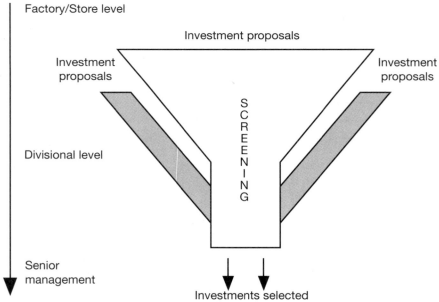

Figure 10.2   The investment appraisal filter

The capital budgeting approach is not, however, just a bottom-up approach. Depending on the corporate culture and the management style of the company, it may in fact be more of a top-down approach especially if the senior management has a clear idea of the strategy that they wish to pursue. This may lead them to champion projects of a broad strategic nature which are less likely to be filtered up from within the company. Similarly, investments coming from store level within a retail chain are likely to revolve around expansion or diversification opportunities for the store or organisational and cost-saving investments. However, a regional manager of the retail chain may be considering an investment in new store locations, his or her area of expertise. So the process of capital investment should not be seen as a single funnel as in Figure 10.2 but rather as a delta with many channels providing investment proposals.

How to avoid common problems with capital budgeting systems

As a manager with an investment proposal you will often need to gain supporters for the investment throughout the company if it is going to be accepted. Knowing how the capital budgeting process can be distorted, so that managers do not always accept the most profitable investments, can help you to avoid such problems or at least work around them as best you can. So what are the common problems?

Imposing soft ceilings for the wrong reasons

The capital budgeting systems in many companies have evolved in response to some of the problems that are associated with investment appraisal, namely, errors in forecasting through inaccurate cashflow assumptions, through inaccurate use of appraisal methods or over-optimism or exaggeration on the part of the project champions. One common response to the latter problem is to put a soft ceiling on capital investment either for the company or for each business unit or division of the company. In this way senior management tries to reduce exaggerated investment claims. However, this can lead to a 'chicken and egg' situation. The senior management imposes a ceiling on capital budgets and in order to raise this ceiling for the following year, managers within a division or department propose a series of investment proposals with strongly positive NPVs so as to justify such an increase. Some of these investments may have over-optimistic forecasts.

A short-term outlook

In an ideal world, senior managers would accept all investments which will increase shareholder value. However, sometimes capital investments which fulfil this objective can conflict with senior managers' desire to maintain current levels of profitability. Figure 10.3 indicates the different short-term and long-term impacts an investment project can have.

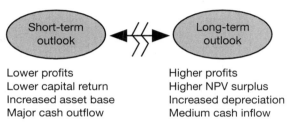

Short-term outlook	Long-term outlook
Lower profits	Higher profits
Lower capital return	Higher NPV surplus
Increased asset base	Increased depreciation
Major cash outflow	Medium cash inflow

Figure 10.3   Short-term vs long-term outlook

Such conflicts can be particularly acute if managers are being rewarded on short-term financial objectives (see next section).

Example

Quick-Quick Ltd are considering an investment project which has an NPV of £1 million and an Internal Rate of Return of 32 per cent. This major investment will draw on reserves for two years, produce only moderate net cashflow in Year Two and significant cashflows in Years Three to Six. But the managers of Quick-Quick Ltd are being evaluated on the annual Return on Capital Employed (ROCE). They have set an objective that ROCE must not fall below 15 per cent. This investment project violates that objective and thus they reject the investment even though it would have increased shareholder wealth.

Year	Total capital employed	New investment	Profit	ROCE
−1	£6 million		£1 million	16.7%
0	£7 million	£1 million	£1 million	14.3%
1	£8 million	£1 million	£1 million	12.5%
2	£8 million		£1.5 million	18.8%
3	£8 million		£2 million	25%

Remuneration systems

This problem can be exacerbated if the reward and remuneration system throughout the company is not in line with the objectives of the capital budget. If managers are rewarded on the basis of this year's performance rather than on a more medium-term performance basis, it is human nature that they will propose investments that achieve a fast payback regardless of whether they are the most cash-generating in the long run of all the potential investments. Similarly, even if the company does not necessarily reward a short-term focus in the remuneration package, there is often a culture of moving jobs within the company every two to three years. In such cases the manager will seek to demonstrate 'results' within this time period.

> In a perfect capital market, economic theory would suggest that every investment should earn its opportunity cost of capital and no more. If this was not the case, then competitors would enter the market and competition would force down profit margins to the point when the return is equal to the opportunity cost of capital.

If the remuneration system of the company is to reward successful investments or achievement of the budget forecasts rather than to reward good decisions (and not just good luck), then human nature will often lead to managers under-estimating the upside potential of an investment so as to ensure that the budget is met and exceeded.

Where does the positive NPV come from?

You have completed your analysis and the investment project is showing a healthy positive NPV at its opportunity cost of capital. But where does this positive NPV come from? In a perfect capital market, economic theory would suggest that every investment should earn its opportunity cost of capital and no more. If this was not the case, then competitors would enter the market and competition would force down profit margins to the point when the return is equal to the opportunity cost of capital. This is an equilibrium position. (If the profit margin was less than the opportunity cost of capital, some companies would leave the industry in order to gain a higher return through employing their assets differently, and margins would again rise.) So if you have an investment project in a mature industry with a positive NPV, there can be only two alternatives: you have got it wrong or the investment enables the company to earn 'economic rents'. I will explain what I mean by this in a minute but first let's look at the less satisfactory option – being wrong!

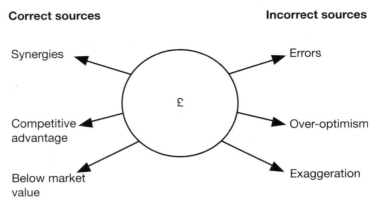

Figure 10.4   Sources of positive NPV investments

CHECKLIST OF COMMON MISTAKES

Errors can, and frequently do, happen, especially if the investment proposal is a complex one. Here is a checklist of the most common mistakes that investment appraisers can make. It is useful to read it through and mentally check off each one.

❏ Have you used nominal cashflows with a nominal opportunity cost of capital?

❏ If you have used real cashflow forecasts and a real opportunity cost of capital, are you confident that inflation will affect all of your cashflows in exactly the same way? This will not be the case if any capital allowances are part of your calculations.

❏ Have you used only cashflows in your forecasts, i.e. you have not included depreciation charges?

❏ Is the timing of your cashflows correct? For example, have you included tax only when it is likely to be paid and not when it will be recorded as 'Tax Payable'?

❏ Have you included only incremental cashflows and not sunk costs (costs already incurred)?

❏ Have you considered the alternatives to this investment and costed in any opportunity costs?

❏ Have you tested any areas of uncertainty in your cashflows, and identified the Expected Net Present Value which is the weighted average of the NPV of each of the alternative outcomes?

❏ Have you fully utilised tools to identify the specific drivers of your NPV such as sensitivity testing, scenario modelling and decision trees?

❏ Is the discount rate chosen specific to this investment, taking into account the market risk of this investment rather than the company as a whole?

❏ If the investment does not have a clear-cut end to its economic life, or an extended life of many years, have you decided what is the most appropriate way to assess its terminal value and included that value in your NPV for the investment?

Another important step in avoiding needless errors is to ensure that, if cashflow forecasts are originating from different sources, they are at least based on the same fundamental assumptions. For example, if you are the project leader co-ordinating the investment appraisal of a new product line, you may be asking for sales forecasts from the sales and marketing expert, variable production costs per unit from the production engineer and an estimate of fixed overheads from the production manager. If each of these experts devises their forecasts using their own assumptions concerning the inflation rate and the exchange rate and so on, then the cashflows will probably show some discrepancies.

Formulate some common assumptions on the macro-environment such as inflation, interest rates, GDP growth and exchange rates and then leave each of the functional experts to build their cashflow forecasts using these as a base. There is no point in asking for a pessimistic and an optimistic forecast from individual project team members without first discussing exactly *how* pessimistic and *how* optimistic these scenarios should be. One person's pessimistic forecast might be another person's base-case scenario! Preferably a common scenario should be agreed upon, such as the following example:

Pessimistic scenario: Recession deepens with real economic growth falling to –1 per cent. Inflation continues high at 8 per cent with government increases in interest rates in an attempt to curb inflation bringing interest rates up to 12 per cent by the end of next year.

Of course, you will never be able to eradicate all the errors and/or omissions. But, by thinking widely around the investment and checking all the steps, you will avoid the most glaring errors which might otherwise be picked up in a review meeting.

Optimism and exaggeration

Optimism is when your enthusiasm for an investment, or your natural state of mind, leads you to over-emphasise the positive benefits of the investment or the upside potential, without fully investigating the possible risks or pessimistic scenarios. To some degree there is little you can do to change human nature but if you know that optimism is your natural state then take care to investigate fully all the possible outcomes of the investment. The next section reviews this.

Exaggeration is a more deliberate manipulation of the analysis to produce a favourable 'result'. This can be done, for example, either by inflating the cashflow forecasts or by lowering the discount rate. A company's review process will be aimed at trying to minimise over-exaggeration through budget committees and the use of post-audits.

A note for reviewers

There are several ways to deal with exaggeration on the part of investment proposers. One way is to set the opportunity cost of capital at the outset for a division which will have investment opportunities of similar risk (in terms of exposure to market trends). This will reduce the opportunity for individuals to manipulate the discount rate and will also save them time and effort. However, what might happen is that the cashflows are then manipulated instead!

An alternative is to ask for the analysis to be completed with several discount rates without communicating the opportunity cost of capital that the investment will be discounted at. However this does reduce the involvement and the motivation of the investment appraisers.

A third option is to ensure that accuracy of forecasting is rewarded even if it does not result in a stream of positive NPV investments. This is more difficult than it sounds given our natural inclination to reward good results regardless of whether they were forecasted or not, and vice versa.

Figure 10.5 contrasts the normal company reward system with an alternative approach.

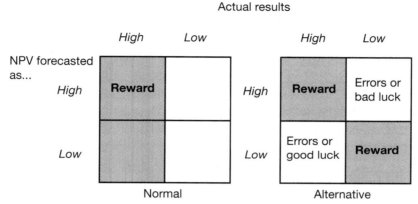

Figure 10.5   Rewarding accuracy

The investment appraiser could be asked to take part in the post-audit process and to justify their forecasts when compared with actual results. Even suggesting this could curb the worst cases of exaggeration. But it may lead to too great a degree of conservatism as project teams shy away from risky investments, even those investments with positive NPVs at high discount rates.

Getting it right – economic rents

Earlier on we discussed that in a perfect world most investments should earn their opportunity cost of capital, no more, no less. But there are a number of exceptions to this rule. If an investment earns more than its opportunity cost of capital, it is said to be earning economic rents. The positive NPV is the present value of these economic rents.

These rents could be temporary as in the case of a company moving into an attractive new market. As the attractiveness of the market becomes clear, other companies will also enter and margins may fall. Or the economic rents could be more permanent as in the case of a natural or created monopoly. So if your investment proposal has a positive NPV you must try to establish the source of these economic rents. If you cannot identify the source, then perhaps an error has been made or possibly you have been too optimistic in your cashflow forecasts.

A new technology or market

If the investment will lead to the development of a new market and/or an improved product, you may be able to charge a premium price for the product. You may have some proprietary technology that can be patented or which will allow you to produce your product at a lower cost than your competitors. You may be able to patent the product itself. All such advantages will give you a time advantage and the NPV of the investment is the present value of these above-average profits in the first few years.

Competitive response

However, no gold mine continues for ever. In many investments the positive NPV is the present value of the additional cash to be made by an investment *before competitors enter* and the profitability of the investment is driven down. Investment appraisal will often involve an analysis of *when the competitors will enter* and this may be one of the key assumptions, along with its impact on your selling price and market share, that determines the NPV of the investment.

Competitive advantage

This leads me on to the general rule that you are more likely to find positive NPV projects if you search for new investment ideas in the areas where your company has a competitive advantage. Are you a low-cost producer? Do you have an excellent service reputation in your industry? The objective is to find investments that are cheaper for you than for other potential investors or sales opportunities that you will be able to exploit to a greater extent than anyone else. The emphasis should be on your *competitive* stance – what you can do that no-one else can do as well or as cheaply.

This method will help to ensure that you don't miss positive NPV investments that, due to forecasting errors, have not been considered viable. If you are a profitable low-cost producer in a growing market then an investment in expansion to grow

> This leads me on to the general rule that you are more likely to find positive NPV projects if you search for new investment ideas in the areas where your company has a competitive advantage. Are you a low cost producer? Do you have an excellent service reputation in your industry?

with the market should be a positive NPV investment. If your cashflow forecasts show otherwise, perhaps a mistake has been made.

Part II – Selling the investment proposal
Who is your audience?

Typically an investment proposal of any size will involve a series of formal and informal presentations through the company up to senior management. The number of such selling meetings will depend on the size and complexity of both the investment proposal and the company. The same checklist can be adapted to suit the style of each of these meetings.

PRACTICAL TIPS: KNOW YOUR AUDIENCE

Regardless of who you are presenting the investment to, you must always spend time considering the background of your audience:

1   What is their preference for investment criteria?

– Are they familiar with the concept of Net Present Value or Internal Rate of Return? Or do they prefer the more traditional investment appraisal methods such as Payback or Return on Investment?

2   If they are not familiar with Net Present Value, what would be their attitude to being introduced to such concepts?

– Many managers would feel uncomfortable being introduced to new concepts in the meeting. They might feel that they are struggling to come to terms with the new methods and this might affect their ability to look at the investment in detail and to use their judgement to think widely about the proposal.

Communication

In Chapter 3, we looked briefly at how using the right language can help you to present the investment in its best light. I will summarise some of those points here:

- Conduct the analysis using the Net Present Value method but use the language of Payback or Internal Rate of Return if this will make your reviewers feel more comfortable.

- If your company uses a standard method to evaluate investments, gradually try to introduce refinements that will make the appraisal more complete. For example, introduce the discounting of cashflows to their present values in Payback or Return on Book Value.

- The more people you have to convince, the simpler your message must be. Work at reducing your argument down to its barest components and leaving the further detail for questions. In this way you can focus on your audience's concerns in the most direct way.

- You can provide a two or three-page summary of the investment which gives some further detail for the reviewers to take away from the meeting and digest at their leisure.

A proposal

All proposals should include the following information:

- A brief description of the investment project and your recommendation.

- A brief summary of the appraisal methods used and the main financial highlights: sales, cost savings, cashflow etc.

- Detailed working of the net cashflows together with your main assumptions.

- A review of the investment project using different criteria, such as its Internal Rate of Return, its Payback period.

- Schedule for the investment.

- Major outstanding issues to discuss at the meeting.

Appendix

- Main results of any sensitivity testing (see next section).

How to support your case to your best advantage

The overriding principle in selling an investment is to keep it simple. Make sure you can still see the wood for the trees and preferably the lie of the land as well! However, this does not mean that background analysis in the form of sensitivity testing and scenario forecasting should not have been conducted. Such additional analyses can serve two purposes:

■ Firstly, it can help to ensure that your analysis has looked at all the probable outcomes and thus minimised the possibility of error.

■ Secondly, you will be fully prepared for 'what if' questions during the investment review meetings.

We have looked at these analyses in detail in Chapter 5 so I shall merely summarise them here. Please re-read these sections if you are not clear about the use of these techniques and, as importantly, their advantages and inadequacies.

Sensitivity analysis

Take each of the major components of the cashflow forecasts and consider what would happen to the overall NPV of the investment project if any of these components were changed. Sensitivity analysis helps to identify those variables which particularly affect the NPV result.

Example

Today Corinne Brown has a review meeting for a brand extension investment that she is proposing. She has already received approval from her commercial director but now she is presenting her case to her senior management. Present at the meeting are the finance director, the commercial director, the production director and the managing director. Her base-case scenario would suggest that the investment has a positive NPV of £60,000 with an opportunity cost of capital of 14 per cent. She has completed a sensitivity analysis of the major components and has identified that each component would have to change by the following percentages for the NPV of the investment to be reduced to zero.

	Change from base case to reduce NPV to zero	Effect of a 1% change on the NPV
Initial capital outlay	Up by 25%	±£2,400
Selling price	Down by 8%	±£7,500
Sales volumes	Down by 12%	±£5,000
Production cost per unit	Up by 14%	±£4,285

Corinne believes that there is little likelihood that any of these changes will take place and so does not bring them into her presentation. At the meeting the finance director asks her how she believes that a possible devaluation of the pound against the US dollar would affect her figures. She replies that, as the US market comprises 20 per cent of the forecast sales, a 10 per cent devaluation in the pound-dollar exchange rate would effectively increase the average selling price of the product by 2 per cent which would increase the NPV by £15,000.

Scenarios

Of course in many situations it is unlikely that just one of the variables will change by itself. If inflation is higher than in the base-case scenario, this might affect both production costs and the selling price though not necessarily to the same degree or over the same time period. In such cases an alternative way of deepening your understanding of the investment is to formulate two or three possible and realistic scenarios.

Example

Robert Jenkins is considering an investment proposal he is due to put forward to his divisional finance director tomorrow. It is for a new piece of machinery that will result in cost savings in five of the plants in the division. The base-case scenario has shown an NPV of £30,000. This is based on a capital outlay of £200,000 over the first two years (Present Value of £190,000), and on Present Value cost savings of £220,000 over the next six years. He is now considering two alternative scenarios: a recession scenario where costs increase at a slightly faster rate than forecast sales, and where output is down on the last three years; and an upside scenario where the machinery actually leads to a greater level of savings and output is slightly up on the last three years. He feels that his base-case scenario is still the most likely with a probability of 60 per cent, the downside

	Capital	PV cashflows	NPV	Probability
Upside scenario	£190,000	£240,000	£50,000	15%
Base-case scenario	£190,000	£220,000	£30,000	60%
Downside scenario	£195,000	£200,000	£5,000	25%
Expected Net Present Value			£26,750	

scenario has a 25 per cent likelihood and the upside scenario a 15 per cent possibility. He computes the alternative cashflows and their PVs as below:

The Expected Net Present Value is not much lower than the base-case scenario. He presents the base case to the finance director and leaves the two scenarios and the ENPV as appendices.

Part III – After your investment proposal is accepted

To some degree it is a moot point as to when an investment of any size finally gets accepted. Even after the investment proposal has been authorised by the senior management of a company, it is still subject to review as the actual cash for the capital outlay of the investment is asked for.

Post-acceptance monitoring

Broadly there are three types of post-acceptance monitoring:

- First, a company will seek to check that the authorised investment is not running over budget. Each of the main components of expenditure will be checked against the budgeted expenditure in the capital investment plan, usually on a quarterly or bi-annual basis.

- Later, once the initial cash outlay has taken place and the net cash inflows are beginning, a post-audit takes place. This is the most useful audit for the investment appraiser as it reviews the early stages of the investment. It compares actual cashflows with forecasted cashflows and can give useful feedback to the investment appraiser or the project team which analysed the investment on how they could have improved their appraisal process.

■ Finally, once the cash from the investment is flowing steadily, the investment is subject to the normal financial and commercial reviews that are used by the company in question.

Focusing on the post-audit

There are many valuable lessons that can be learnt from a well thought-out post-audit. It should not aim merely to compare the budgeted cashflows with the actual cashflows but to delve deeper and understand how realistic were the assumptions that supported the investment proposal.

This aids the analysis of other potential investments. However, post-audits do have some problems. On the one hand, they may provide a stimulus to those conducting investment appraisals to forecast cashflows as accurately as possible because of the perceived 'threat' of the post-audit. On the other hand, this threat may lead to under-estimation of the potential value of an investment project as appraisers err on the cautious side.

The timing of the post-audit

It is not always easy to determine when a post-audit should take place. If it is conducted too early, then not all of the cashflows will have begun and the investment may be perceived unfairly as unsuccessful or lagging. On the other hand, it is at this early stage that post-audits are most useful especially for giving feedback to project teams. If you leave it for two or three years, it loses its newsworthiness rather like last week's paper.

Flow chart summary

Figure 10.6 summarises some of the questions to ask once you have completed your investment appraisal as you consider how to sell the proposal within your company, or to outsiders such as banks or other investors.

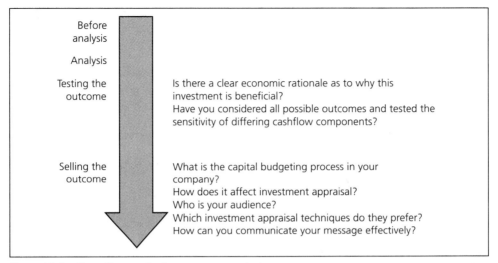

Figure 10.6   Flow diagram for investment appraisal

CASE STUDY 10.1

Case 1

William Johnson is a production engineer for a firm of furniture manufacturers. He has been asked by his production manager to look into an investment into a new cutting machine which will save costs. He has reviewed three machines and two have emerged as possibilities. Both have a positive NPV when he discounts the cashflows using the opportunity cost of capital of 14 per cent which has been established by the firm's finance department. He prefers Machine B: it has the highest NPV and it also has the intangible benefit of being straightforward to use and pleasant to operate as it is quieter and creates less dust. He believes that its greater simplicity will also reduce the time it takes to train operators leading to a saving of approximately £5,000 in downtime and training materials. He must now present his proposal to an investment committee. He is somewhat concerned about this meeting as he knows that the investment appraisal methods used in the past have been a mixture of Payback (using three years as the cut-off point) and Return on Book Value (with a return on book value of 20 per cent being considered acceptable). Furthermore Jack Keggins, the factory supervisor, can be awkward and obstreperous. However William believes that the factory manager, David Bartholomew, is the key decision-maker. He is an intelligent and practical man and prefers a no-nonsense approach to meetings and to decisions. He is not familiar with the Net Present Value method. It is now Monday and the meeting is set for Wednesday.

What would you do?

Some possibilities

- He should use familiar language – say how many years it takes to achieve payback or what the IRR is, so long as these answers conform to the company's existing criteria.

- He should keep it short and sweet in line with the factory manager's preferences.

- He could send them a two-page summary of the method that he used to evaluate the investment so that they can familiarise themselves with Net Present Value.

- He should ensure that he is familiar with the main advantages of Net Present Value and the main disadvantages of the methods used so as to deal effectively with any criticism.

- Given the nature of his audience, he should probably present the base-case NPV and include any additional savings in training as an upside potential. This is especially the case as his preferred choice is showing a positive NPV under the base case.

- He could try to get a firmer estimate of any cost savings in training time so as to give a clear-cut case.

- He could do some reality checks. He could compute how low the savings would have to be for each machine to show a zero NPV. He could try to establish from others the likelihood of this happening. Otherwise it could be a topic for discussion at the meeting.

Case 2

Emma Marshall is in charge of a small project team looking at a sales expansion investment. It has been quite a complex process as they have had to canvass opinions and information from many sources within the company in order to put together realistic and detailed cashflow forecasts based on market trends, marketing strategy, production capacity and a myriad of other issues. Furthermore, it is clear to Emma that there is not just one decision. If the sales expansion is a success it can lead to many exciting new opportunities in related markets. She has looked at several possible outcomes and assigned probabilities to them.

She thinks she has done a competent appraisal, especially given the time she had! But now her concerns are how to simplify the forecasts and assumptions into a manageable presentation. She will only have 30 minutes to present. She doesn't want to emphasise the uncertainties but on the other hand, she doesn't want to simplify it too much.

What would you do?

Some possibilities

- Emma should ensure that she doesn't get bogged down in irrelevant detail during her presentation – keep it simple and clear with the supporting evidence in the background.

- She should outline either her base-case scenario or her expected NPV if it differs significantly from the base case. The base-case scenario should be based predominantly on tangible costs and benefits so that the meeting is not taken up with a discussion about assumptions.

- Next she could take them through three scenarios: base-case, downside and upside scenarios.

- She should outline the major strategic benefits to be gained from the investment.

- She could also indicate the main actions which can be taken once the investment is started such as expansion or contraction options to highlight that this is not a one-off decision.

- She can provide a detailed plan of the main assumptions behind each scenario at the meeting and an appendix with some sensitivity analysis of the base-case NPV for the main components of the cashflows.

CHECKLIST OF PRACTICAL TIPS

1 Have you followed the checklist on pages 242–43 to ensure that the base-case NPV of the investment is free from errors?

2 Have you looked at all the probable outcomes of the investment and calculated an ENPV?

3 Have you conducted some reality tests?

4 Have you looked at the possibility of something going wrong and the impact on the NPV? This can be done through sensitivity testing and scenario modelling.

5 Have you thought about who your audience is and what their preferences are in terms of investment criteria?

6 Have you thought about changes in the way you communicate in order to sell your investment as effectively as possible?

I hope that this book has convinced you that the most appropriate method to use for investment appraisal is either the Net Present Value method or another method that uses cashflow techniques.

CHAPTER ELEVEN

Conclusion

- The most appropriate method to use

- The information inputs into the investment appraisal

- The best way to sell the investment appraisal

- Cutting out irrelevant detail

- The importance of judgement

- When you cannot use the NPV method

- An alternative: option pricing

The purpose of this book has been to acquaint the Non-Financial Manager with the basic knowledge and tools with which to conduct an appraisal of a potential investment, opening up the black box of investment appraisal that has so often been kept under lock and key by the financial specialists. It has focused on three main questions:

- What is the most appropriate method to use to evaluate investments?

- What information needs to be collected for use in the investment appraisal?

- What is the best way to sell the investment appraisal once it has been conducted?

The most appropriate method to use

I hope that this book has convinced you that the most appropriate method to use for investment appraisal is either the Net Present Value method or another method that uses discounted cashflow techniques. The NPV method is the most flexible and robust investment appraisal method. Its basic approach is logical and simple to understand, but it can also cope with much complexity. It takes into account the time value of money and compares today's investment with the future cashflows in today's money. It takes the risk of the investment into account through the choice of cost of capital or discount rate – the greater the risk, the higher the discount rate. It considers the whole of the economic life of the investment, not just an arbitrary number of years. Finally it focuses on cashflow and not simply accounting profit.

> If there are no budget constraints for your investment appraisal then the NPV method is preferable to the other related methods of investment appraisal: the Internal Rate of Return method and the Profitability Index.

If there are no budget constraints for your investment appraisal then the NPV method is preferable to the other related methods of investment appraisal: the Internal Rate of Return method and the Profitability Index. These methods are not able to indicate the most attractive investment when they are comparing two mutually exclusive investment projects of differing size or scope. This factor is often overlooked by managers who implicitly assume that there is a capital constraint and choose the investment which gives the greatest number of pounds back per pound invested. If your company can afford to take either an investment project of £500,000 capital outlay with a Present Value of £650,000, or one of £250,000 capital outlay with a Present Value of £350,000, it should always take the project which gives the highest Net Present Value, rather than the one with the highest Profitability Index.

However, in cases where the company *is* under a budget constraint, the use of the Profitability Index to rank projects whose Present Value has already been estimated will highlight the most attractive investment or group of investments.

The information inputs into the investment appraisal

There are four main categories of information inputs:

1 The estimated cash outlay for the investment (addressed in Chapter 4).

2 The estimated cashflows coming back from the investment (addressed in Chapters 4 and 5).

3 The appropriate cost of capital or discount rate (addressed in Chapters 7 and 8).

4 The length of the investment's economic life (addressed in Chapter 9).

The first component, the cash outlay, is usually the easiest to estimate given that it is based on real prices today or in the near future. The main concern is to ensure that you are including all the relevant costs for the investment project and excluding all irrelevant costs. Examples of the former are the initial working capital costs, any 'opportunity' costs (if existing assets would have been sold or used in an alternative investment) and incidental costs, such as managers' time spent on development which has led to a temporary downturn in the business elsewhere. An example of the latter is allocated overhead cost that would have occurred anyway even if the investment had not taken place.

In many ways, estimation of the second element, the future cashflows, is the most difficult part of the analysis. Not only do you have to focus on the relevant costs to include, you will also have to consider how to deal with inflation and taxation. There may not be only one set of cashflow forecasts, but several possible outcomes that have to be considered, with a probability attached to each scenario. You will need to identify areas of uncertainty and test your results rigorously. Finally it may be appropriate to factor in management's option to increase or decrease the scope of the investment depending on its initial success (or lack of it).

The third component, the cost of capital, is dependent on the systematic risk of the investment project. It is the 'opportunity' cost of the capital involved in the investment and it reflects the interest rate achievable in the capital markets for an investment with a *similar risk level*. Depending on the size and strategic importance of the investment project, the discount rate can be calculated with a greater or lesser degree of accuracy. The important issue is to make some adjustment for the risk of each investment – not just use the same cost of capital for every project whether it is a diversification into a new market or a straightforward machine replacement.

Finally, the number of years that are included in the appraisal model will depend on the economic life of the investment project and the certainty of the cashflows in the later years. In many cases it is appropriate to take a set number of years: either the investment has a discrete end or its economic life cannot be certain after that time, or technological advances make future cashflows highly speculative. In other investment projects, you will need to give a terminal value that accounts for the residual value in the investment.

> **Practical tip:** As you conduct your analysis, take into consideration the required detail needed – the stage of the investment, the size and importance of the investment and who you will need to sell the investment to. Do not make your analysis more complicated than it needs to be.

The best way to sell the investment appraisal

I'm not going to dwell on this stage as it was the subject of the last chapter and so should be reasonably fresh in your minds. My only point is that successful selling should be considered a discrete part of your investment appraisal not a natural end-point of a well-conducted investment analysis. You can choose the most appropriate method; you can conduct the analysis thoroughly and logically, but if you don't allow time to step back from the process and decide which issues to highlight, you run the risk of making the investment appraisal seem more complicated than it is and presenting a jumble of information rather than a recommendation.

Cutting out irrelevant detail

Most of the chapters in this book have concentrated on what information should go into the investment appraisal process. Two points should be made here: firstly, not every investment appraisal will require all of the detailed analysis that has been outlined in Chapters 4 to 9 – you must use your judgement to know what information to collect and what information to test rigorously. Secondly, the investment appraiser will be able to contract out some of the inputs. Use specialists to aid your cashflow forecast development. The computer can also cut out much of the number-crunching work and can conduct sensitivity tests in a matter of minutes rather than hours. But even if you don't do all the analysis yourself, you do need to know how everything is done if you are going to be confident of your investment proposition. For example, you may use your company's cost of capital as a starting point to estimate your investment's cost of capital and adjust it to take into account the market risk of the proposed investment. Though you do not need to calculate the company cost of capital again, you do need to know how the accountants have calculated it in the first place.

The importance of judgement

The chapters have necessarily focused on the methods and tools to use in investment appraisal. But this must never be taken as an alternative for management insight and judgement. Early on in the book, I said that investment appraisal was an art not a science. The book has inevitably dwelled on the *process* of investment appraisal, but through the chapters it should be clear that there are no magic formulae, no mechanical application of set rules that are set in stone. From the moment that you first consider the investment project, you are required to use your judgement. Investment appraisal is the process of using your experience and judgement to know how to use the investment appraisal method such as Net Present Value.

> You can choose the most appropriate method; you can conduct the analysis thoroughly and logically, but if you don't allow time to step back from the process and decide which issues to highlight, you run the risk of making the investment appraisal seem more complicated than it is and presenting a jumble of information rather than a recommendation.

When you cannot use the NPV method

As we have seen, many of the criticisms levelled at the NPV method of investment appraisal can be dismissed on closer inspection. But it would be naïve to insist that all criticisms can be cast aside. The NPV method relies on managers being able to predict, with some certainty, the outcome of their investment decisions. Net Present Value was originally a method used to value bond prices, which has been adapted by managers to value capital investments. If we picture a continuum of investments (see Figure 11.1) from a portfolio of stocks and shares, through a range of capital investments through to an investment in, say, a highly speculative natural resource exploration, the use of NPV, and indeed all common investment appraisal methods discussed in this book, becomes increasingly risky.

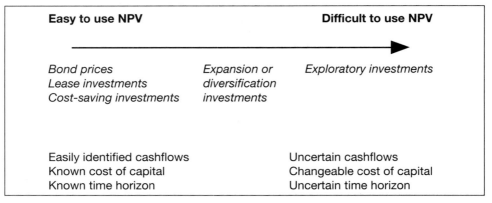

Figure 11.1 When you cannot use the NPV method

Why is this? Let us return to the basis for the NPV method and other discounted cashflow methods. They rest on some tacit assumptions:

■ That uncertain future cashflows can be replaced by their expected values. Those expected values can then be treated as given within the investment analysis.

■ That the discount rate is known and constant and is based on the risk of the project.

Let us address each one of these in turn.

Uncertain future cashflows can be replaced by their expected values

Any book on investment appraisal spends much time considering how uncertain future cashflows can be converted into their 'expected values'. The use of probability assessment with scenario modelling gives Expected NPVs. The use of simulation models and decision trees help managers consider the ramifications of each investment decision. But there is only so far you can reasonably go. Decision trees can become very complex, very quickly. A more fundamental problem is that simulation models and decision trees can only consider the future decisions that managers *know about today.* In every investment, especially large complex ones there is a range of future decisions to be made which are not even formulated at the time of investment appraisal. The further you go along the continuum towards highly speculative investments, the greater those future unknown decisions become.

That the discount rate is known and constant is based on the risk of the project

The determination of the discount rate, as was seen in Chapters 7 and 8, is based on some useful models but also a healthy dose of pragmatism. Many investment appraisals are based on the company cost of capital, perhaps arbitrarily adjusted upwards or downwards for risk. But this is a problem with execution, not with the theory itself. More serious is the claim that the use of one discount rate throughout the estimated life of the investment is highly unrealistic. If this assumption will lead to unrealistic valuations in your investment, a consideration of how the investment's risk changes over its life must be entertained.

In my opinion, the rational use of the NPV method and other discounted cashflow methods will allow you to make useful decisions for most capital investments. But if the investment you are considering is highly speculative, you should be aware of the limitations of all classical investment methods.

An alternative: option pricing

If the investment *is* highly speculative, such as in the case of oil and gas exploration, or very early research and development, such as the exploratory development undertaken by the pharmaceutical industry, some form of option pricing could be an alternative way of valuing an investment.

The appraiser of an investment project is trying to establish the value of the investment, the future asset. They use what they know about known assets to estimate the value of this potential future asset. In discounted cashflow methods, the known assets are stocks in the market place which are considered to have the same risk profile as the investment being considered. As the potential investment becomes less and less like an investment on the stock market, that is to say, more complex, more uncertain, with variable risk across its lifetime, so the investment appraiser should look around for other assets of known value which are closer in their characteristics to the potential asset which is being valued. For example, when natural resource investments are being evaluated, the most relevant comparison to consider is a portfolio of riskless bonds together with a futures contract on the commodity which the investment would produce. The future output will be a function of a number of factors that are unknown when the investment appraisal is taking place: the geological features which determine the size and quality of the output, the future market conditions and most notably the future price. The NPV method of investment appraisal cannot deal with this level of uncertainty but the investment can be valued *if it is considered as an option on the underlying commodity.*

For further information, you may like to read the following papers:
'A New Approach to Evaluating Natural Resource Investments', Brennan & Schwartz.
'Evaluating Natural Resource Investments', Brennan & Schwartz, *Journal of Business* 1985.
'Theory of Rational Option Pricing', *Bell Journal of Economics & Management Science* 1973.

Appendices

Appendix 1: DISCOUNT TABLE

Present Value of £1 to be received after X years

Year	1%	2%	3%	4%	5%	6%	7%	8%	9%	10%	11%	12%	13%	14%
0	1.000	1.000	1.000	1.000	1.000	1.000	1.000	1.000	1.000	1.000	1.000	1.000	1.000	1.000
1	0.990	0.980	0.971	0.962	0.952	0.943	0.935	0.926	0.917	0.909	0.901	0.893	0.885	0.877
2	0.980	0.961	0.943	0.925	0.907	0.890	0.873	0.857	0.842	0.826	0.812	0.797	0.783	0.769
3	0.971	0.942	0.915	0.889	0.864	0.840	0.816	0.794	0.772	0.751	0.731	0.712	0.693	0.675
4	0.961	0.924	0.888	0.855	0.823	0.792	0.763	0.735	0.708	0.683	0.659	0.636	0.613	0.592
5	0.951	0.906	0.863	0.822	0.784	0.747	0.713	0.681	0.650	0.621	0.593	0.567	0.543	0.519
6	0.942	0.888	0.837	0.790	0.746	0.705	0.666	0.630	0.596	0.564	0.535	0.507	0.480	0.456
7	0.933	0.871	0.813	0.760	0.711	0.665	0.623	0.583	0.547	0.513	0.482	0.452	0.425	0.400
8	0.923	0.853	0.789	0.731	0.677	0.627	0.582	0.540	0.502	0.467	0.434	0.404	0.376	0.351
9	0.914	0.837	0.766	0.703	0.645	0.592	0.544	0.500	0.460	0.424	0.391	0.361	0.333	0.308
10	0.905	0.820	0.744	0.676	0.614	0.558	0.508	0.463	0.422	0.386	0.352	0.322	0.295	0.270
11	0.896	0.804	0.722	0.650	0.585	0.527	0.475	0.429	0388	0.350	0.317	0.287	0.261	0.237
12	0.887	0.788	0.701	0625	0.557	0.497	0.444	0.397	0.365	0.319	0.286	0.257	0.231	0.208
13	0.879	0.773	0.681	0.601	0.530	0.469	0.415	0.368	0.326	0.290	0.258	0.229	0.204	0.182
14	0.870	0.758	·0.661	0.577	0.505	0.442	0.388	0.340	0.299	0.263	0.232	0.205	0.181	0.160
15	0.861	0.743	0.642	0.555	0.481	0.417	0.362	0.315	0.275	0.239	0.209	0.183	0.160	0.140
16	0.853	0.728	0.623	0.534	0.458	0.394	0.339	0.292	0.252	0.218	0.188	0.163	0.141	0.123
17	0.844	0.714	0.605	0.513	0.436	0.371	0.317	0.270	0.231	0.198	0.170	0.146	0.125	0.108
18	0.836	0.700	0.587	0.494	0.416	0.350	0.296	0.250	0.212	0.180	0.153	0.130	0.111	0.095
19	0.828	0.686	0.570	0.475	0.396	0.331	0.277	0.232	0.194	0.164	0.138	0.116	0.098	0.083
20	0.820	0.673	0.554	0.456	0.377	0.312	0.258	0.215	0.178	0.149	0.124	0.104	0.087	0.073
21	0.811	0.660	0.538	0.439	0.359	0.294	0.242	0.199	0.164	0.135	0.112	0.093	0.077	0.064
22	0.803	0.647	0.522	0.422	0.342	0.278	0.226	0.184	0.150	0.123	0.101	0.083	0.068	0.056
23	0.795	0.634	0.507	0.406	0.326	0.262	0.211	0.170	0.138	0.112	0.091	0.074	0.060	0.049
24	0.788	0.622	0.492	0.390	0.310	0.247	0.197	0.158	0.126	0.102	0.082	0.066	0.053	0.043
25	0.780	0.610	0.478	0.375	0.295	0.233	0.184	0.146	0.116	0.092	0.074	0.059	0.047	0.038
30	0.742	0.552	0.412	0.308	0.231	0.174	0.131	0.099	0.075	0.057	0.044	0.033	0.026	0.020
35	0.706	0.500	0.355	0.253	0.181	0.130	0.094	0.068	0.049	0.036	0.026	0.019	0.014	0.010
40	0.672	0.453	0.307	0.208	0.142	0.097	0.067	0.046	0.032	0.022	0.015	0.011	0.008	0.005

Note: The above calculations are based on year-end interest calculations

15%	16%	17%	18%	19%	20%	21%	22%	23%	24%	25%	30%	35%	40%
1.000	1.000	1.000	1.000	1.000	1.000	1.000	1.000	1.000	1.000	1.000	1.000	1.000	1.000
0.870	0.862	0.855	0.847	0.840	0.833	0.826	0.820	0.813	0.806	0.800	0.769	0.741	0.714
0.756	0.743	0.731	0.718	0.706	0.694	0.683	0.672	0.661	0.650	0.640	0.592	0.549	0.510
0.658	0.641	0.624	0.609	0.593	0.579	0.564	0.551	0.537	0.524	0.512	0.455	0.406	0.364
0.572	0.552	0.534	0.516	0.499	0.482	0.467	0.451	0.437	0.423	0.410	0.350	0.301	0.260
0.497	0.476	0.456	0.437	0.419	0.402	0.386	0.370	0.355	0.341	0.328	0.269	0.223	0.186
0.432	0.410	0.390	0.370	0.352	0.335	0.319	0.303	0.289	0.275	0.262	0.207	0.165	0.133
0.376	0.354	0.333	0.314	0.296	0.279	0.263	0.249	0.235	0.222	0.210	0.159	0.122	0.095
0.327	0.305	0.285	0.266	0.249	0.233	0.218	0.204	0.191	0.179	0.168	0.123	0.091	0.068
0.284	0.263	0.243	0.225	0.209	0.194	0.180	0.167	0.155	0.144	0.134	0.094	0.067	0.048
0.247	0.227	0.208	0.191	0.176	0.162	0.149	0.137	0.126	0.116	0.107	0.073	0.050	0.035
0.215	0.195	0.178	0.162	0.148	0.135	0.123	0.112	0.103	0.094	0.086	0.056	0.037	0.025
0.187	0.168	0.152	0.137	0.124	0.112	0.102	0.092	0.083	0.076	0.069	0.043	0.027	0.018
0.163	0.145	0.130	0.116	0.014	0.093	0.084	0.075	0.068	0.061	0.055	0.033	0.020	0.013
0.141	0.125	0.111	0.099	0.088	0.078	0.069	0.062	0.055	0.049	0.044	0.025	0.015	0.009
0.123	0.108	0.095	0.084	0.074	0.065	0.057	0.051	0.045	0.040	0.035	0.020	0.011	0.006
0.107	0.093	0.081	0.071	0.062	0.054	0.047	0.042	0.036	0.032	0.028	0.015	0.008	0.005
0.093	0.080	0.069	0.060	0.052	0.045	0.039	0.034	0.030	0.026	0.023	0.012	0.006	0.003
0.081	0.069	0.059	0.051	0.044	0.038	0.032	0.028	0.024	0.021	0.018	0.009	0.005	0.002
0.070	0.060	0.051	0.043	0.037	0.031	0.027	0.023	0.020	0.017	0.104	0.012	0.005	0.002
0.061	0.051	0.043	0.037	0.031	0.026	0.022	0.019	0.016	0.104	0.012	0.005	0.002	0.001
0.053	0.044	0.037	0.031	0.026	0.022	0.018	0.015	0.013	0.011	0.009	0.004	0.002	0.001
0.046	0.038	0.032	0.026	0.022	0.018	0.015	0.013	0.011	0.009	0.007	0.003	0.001	0.001
0.040	0.033	0.027	0.022	0.018	0.015	0.012	0.010	0.009	0.007	0.006	0.002	0.001	0.000
0.035	0.028	0.023	0.019	0.015	0.013	0.010	0.008	0.007	0.006	0.005	0.002	0.001	0.000
0.030	0.024	0.020	0.016	0.013	0.010	0.009	0.007	0.006	0.005	0.004	0.001	0.001	0.000
0.015	0.012	0.009	0.007	0.005	0.004	0.003	0.003	0.002	0.002	0.001	0.000	0.000	0.000
0.008	0.006	0.004	0.003	0.002	0.002	0.001	0.001	0.001	0.001	0.000	0.000	0.000	0.000
0.004	0.003	0.002	0.001	0.001	0.001	0.000	0.000	0.000	0.000	0.000	0.000	0.000	0.000

Appendix 2: ANNUITY TABLE

Cumulative Present Value of £1 after X years

Year	1%	2%	3%	4%	5%	6%	7%	8%	9%	10%	11%	12%	13%	14%
1	0.990	0.980	0.971	0.962	0.952	0.943	0.935	0.926	0.917	0.909	0.901	0.893	0.885	0.877
2	1.970	1.942	1.913	1.886	1.859	1.833	1.808	1.783	1.759	1.736	1.713	1.690	1.668	1.647
3	2.941	2.884	2.829	2.775	2.723	2.673	2.634	2.577	2.531	2.487	2.444	2.402	2.361	2.322
4	3.902	3.808	3.717	3.630	3.546	3.465	3.387	3.312	3.240	3.170	3.102	3.037	2.974	2.914
5	4.853	4.713	4.580	4.452	4.329	4.212	4.100	3.993	3.890	3.791	3.696	3.605	3.517	3.433
6	5.795	5.601	5.417	5.242	5.076	4.917	4.767	4.623	4.486	4.355	4.231	4.111	3.998	3.889
7	6.728	6.472	6.230	6.002	5.786	5.582	5.389	5.206	5.033	4.868	4.712	4.564	4.423	4.288
8	7.652	7.325	7.020	6.733	6.463	6.210	5.971	5.747	5.535	5.335	5.146	4.968	4.799	4.639
9	8.566	8.162	7.786	7.435	7.108	6.802	6.515	6.247	5.995	5.795	5.537	5.328	5.132	4.946
10	9.471	8.983	8.530	8.111	7.722	7.360	7.024	6.710	6.418	6.145	5.889	5.650	5.426	5.216
11	10.368	9.787	9.253	8.760	8.306	7.887	7.499	7.139	6.805	6.495	6.207	5.938	5.687	5.453
12	11.255	10.575	9.954	9.385	8.863	8.384	7.943	7.536	7.161	6.814	6.492	6.194	5.918	5.660
13	12.134	11.348	10.635	9.986	9.394	8.853	8.358	7.904	7.487	7.103	6.750	6.424	6.122	5.842
14	13.004	12.106	11.296	10.563	9.899	9.295	8.745	8.244	7.786	7.367	6.982	6.628	6.302	6.002
15	13.865	12.849	11.938	11.118	10.380	9.712	9.108	8.559	8.061	7.606	7.191	6.811	6.462	6.142
16	14.718	13.578	12.561	11.652	10.838	10.106	9.447	8.851	8.313	7.824	7.379	6.974	6.604	6.265
17	15.562	14.292	13.166	12.166	11.274	10.477	9.763	9.122	8.544	8.022	7.549	7.120	6.729	6.373
18	16.398	14.992	13.754	12.659	11.690	10.828	10.059	9.372	8.756	8.201	7.702	7.250	6.840	6.467
19	17.226	15.678	14.324	13.134	12.085	11.158	10.336	9.604	8.950	8.365	7.839	7.366	6.938	6.550
20	18.046	16.351	14.877	13.590	12.462	11.470	10.594	9.818	9.129	8.514	7.963	7.469	7.025	6.623
21	18.857	17.011	15.415	14.029	12.821	11.764	10.836	10.017	9.292	8.649	8.075	7.562	7.102	6.687
22	19.660	17.658	15.937	14.451	13.163	12.042	11.061	10.201	9.442	8.772	8.176	7.645	7.170	6.743
23	20.456	18.292	16.444	14.857	13.489	12.303	11.272	10.371	9.580	8.883	8.266	7.718	7.230	6.792
24	21.243	18.914	16.936	15.247	13.799	12.550	11.469	10.529	9.707	8.985	8.348	7.784	7.283	6.835
25	22.023	19.523	17.413	15.622	14.094	12.783	11.654	10.675	9.823	9.077	8.422	7.843	7.330	6.873
30	25.808	22.396	19.600	17.292	15.372	13.765	12.409	11.258	10.274	9.427	8.694	8.055	7.496	7.003
35	29.409	24.999	21.487	18.665	16.374	14.498	12.948	11.655	10.567	9.644	8.855	8.176	7.586	7.070
40	32.835	27.355	23.115	19.793	17.159	15.046	13.332	11.925	10.757	9.779	8.951	8.244	7.634	7.105

Note: The above calculations are based on year-end interest calculations

15%	16%	17%	18%	19%	20%	21%	22%	23%	24%	25%	30%	35%	40%
0.870	0.862	0.855	0.847	0.840	0.833	0.826	0.820	0.813	0.806	0.800	0.769	0.741	0.714
1.626	1.605	1.585	1.566	1.547	1.528	1.509	1.492	1.474	1.457	1.440	1.361	1.289	1.224
2.283	2.246	2.210	2.174	2.140	2.106	2.074	2.042	2.011	1.981	1.952	1.816	1.696	1.589
2.855	2.798	2.743	2.690	2.639	2.589	2.540	2.494	2.448	2.404	2.362	2.166	1.997	1.849
3.352	3.274	3.199	3.127	3.058	2.991	2.926	2.864	2.803	2.745	2.689	2.436	2.220	2.035
3.784	3.685	3.589	3.498	3.410	3.326	3.245	3.167	3.092	3.020	2.951	2.643	2.385	2.168
4.160	4.039	3.922	3.812	3.706	3.605	3.508	3.416	3.327	3.242	3.161	2.802	2.508	2.263
4.487	4.344	4.207	4.078	3.954	3.837	3.726	3.619	3.518	3.421	3.329	2.952	2.598	2.331
4.772	4.607	4.451	4.303	4.163	4.031	3.905	3.786	3.673	3.566	3.463	3.019	2.665	2.379
5.019	4.833	4.659	4.494	4.339	4.192	4.054	3.923	3.799	3.682	3.571	3.092	2.715	2.414
5.234	5.029	4.836	4.656	4.486	4.327	4.177	4.035	3.902	3.776	3.656	3.147	2.752	2.438
5.421	5.197	4.988	4.793	4.611	4.439	4.278	4.127	3.985	3.851	3.725	3.190	2.779	2.456
5.583	5.342	5.118	4.910	4.715	4.533	4.362	4.203	4.053	3.912	3.780	3.223	2.799	2.469
5.724	5.468	5.229	5.008	4.802	4.611	4.432	4.265	4.108	3.962	3.824	3.249	2.814	2.478
5.847	5.575	5.324	5.092	4.876	4.675	4.489	4.315	4.153	4.001	3.859	3.268	2.825	2.484
5.954	5.668	5.405	5.162	4.938	4.730	4.536	4.357	4.189	4.033	3.887	3.283	2.834	2.489
6.047	5.749	5.475	5.222	4.990	4.775	4.576	4.391	4.219	4.059	3.910	3.295	2.840	2.492
6.128	5.818	5.534	5.273	5.033	4.812	4.608	4.419	4.243	4.080	3.928	3.304	2.844	2.494
6.198	5.877	5.584	5.316	5.070	4.843	4.635	4.442	4.263	4.097	3.942	3.311	2.848	2.496
6.259	5.929	5.628	5.353	5.101	4.870	4.657	4.460	4.297	4.110	3.954	3.316	2.850	2.497
6.312	5.973	5.665	5.384	5.127	4.891	4.675	4.476	4.292	4.121	3.963	3.320	2.852	2.498
6.359	6.011	5.696	5.410	5.149	4.909	4.690	4.488	4.302	4.130	3.970	3.323	2.853	2.498
6.399	6.044	5.723	5.432	5.167	4.925	4.703	4.499	4.311	4.137	3.976	3.325	2.854	2.499
6.434	6.073	5.746	5.451	5.182	4.937	4.713	4.507	4.318	4.143	3.981	3.327	2.855	2.499
6.464	6.097	5.766	5.467	5.195	4.948	4.721	4.514	4.323	4.147	3.985	3.329	2.856	2.499
6.566	6.177	5.829	5.517	5.235	4.979	4.746	4.534	4.399	4.160	3.995	3.332	2.857	2.500
6.617	6.215	5.858	5.539	5.521	4.992	4.756	4.541	4.345	4.164	3.998	3.333	2.857	2.500
6.642	6.233	5.871	5.548	5.258	4.997	4.760	4.544	4.347	4.166	3.999	3.333	2.857	2.500

Appendix 3: FUTURE VALUE TABLE

Future Value of £1 after X years

Year	1%	2%	3%	4%	5%	6%	7%	8%	9%	10%	11%	12%	13%	14%
0	1.000	1.000	1.000	1.000	1.000	1.000	1.000	1.000	1.000	1.000	1.000	1.000	1.000	1.000
1	1.010	1.020	1.030	1.040	1.050	1.060	1.070	1.080	1.090	1.100	1.110	1.120	1.130	1.140
2	1.020	1.040	1.061	1.082	1.103	1.124	1.145	1.166	1.188	1.210	1.232	1.254	1.277	1.300
3	1.030	1.061	1.093	1.125	1.158	1.191	1.225	1.260	1.295	1.331	1.368	1.405	1.443	1.482
4	1.041	1.082	1.126	1.170	1.216	1.262	1.311	1.360	1.412	1.464	1.518	1.574	1.630	1.689
5	1.051	1.104	1.159	1.217	1.276	1.338	1.403	1.469	1.539	1.611	1.685	1.762	1.842	1.925
6	1.062	1.126	1.194	1.265	1.340	1.419	1.501	1.587	1.677	1.772	1.870	1.947	2.082	2.195
7	1/072	1.149	1.230	1.316	1.407	1.504	1.606	1.714	1.828	1.949	2.076	2.211	2.353	2.502
8	1.083	1.172	1.267	1.369	1.477	1.594	1.718	1.851	1.993	2.114	2.305	2.476	2.658	2.853
9	1.094	1.195	1.305	1.423	1.551	1.689	1.838	1.999	2.172	2.358	2.558	2.773	3.004	3.252
10	1.105	1.219	1.344	1.480	1.629	1.791	1.967	2.159	2.367	2.594	2.839	3.106	3.395	3.707
11	1.116	1.243	1.384	1.539	1.710	1.898	2.105	2.332	2.580	2.853	3.152	3.479	3.836	4.226
12	1.127	1.268	1.426	1.601	1.796	2.012	2.252	2.518	2.813	3.138	3.498	3.896	4.335	4.818
13	1.138	1.294	1.469	1.665	1.886	2.133	2.410	2.720	3.066	3.452	3.883	4.363	4.898	5.492
14	1.149	1.319	1.513	1.732	1.980	2.261	2.579	2.937	3.342	3.797	4.310	4.887	5.535	6.261
15	1.161	1.346	1.558	1.801	2.079	2.397	2.759	3.172	3.642	4.177	4.785	5.474	6.254	7.138
16	1.173	1.373	1.605	1.873	2.183	2.540	2.952	3.426	3.970	4.595	5.311	6.130	7.067	8.137
17	1.184	1.400	1.653	1.948	2.292	2.693	3.159	3.700	4.328	5.054	5.895	6.866	7.986	9.276
18	1.196	1.428	1.702	2.026	2.407	2.854	3.380	3.996	4.717	5.560	6.544	7.690	9.024	10.575
19	1.208	1.457	1.754	2.107	2.527	3.026	3.617	4.316	5.142	6.116	7.263	8.613	10.197	12.056
20	1.220	1.486	1.806	2.191	2.653	3.207	3.870	4.661	5.604	6.727	8.062	9.646	11.523	13.743
21	1.232	1.516	1.860	2.279	2.786	3.400	4.141	5.034	6.109	7.400	8.949	10.804	13.021	15.668
22	1.245	1.546	1.916	2.370	2.925	3.604	4.430	5.437	6.659	8.140	9.934	12.100	14.714	17.861
23	1.257	1.577	1.974	2.465	3.072	3.820	4.741	5.871	7.258	8.954	11.026	13.552	16.627	20.362
24	1.270	1.608	2.033	2.563	3.225	4.049	5.072	6.341	7.911	9.850	12.239	15.179	18.788	23.212
25	1.282	1.641	2.094	2.666	3.386	4.292	5.427	6.848	8.623	10.835	13.585	17.000	21.231	26.462
30	1.348	1.811	2.427	3.243	4.322	5.743	7.612	10.063	13.268	17.449	22.892	29.960	39.116	50.950
35	1.417	2.000	2.814	3.946	5.516	7.686	10.677	14.785	20.414	28.102	38.575	52.800	72.069	98.100
40	1.489	2.208	3.262	4.801	7.040	10.286	14.974	21.725	31.409	45.259	65.001	93.051	132.78	188.88

Note: The above calculations are based on year-end interest calculations

15%	16%	17%	18%	19%	20%	21%	22%	23%	24%	25%	30%	35%	40%
1.000	1.000	1.000	1.000	1.000	1.000	1.000	1.000	1.000	1.000	1.000	1.000	1.000	1.000
1.150	1.160	1.170	1.180	1.190	1.200	1.210	1.220	1.230	1.240	1.250	1.300	1.350	1.400
1.323	1.346	1.369	1.392	1.416	1.440	1.464	1.488	1.513	1.538	1.563	1.690	1.823	1.960
1.521	1.561	1.602	1.643	1.685	1.728	1.772	1.816	1.861	1.907	1.953	2.197	2.460	2.744
1.749	1.811	1.874	1.939	2.005	2.074	2.144	2.215	2.289	2.364	2.441	2.856	3.322	3.842
2.011	2.100	2.192	2.288	2.386	2.488	2.594	2.703	2.815	2.932	3.052	3.713	4.484	5.378
2.313	2.436	2.565	2.700	2.840	2.986	3.138	3.297	3.463	3.635	3.815	4.827	6.053	7.530
2.660	2.826	3.001	3.185	3.379	3.583	3.797	4.023	4.259	4.508	4.768	6.275	8.172	10.541
3.059	3.278	3.511	3.759	4.021	4.300	4.595	4.908	5.239	5.590	5.960	8.157	11.032	14.758
3.518	3.803	4.108	4.435	4.785	5.160	5.560	5.987	6.444	6.931	7.451	10.604	14.894	20.661
4.046	4.411	4.807	5.234	5.695	6.192	6.727	7.305	7.926	8.594	9.313	13.786	20.107	28.925
4.652	5.117	5.624	6.176	6.777	7.430	8.140	8.912	9.749	10.657	11.642	17.922	27.144	40.496
5.350	5.936	6.580	7.288	8.064	8.916	9.850	10.872	11.991	13.215	14.552	23.298	36.644	56.694
6.153	6.886	7.699	8.599	9.596	10.699	11.918	13.264	14.749	16.386	18.190	30.288	49.470	79.371
7.076	7.988	9.007	10.147	11.420	12.839	14.421	16.182	18.141	20.319	22.737	39.374	66.784	111.12
8.137	9.266	10.539	11.974	13.590	15.407	17.449	19.742	22.314	25.196	28.422	51.186	90.158	155.57
9.358	10.748	12.330	14.129	16.172	18.488	21.114	24.086	27.446	31.243	35.527	66.542	121.71	217.80
10.761	12.468	14.426	16.672	19.244	22.186	25.548	29.384	33.759	38.741	44.409	86.504	164.31	304.91
12.375	14.463	16.879	19.673	22.901	26.623	30.913	35.849	41.523	48.039	55.511	112.46	221.82	426.88
14.232	16.777	19.748	23.214	27.252	31.948	37.404	43.736	51.074	59.568	69.389	146.19	299.46	597.63
16.367	19.461	23.106	27.393	32.429	38.338	45.259	53.358	62.821	73.864	86.736	190.05	404.27	836.68
18.822	22.574	27.034	32.324	38.591	46.005	54.764	65.096	77.269	91.592	108.42	247.06	545.77	1171.4
21.645	26.186	31.629	38.142	45.923	55.206	66.264	79.418	95.041	113.57	135.53	321.18	736.79	1639.9
24.891	30.376	37.006	45.008	54.649	66.247	80.180	96.889	116.90	140.83	169.41	417.54	994.66	2295.9
28.625	35.236	43.297	53.109	65.032	79.497	97.017	118.21	143.79	174.63	211.76	542.80	1342.8	3214.2
32.919	40.874	50.658	62.669	77.388	95.396	117.39	144.21	176.86	216.54	264.70	705.64	1812.8	4499.9
66.212	85.850	111.06	143.37	184.68	237.38	304.48	389.76	497.91	634.82	807.79	2620.0	8128.5	24201
133.18	180.31	243.50	328.00	440.70	590.67	789.75	1053.4	1401.8	1861.1	2465.2	9727.9	36449	130161
267.86	378.72	533.87	750.38	1051.7	1469.8	2048.4	2847.0	3946.4	5455.9	7523.2	36119	163437	700038

Glossary

Accelerated depreciation   A depreciation method which leads to greater deductions for depreciation in the early part of the asset's life, such as reducing balance depreciation.

Accounting rate of return on book value   See Rate of Return.

Adjusted cost of capital   The cost of capital which already reflects the financing side-effects of an investment project.

Adjusted Present Value (APV) method   The Net Present Value of an investment project assuming it is financed solely by shareholders' equity together with the Present Value of any financing side-effects such as issuing costs or the tax benefits of using borrowed capital.

Annuity   An investment that results in a level stream of cashflows for a fixed period of time.

Balance sheet   A statement of the financial position of the company at a particular point in time showing the assets and the liabilities of the company, and its sources of finance.

Beta factor   A measurement of risk which indicates an investment project's degree of exposure to general market risk such as a downturn in the economy. It is used in the calculation of an appropriate cost of capital for an investment appraisal.

Capital allowance   The Inland Revenue's equivalent of a company depreciation charge. Allowances are granted for particular capital assets and can be set against taxable profit thus reducing the amount of tax payable.

Capital Asset Pricing Model (CAPM)   A model which calculates an appropriate cost of capital for an investment relating the market risk of the investment to its cost of capital.

Capital budget   A formal assessment of all the planned investment projects for a company. It is usually prepared on an annual basis.

Capital expenditure   Expenditure on fixed assets which have an economic life of more than one year.

Capital lease   See Financial lease.

Capital rationing   A shortage of funds either due to an inability to raise additional capital (a 'hard ceiling'), or a decision by senior management to limit capital available for new investment projects (a 'soft ceiling'). It may force the company to choose between investment projects which have positive Net Present Values.

Compound interest   A reinvestment of each interest payment as well as the capital investment itself.

Corporation tax   The tax payable on a limited company's profits. Small companies with profits up to £250,000 pay a reduced rate of 25 per cent but the standard rate is 33 per cent.

Cost-Benefit Analysis (CBA)   An investment appraisal method which takes a broad approach in considering not only the costs and benefits of an investment project to the company concerned, but also to other interested parties or stakeholders such as the workforce, the community, local government etc. It is often used on large public sector investment projects.

Cost of capital   The annual percentage cost of a particular source of capital. Also known as the Composite Cost of Capital. See also Opportunity cost of capital, and Weighted Average Cost of Capital.

Decision tree   A diagram which shows alternative courses of action for an investment and alternative outcomes as branches of a tree. It is usually sequential showing how managers can respond to different 'states of nature' in the environment and the possible monetary outcomes of their decisions. See also States of nature.

Depreciation   The proportion of a fixed asset which is charged as an expense in a company's profit and loss account and which cumulatively reduces the value of the fixed asset as shown on the balance sheet.

Discount factor   The present value of £1 received at a stated future date.

Discount rate   The rate used to convert cash received in future years to its present value today.

Discounted cashflow   Future cashflows which have been multiplied by discount factors to obtain their present values.

Discounted Cashflow (DCF) Yield   See Internal Rate of Return.

Earnings   The profit attributable to ordinary shareholders after interest on any loans, corporation tax and preference dividends. These profits can then be retained or given out as dividends.

Earnings per share (EPS)   The earnings divided by the number of ordinary shares issued.

Economic rents   Profits which are made in excess of the general competitive level. All investment projects with positive Net Present Values will earn economic rents.

Equity   See Shareholders' equity.

Equivalent Annual Cost (EAC)   An annuity with the same Net Present Value as the investment project. It can then be used to compare two investment projects with differing lifetimes.

Expected Net Present Value (ENPV)   A method used in evaluating investments whereby the Net Present Value (NPV) of all cash outflows and cash inflows is calculated using a given discount rate.

Financial lease   A long-term non-cancellable lease. (Also called Capital lease.)

Fixed assets   Land, buildings, machinery, vehicles which are owned and used by the company in its operations and not for resale to the public.

Gearing   The ratio of borrowed capital to capital owned by the shareholders (the initial paid-up share capital plus any retained profits). An alternative measure of gearing is the ratio of borrowed capital to total capital employed.

Hurdle rate   The minimum acceptable rate of return on an investment project for that project to be accepted by senior management.

Income tax   The tax payable on the income of all employees including the profits of self-employed business people.

Internal Rate of Return (IRR)   Also known as the Discounted Cashflow Yield (DCF Yield). It is a measure of the rate of profitability expected from an investment project. At this rate of profitability, the investment will have a Net Present Value of zero when its cashflows are discounted.

Investment appraisal   The process of assessing the viability of investing money, and other resources, in a particular investment project. The appraisal comprises both a financial assessment and an operational assessment which incorporates both quantitative and qualitative judgement.

Lease   See Financial lease.

Leverage   See Gearing.

Life-Cycle Costing (LCC)   The total cost of a physical asset from the design to the scrap heap. It includes the initial capital outlay net of any residual salvage value, maintenance and running costs.

Linear Programming (LP)   A computer program and method used by companies that wish to maximise the value of resources when those resources are subject to a set of constraints. These constraints are converted into a set of equations which provide the parameters for investment decision. Linear Programming is often used when a company is facing a capital budget constraint.

Liquidation Value (LV)   Net amount that could be realized by selling the assets of a firm after paying the debt.

Market risk   Also known as Systematic risk. It is risk that cannot be diversified away as it relates to possible changes in the overall macro-economic environment.

Mutually exclusive projects   Investment projects are said to be mutually exclusive when they are assessed as alternative projects, only one of which can be accepted. This usually comprises two alternative methods of achieving the same overall objective, for example, alternative machinery designs. Occasionally the term is used when different investment projects are competing for a limited supply of cash and only one project can be funded.

Net cashflow   The net cashflow from an investment is the cash inflows minus the cash outflows for each year of the investment project.

Net Present Value (NPV)   An investment project's *net* contribution to the value of a company. It is the total cashflow from an investment project when all yearly cashflows have been expressed in terms of their present value by discounting the cashflows at their Opportunity cost of capital.

Nominal return   The apparent rate of return on an investment project where the periodic cashflows have been inflated to take into account the effect of inflation.

Operating leverage   The ratio of fixed operating costs to variable operating costs. It is a similar term to financial gearing as a high ratio of fixed operating costs accentuates variations in profitability and thus increases the *risk* of an investment project.

Opportunity cost   The value of the best alternative use of the resource in question. This is the lost opportunity hence the name.

Opportunity cost of capital   The expected rate of return that can be earned on the best alternative use of the cash, usually by investing in stocks with a comparable risk profile. Also known as Cost of capital or Hurdle rate.

Payback period   The period of time, whether it is measured in years or months, that it takes to recoup the money invested in an investment project.

Price Earnings (P/E) ratio   The share price divided by the Earnings Per Share (EPS).

Perpetuity   An investment that results in a level stream of cashflows in perpetuity.

Post-audit   An assessment of an investment after it has been undertaken. It is usually six months to one year after the main capital outlay.

Present Value (PV)   The value of cash coming from an investment project when it is converted into today's money.

Profit and loss account   An account of trading performance which considers the sales and expenses over a period of time, usually one year.

Profitability Index   A means of ranking alternative investment projects after they have been assessed using the Net Present Value method. The total present value of each investment project is divided by the initial cash outlay (or the present value of the initial cash inflow if the investment takes place over several years). The investment project with the highest Profitability Index should be the one chosen by managers if they are facing a capital budget constraint. All Profitability Indices of over one indicate a positive Net Present Value for the investment project.

Rate of return   Also known as Accounting Rate of Return on Book Value. It is an investment appraisal method which divides the average yearly profit received from an investment project by the average yearly capital invested in the project.

Real return   The nominal rate of return for an investment project minus the inflation rate.

Return on Capital Employed (ROCE)   A company performance ratio also known as Return on Investment (ROI) or Return on net assets; the return on capital invested.

Rights issue   One method of raising additional capital for a company. The company invites existing and potential shareholders to buy new shares issued for the company.

Risk   The variability of potential returns gives a measure of the overall risk. However, risk can be divided into market risk and unique risk, which can be diversified away.

Risk premium   An additional premium which is added to a market or company cost of capital to account for the added risk of this investment.

Return on Investment (ROI)   See Rate of return.

Scenario modelling   A method used to examine alternative cashflow scenarios and their influence on the Net Present Value or profitability of an investment project. These scenarios may be either different States of nature or Upside/Downside scenarios.

Security Market Line   The graphical representation of the relationship between expected return and market risk.

Sensitivity analysis   An analysis of the sensitivity of the Net Present Value of an investment to changes in the main components which make up the yearly cashflows, such as sales and costs.

Shareholders' equity   The current value of the shareholders' investment in a company which comprises the initial capital invested, retained profit and any other reserves. It is equivalent to the net assets of the company, i.e. all the assets of the company minus any outstanding debts owed by the company such as loans, taxes due for payment and creditors due for payment.

States of nature   The prevailing economic environment in which the investment project is being considered, such as the current inflation rate, unemployment, the exchange rate with key markets or supply countries, the interest rates, and so forth.

Sunk cost   A cost which has already occurred and which, for the purpose of investment appraisal now, is irrelevant to the decision.

Systematic risk   See Market risk.

Terminal value   The residual value of an investment project after the first five to ten years of cashflows from the investment project have been forecasted.

Unique risk   Risk which can be eliminated through diversification. Also called Unsystematic risk.

Unsystematic risk   See Unique risk.

Weighted Average Cost of Capital (WACC)   The overall *expected* cost of capital for a company. It is the weighted average of the various costs of capital from the different sources of that capital, usually shareholders' or equity cost of capital, and the cost of debt. It is often used as the Hurdle rate of new investment projects.

Working capital   The capital for an investment project or a company which is tied up in the investment, in the stock of the company, in work-in-progress and in credit sales to customers. It is computed by taking the stock and the trade debtors (money that is owed to you from customers) and taking away trade creditors (money that you owe to your suppliers).

Index

Page numbers in italics indicate diagrams and tables.